The Interpretation of Roman Poetry: Empiricism or Hermeneutics?

Studien zur klassischen Philologie

Herausgegeben von Prof. Dr. Michael von Albrecht

Band 67

Peter Lang

Frankfurt am Main · Bern · New York · Paris

Karl Galinsky (Ed.)

The Interpretation of Roman Poetry: Empiricism or Hermeneutics?

Peter Lang

Frankfurt am Main · Bern · New York · Paris

Die Deutsche Bibliothek - CIP-Einheitsaufnahme

The interpretation of Roman poetry: empiricism or
hermeneutics? / Karl Galinsky (ed.). - Frankfurt am Main ;
Bern ; New York ; Paris : Lang, 1992
  (Studien zur klassischen Philologie ; Bd. 67)
  ISBN 3-631-44741-8

NE: Galinsky, Karl [Hrsg.]; GT

ISSN 0172-1798
ISBN 3-631-44741-8

CONTENTS

Preface   i x

1. KARL GALINSKY (University of Texas at Austin)
   Introduction: The Interpretation of Roman
   Poetry and the Contemporary Critical Scene   1

   1. What to do about multiple
      interpretations?   4
   2. The legacy of the New Criticism   13
   3. The role of historicism   16
   4. Resistance to theory   21
   5. Convergences   27
   6. Some conclusions and challenges   31
   7. The contributions to this volume   33
      Bibliography   37

2. JAMES E. G. ZETZEL (Columbia University)
   Roman Romanticism and Other Fables   41

3. T. P. WISEMAN (University of Exeter)
   Erridge's Answer
   Response to James Zetzel   58

4. FRANCIS CAIRNS (University of Leeds)
   Propertius 4.9: "Hercules Exclusus"
   and the Dimensions of Genre   65

5. WILLIAM S. ANDERSON (University of California,
   Berkeley)
   The Limits of Genre
   Response to Francis Cairns   96

6. GIAN BIAGIO CONTE (University of Pisa)
   Empirical and Theoretical Approaches
   to Literary Genre   104

7. JASPER GRIFFIN (Balliol College, Oxford)
   Of Genres and Poems
   Response to Gian Biagio Conte   124

8. GIAN BIAGIO CONTE
   Response to Griffin's Response   134

9. CHARLES SEGAL (Harvard University)
   Boundaries, Worlds, and Analogical Thinking,
   or How Lucretius Learned to Love Atomism
   and Still Write Poetry   137

10. FREDERICK AHL (Cornell University)
    Moenia Mundi: the Akritic Poet
    Response to Charles Segal   157

11. DISCUSSION following Segal and Ahl   170

12. MICHAEL VON ALBRECHT (Universität Heidelberg)
    Ovidian Scholarship: Some Trends and
    Perspectives   176

13. ELAINE FANTHAM (Princeton University)
    Strengths and Weaknesses of Current
    Ovidian Criticism
    Response to Michael von Albrecht   191

14. W. R. JOHNSON (University of Chicago)
    The Death of Pleasure. Literary Critics
    in Technological Societies   200

15. MARILYN SKINNER (Northern Illinois University)
Literary Theorists at Second-Rate
Universities
Response to W.R. Johnson   215

16. THOMAS N. HABINEK (University of California,
Berkeley)
Grecian Wonders and Roman Woe: the Romantic
Rejection of Rome and its Consequences for
the Study of Roman Literature   227

Index of Greek and Roman Authors   243

Index of Modern Authors   246

PREFACE

The interpretation of Roman poetry, especially in America, has had a highly idiosyncratic history. Definitions of hermeneutic principle and reflections on method have been less than sporadic, in marked contrast to their ubiquity in literary criticism and theory outside of classics. It could be argued that so long as the practice is good, no theory is needed, but that would amount to unjustified complacency on several counts. For whatever small comfort this provides, the situation at least is not unparalleled, and Dominick LaCapra's recent comments on current historiography are equally applicable to the contemporary interpretation of Roman poetry: "I would not deny that history is in important respects a craft or, indeed, an art that is learned and plied on the basis of tacit knowledge and subtle know-how. But I would resist the complacent if not reactionary version of this idea that enjoins the historian to 'imbibe' the wisdom of eminent ⁶practitioners and bask in the light of sun-drenched exemplars."[1] Modern theory may be excessive, among other things, in the amount of verbiage it spends on explaining its presuppositions and procedures. But the virtual silence of Latinists about such matters is another extreme, and there is a broad *via media*.

This collection of essays by fourteen well-known Latinists from Europe and the U.S. has, therefore, two primary purposes and audiences. One is to provide some up-to-date, representative examples of work that is currently being done in the area of Roman poetry in order to inform those who are working in other literatures about the present state of its interpretation. The other is to engage, mostly for the benefit of classicists, in some methodological reflection and the discussion of related issues. Both aspects are enhanced by the familiarity of most of the contributors with recent developments in literary criticism and theory. I will discuss all these perspectives more fully in the Introduction.

---

1   *History & Criticism* (Ithaca 1985) 12.

The papers are based on a conference that was held at the University of Texas at Austin in the spring of 1990. They were substantially revised especially in the light of the ensuing discussions of which only one, that after the presentations of Professors Segal and Ahl, is included in this volume. The speaker/respondent format is the time-honored one of the *controversia* and improved on its model by producing substantive rather than rhetorical results. It is my pleasure to thank the Department of Classics and the College of Liberal Arts for their sponsorship, and to acknowledge gratefully the financial support of the Mobil Foundation, the Floyd A. Cailloux Centennial Professorship in Classics, Mr. and Mrs. Dixie Smith of Fulbright&Jaworski in Houston, Mr. and Mrs. Kenneth Keller of Plano, Mr. and Mrs. Mark Finley of Austin, and Mr. and Mrs. George Nalle, Jr. of Austin. I am indebted to several of my colleagues, especially David Armstrong, Peter Green, and Thomas Hubbard for their encouragement and helpful suggestions; to Christopher Francese, Ruth Rothaus, and Shawn O'Bryhim for technical and research assistance; and to Cate Fowler for her invaluable help with my Roman desire for order and with the production of the manuscript. Finally, I am grateful to Michael von Albrecht for accepting this volume for expeditious publication in the series *Studien zur Klassischen Philologie*.

Austin, November 1991

INTRODUCTION: THE CURRENT STATE OF THE INTERPRETATION OF ROMAN POETRY AND THE CONTEMPORARY CRITICAL SCENE

In the very first decade of this century, Richard Heinze, one of the great Latinists of our time, wrote an eloquent article on "The present tasks of the history of Roman literature." In it, he laid stress on two basic perspectives whose interplay, whenever it is pursued vigorously, is essential to the dynamics of the interpretation of literature in general and of Roman poetry in particular. First, he urged, as he had in other fundamental articles, the need for attentiveness to the historical and social setting of a literary work, but he now reformulated such aspects in strikingly modern terms, such as the "aesthetic demands of the public" and the relationship between "producers" and "recipients." Secondly, instead of holding classical philology up as a model for literary research and interpretation—and this was only twenty years after the appearance of the revised edition of Boeckh's monumental *Encyklopädie und Methodologie der Philologischen Wissenschaften*—Heinze faulted classical philology for having let itself be overtaken by the kind of work that was being done on modern literatures. Instead of contentment with mere historical positivism, he emphasized the importance of the later reception of Roman literature because that literature "did not die with its creators; its works have continued to live on and to have an effect." He then went on to ask for cooperation between scholars of classical, medieval, and modern literature (Heinze 161ff., esp. 174f.).

Now, any savvy reader of a book written by a classicist is conditioned, as part of his or her horizon of expectations, to await the moment when the old shoe of *déjà vu* is being dropped. Part of my reason for beginning with a reference to Heinze, therefore, is not to transgress such generic codes and, in fact, to get them over with as quickly as possible. More important, of course, is the essence of Heinze's exhortation. Had it been followed, the course of the interpretation of Roman literature in this century might well have been different. From being active participants in hermeneutic discussions Latinists have turned into mere bystanders, a situation that does not apply to Graecists whose work increasingly is fruitfully incorporating modern anthropological and literary approaches, all in combination with traditional attention to philological nuance and careful historical scholarship.[1] The interpretation of Roman poetry in particular, and especially in the U.S., has been characterized by a virtually complete absence of reflection on method and, most fundamentally, by a lack of explaining its presuppositions. This is not to dismiss it as stale or even bad in qualitative terms, as some good and interesting work is being done and the process of interpretation is anything but standing still. Yet there is an elementary lack in most new interpretations, for instance, of attention to such basic issues as differentiation between authorial meaning (and whether or not it exists), personal reading, and significance in terms of modern sensibilities that may be shaping the interpretation; most of these "horizons of expectation" are merrily commingled and any newly discovered meaning is implicitly identified with that of the poet.

The result is unhealthy and one if its effects has been expressed concisely by a recent European reviewer, Professor Ernst A. Schmidt, of Michael Putnam's study of Horace's fourth book of Odes. Schmidt, who is by no means addicted to any particular literary theory, has these comments (p. 503):

> What concerns me and disturbs me is this: that a sensible, cultivated, and erudite man of approximately my age and with a cultural background (U.S., east coast) not radically different from mine, who teaches the same subject and has similar interests, is able to come up with individual interpretations which I consider as pointless (*abwegig*) and embarrassing and in which I see elementary mistakes of method, while he evidently considers them as having a hermeneutic basis and as plausible. I infer from this that he is coming to similar conclusions about my methods. And I generalize (as this is not my first experience of this sort): are we (philologues, intellectual and cultural historians) still able to be intelligible to one another given the pluralism of opinions and methods, of interests and literary cultures, and given the absence of conditions for a basic consensus, and are we still interesting to

---

1   Gentili's book is a sterling example. Its Appendix on "The Art of Philology" is the kind of methodological statement one would like to see more often. The issue of the orality especially of early Greek literature has provided a major impulse for the greater awareness of method among Graecists.

one another? Obviously not; my resignation has grown after
I read this book.[2]

It is timely, therefore, to address some of the perspectives pertaining to these issues. Hermeneutic is not absent from the current interpretation of Roman poetry; it is simply that often it is not stated. Nor should it be inferred from the title of this book that theory and empiricism be viewed as irreconcilable opposites. They clearly are not, as Tzvetan Todorov, among others, reminds us (p. 173), but it was useful to choose a theme for our discussion that would generate more exact definitions of method instead of the prevailing looseness, which should not be confused with flexibility. Moreover, as is clear from the contributions to this volume, Latinists are quite aware of the ongoing discussion about theory and hermeneutics in the modern literatures, and while any specific debt to them is acknowledged infrequently, absorption of the practices they produce has taken place on an osmotic basis; this applies, for instance, to Stanley Fish's brand of "affective criticism" because it relieves the critic "of the obligation to be right (a standard that simply drops out) and demands only that I be interesting (a standard that can be met without any reference at all to an illusory objectivity)."[3] Or, to give another example, the notion of an infinite plurality of meanings *de facto* is enthusiastically subscribed to by many Anglo-American interpreters of Latin poetry, especially those who make a living by discovering such new meanings, a.k.a. "voices" in Vergilian criticism. One byproduct has been that American scholarship on Roman prose authors, with the occasional exception of cataloguing rhetorical tropes and the like, has declined to less than a subsistence level because the subject requires a relatively higher standard of methodological validation.[4]

In a more positive though similarly unstated fashion, there is, in fact, considerable convergence between the concerns of interpreters of Roman poetry and those of modern theorists who have simply gone to greater, and sometimes excessive, lengths to explain them. Issues such as the multiplicity of possible interpretations and their relation to the text and author, the historicity

[2] It is typical of Professor Putnam's class that Schmidt was subsequently invited to be a visiting professor in his department at Brown University. Schmidt in the meantime has been motivated to further hermeneutic reflection in R. Kannicht, ed., *1838-1988. 150 Jahre Philologisches Seminar der Universtät Tübingen* (Tübingen 1990) 55-67.
[3] "Literature in the Reader: Affective Stylistics" in Fish, 1970, 383ff.; cf. the comments by Abrams, 1979, 580, and Graff, 1977, 473f.
[4] Winkler's study of Apuleius (1985) is a rare and delightful exception.

of both the original setting of a work and of subsequent interpretations, the "burden of the past" borne by poets working in a given tradition, the validity of formalist interpretation like the New Criticism (still much in vogue among American Latinists), and the very resistance to "theory" in favor of a more direct enjoyment of a work of art or literature—these are principal, shared concerns. They provide another illustration, in Frank Lentricchia's words (p. 280), "that the much-touted shift from traditional to contemporary critical theory conceals significant common investments." It is important to discuss them, and some others, and to relate them briefly to the various essays in this volume.

1. *What to do about multiple interpretations?*

Even the traditional philology never entertained the myth of one fixed, immutable meaning of a work of literature. More than a century ago, Boeckh raised, with a succinctness that has found regrettably few imitators, the same epistemological questions (p. 86) on which contemporary theorists like to expatiate at length. Even Boeckh's terminology is strikingly modern. He speaks about "the infinite number of conditions for each individual utterance" and the "impossibility to bring it to discursive clarity." He quotes Gorgias on the impossibility of expressive reality (cf. Belsey 7ff.) and its incommunicability. He concludes by emphasizing, to use Robert Scholes' words (p. 154), that "different, even conflicting assumptions may preside over any reading of a single text by a single person" and that interpretation, therefore, can only be an ongoing process of approximation which is never completed. Or, as John Dryden put it, "no text is ever fully explicated."

Another good intention behind the road to what has been overelaborated into a theoretical inferno is the obvious recognition that great literary works— the much harped-on "classics," for that matter—are classics precisely because they are susceptible to new interpretations by subsequent generations which, due to a changing world, may have cultural sensibilities different from those of the original audience. As teachers of classics, we don't want to treat works like the Homeric epics or Vergil's *Aeneid* as museum pieces that leave us cool and detached. We are also part of a modern audience that wants to react to them directly and find individual meaning in them. Such meanings, of course, can be very subjective and downright anachronistic.

These issues lie at the center of the current theoretical debate, and it is instructive to survey briefly the principal solutions that have been proposed and to assess their utility for the interpretation of Roman poetry. One commendable trend has simply been to differentiate between the original meaning and those developed in the course of interpretative history. E.D. Hirsch, for instance, distinguishes between the "meaning," i.e. the orginal meaning of the text imparted to it in large measure by the author, and the various kinds of "significance" or "relevance" that are products of later values and cultural contexts. The theory takes into account the notions of historicity and historical relativism developed by Gadamer and, from a linguistic orientation, by de Saussure. The recognition of this conditionality is, at root, a common-sensical insight and leads to the further recognition, on the part of a non-charismocratic literary hermeneuticist like the late Peter Szondi, that even our own hermeneutical systems are a product of historical conditions and therefore will be superseded in due historical course (p. 25).

The difference between that liberal attitude and the more autocratic behavior of some of his French and American counterparts could not be more marked (cf. Felperin 203). In line with the paradigm shift from author to text to reader, they celebrate the death of the author in ways rather different from more literal-minded Latinists who find the current decades congenial for congregating on the bimillenaries of the deaths of major Roman poets. The separate existence of author and text was ushered in by the New Criticism; Wimsatt's remarks are fairly typical: "The poem is not the critic's own and not the author's (it is detached from the author at birth and goes about the world beyond his power to control it). The poem belongs to the public" (p. 75). Poststructuralism, with several variants and transitional constructs, has further developed that premise into two principal answers to the question, "What does this text mean?" (cf. Todorov 183). Deconstructionists by and large will answer with "nothing at all" and, in recognition of the historical and linguistic relativism of interpretation, proceed to equate all interpretation with misinterpretation. While this is an insurance policy against hostile critics and relieves the interpreter of the anxiety of possibly being wrong about a text (Graff, 1977, 473), it amounts to a hermeneutic of inconsequentiality. Professor Conte in his paper joins the chorus of those who argue that literary criticism does not need such remedies.

The new literary "pragmatism" reduces the same question to irrelevance by answering it with "anything whatsoever." The paradigm shift is further extended as the authority of literature, which was still acknowledged into the 1970's, was superseded, in a wilful confusion of means and ends, by the authority of criticism. It is only the reader and, especially, the critic who matter: they, and not the *poietes* ("maker"), are the makers of meanings. This puts them in the enjoyable position of making up the rules as they go along; "a track-laying vehicle steered by its own tracks," as Peter Green has characterized the process (p. 8). Validity becomes a moot question or, in Richard Rorty's words, the interpreter "simply beats the text into a shape which will serve his own purposes."[5]

There is, of course, plenty of judicious latitude this side of such extremes. Lest classicist readers get complacent at this point, it is useful to remind them that this seemingly modern *modus interpretandi* has had a long career in the interpretation of Greek and Roman letters. Subjective interpretations are nothing new, no matter what their trappings. Once again, the modern theorists at least explain their presuppositions. Moreover, they do so with unconcealed honesty. We could do worse than learn from that, even if the "method" itself is an incitement to irresponsibility. It is really no method, but, to give only one example, that orientation is hardly different from Wilamowitz' pronouncement on the same subject: "Why, this prized 'philological method'? There simply isn't any—any more than a method to catch fish. The whale is harpooned; the herring caught in a net; minnows are trapped; the salmon speared; trout caught on a fly. Where do you find *the* method to catch fish?"[6] Conversely, critics like R.S. Crane, whom Professor Zetzel prominently cites in his essay, might praise Wilamowitz for his ostensible aversion to the endemic reductionism which has been the curse of theoretical and hermeneutic systems (Graff, 1987, 234-36). The "pragmatic" solution, therefore, is an interesting logical paradox.

It does not, however, obviate the concomitant question of a qualitative hierarchy or validity of multifarious interpretations. One answer, proposed by the advocates of reception theory, is that the meaning of a literary work is concretized over time by various generations of readers. In other words, different, though immanent aspects of a work can be uncovered in the course of time and their sum total, which does not necessarily amount to a synthesis, comprises the meaning of the work. All interpretations, therefore, contribute to the unfolding or development of the *Sinnpotential* of a poem or novel. Careful inspection of such receptions, alas, reveals what one would suspect: it is "the remarkable pliability with which the text follows virtually all predispositions of its interpreters" (Lobsien 28), whether we are dealing with

5   "Nineteenth-Century Idealism and Twentieth-Century Textuality," in *Consequences of Pragmatism* (New York 1982) 151.
6   Cited by William M. Calder III in *Greek, Roman and Byzantine Studies* 16 (1975) 452.

Joyce's *Ulysses* (Lobsien) or the poems of Martial (Sullivan). Texts, after all, "offer no resistance to acts of interpretation."[7]

How, then, should one interpretation be privileged vis-à-vis another? How can myopic interpretations be put in their place by more insightful ones? Here is one solution:

> These blind first readers—they could be replaced for the sake of exposition, by the fiction of a naive reader, though the tradition is likely to provide ample material—then need, in turn, a critical reader who reverses the tradition and momentarily takes us closer to the original insight. The existence of a particularly rich aberrant tradition in the case of writers who can legitimately be called the most enlightened, is therefore no accident, but a constitutive part of all literature, the basis, in fact, of literary history.

One can only marvel how applicable these comments are to Vergil, for instance. Great writers beget "particularly rich aberrant traditions." How refreshing it is to see the confirmation of the value of the critical reader who "takes us closer to the original insight!" No doubt a traditional classicist is speaking, nay, "shouting"[8] here. But no, it is actually Paul de Man himself (p. 141): "For all of its rich poststructuralist texture, de Man's characterization of the best criticism is familiarly traditional" (Lentricchia 306). Similarly, even the Nietzschean Stanley Fish refers to "interpretive communities, rather than the text or the reader, that produce meanings and are responsible for the emergence of formal features" (Fish, 1980, 14). Despite the usual vagueness of the notion (cf. Scholes 152-54), we are back to the concept of the Guild to which Professor Habinek adverted several times during our conference.

Given this sort of traditionalism on the part of even the most avant-garde exponents of literary theory, there is no reason for us as interpreters of Roman poetry to turn our backs on the refined hermeneutic traditionalism of critics such as Hirsch, Graff, and Scholes in judging the quality and validity of various interpretations. There is plenty of latitude between the extremes of "objective" positivism and the egalitarianism of "undecidables." It is in this space that most

---

7   Scholes 158, paraphrasing Fish.

8   Such terminology is not unusual in attempts, such as Don Fowler's in *Greece and Rome* 37 (1990) 106, to dismiss any requests for explanations of method in the current interpretation of Roman poetry. As Fowler himself illustrates by citing E. Lefèvre (in G. Binder, ed., *Saeculum Augustum* 2 [Darmstadt 1988] 178), if American interpreters of the *Aeneid* do not state their procedures, others will do it for them.

of our activities, such as refereeing for journals and supervising dissertations, in fact takes place. The principles these critics invoke largely coincide with those classicists follow in actual practice, but again, it is helpful to see them spelled out[9] and provide an occasion for both critical and self-critical reflection.

The notion that theory alone does not produce good criticism is already found in Boeckh;[10] being a good German, he goes on to mention the importance of such factors as *Gefühl* (perhaps best translated as "intuitive sensibility") and even tact, qualities that are similarly prized by modern non-theoretical critics such as Frederick Crews (p. 1041) and Susan Sontag. More generally, it is common sense (cited, for instance, by Michael von Albrecht) that plays a crucial role in good criticism besides the more specific criteria cited by the traditionalist trio I mentioned in the preceding paragraph, and it is anything but beyond definition. Catherine Belsey spends a whole chapter on defining (and rejecting) it, singling out the reception aesthetics of Iser and Jauss as the culminating example: "Iser's *Act of Reading* is in many ways an excellent theoretical account of what, in all their variety, most liberal humanist readers in the second half of the twentieth century probably *do* when they read" (p. 35). For Belsey, who is a good representative of the advocacy of new theory for the sake of new theory, this is not good enough. She finds Iser's specific readings "very conventional"—a notion that may mildly shock Latinists such as Antonie Wlosok[11]—and proceeds to postulate "a new theoretical framework which makes a fundamental break with the proposition of common sense."

Belsey's characterization, albeit polemical, is another illustration of the "common investments" which are shared by traditional and modern critics and to which I already have referred on several occasions. Jauss in particular exemplifies once more that some modern theorists differ from classicists only in the much greater degree to which they define and articulate hermeneutic issues. I confine myself to one example, his concise distinction between three "horizons of expectation" that critics should use for their interpretations (Jauss, 1981, 473). Jauss usefully differentiates between the following, successive

---

9   See esp. Hirsch, 1967, 127ff. on such issues as critical freedom and interpretive constraint, problems and principles of validation, and objective interpretation; Scholes 149ff. for some basic definitions of interpretation; and Graff, 1987, 247ff. on problems of theory.
10   Cited in full by James Zetzel (p. 42.below).
11   Who blames Iser for much of the relativism and subjectivism of *interpretationes modernae*; see *Würzburger Jahrbücher* 8 (1982) 16ff. *Contra*, see especially P.L. Schmidt and Barner.

kinds of readings that comprise the total interpretation: (1) a first and aesthetic reading, a stage that other theorists identify with "understanding"; (2) a second, "retrospectively explicating" reading; and (3), a third, historical reading "so that we may catch sight of the text in the horizon of its alterity and in its difference from our experience." This historical reading, he continues, "can begin with the reconstruction of the horizon of expectation of the text's original readers; it does full justice, however, to the requisite unity of the hermeneutic triad only when the historical distance between the text and the present is elaborated and when the tradition of readings is clarified that prepared the way for the most recent interpretation."

One concrete example may suffice to illustrate how beneficial this common-sensical three-stage process would be for the interpretation of some of the most debated topics in Roman poetry, such as the ending of the *Aeneid*. A quarter century ago, Michael Putnam reinterpreted the scene in which Aeneas, after hesitating, kills Turnus *furiis accensus et ira terribilis*, as the victory of the dark forces in the *Aeneid*. With a zeal that surpassed even that of the curiously unacknowledged Christian predecessors of this view, Lactantius and Augustine, repetitive assertion of this peculiar interpretation, with a few embroidering accretions, has come to compensate for its intrinsic debility; one indication of the latter is the rather unsophisticated way in which the label "Augustan" or "historicist" is affixed (though not by Putnam) to anyone who doesn't want to buy into it. To move the discussion to higher ground, it is useful to cite Putnam's conclusion in full and then inspect it briefly in the light of Jauss' methodology.

Here is the end of Putnam's chapter on "Tragic Victory" (pp. 200-201):

> When the epic opened, it was Aeneas' turn to shudder with cold as the winds, the first pawns of Juno's anger, threatened imminent death (*solvuntur frigore membra*: I, 92). Now, as the poem reaches its climax, it is one of Virgil's most bitter and cogent ironies that he uses this very phrase at the exact moment Aeneas becomes the personification of avenging wrath and brings death to Turnus. The wheel has come full circle. It should cause little wonder when Juno seems to surrender so readily to Jupiter's plea that she give over her anger in contemplation of future Roman magnificence. For, according to the poet's wishes, it is she, not Aeneas, nor the grandeur for which Augustus seems to stand, who wins the greatest

victory as the soul of Turnus passes with a resentful moan to the
shades below.

This is a textbook example of the confusion or melding (*Verschmelzung*)
of the three interpretive horizons with a resulting lack of precision. When, on
the other hand, we keep them separate at first, the following considerations
emerge:

(1) *Aesthetic reading or "understanding."* What is the methodological
justification for the lexically associative approach by which the repetition of
words or phrases is implicitly considered the key to the "poetry?"[12] This is,
of course, a variant inherited from the New Criticism (to which I shall turn
shortly; see Section 2); hence also the search for "ironies," especially bitter
ones. But is this kind of reading really appropriate for texts that were largely
recited and could not be marked up with verbal grids stretching hither and
yon? How can one say, then, it's "the poet's wishes?" Why not say, "this is my
reading of it" instead of blithely equating one's own aesthetic reading with the
poet's intentions?

(2) *Retrospective explication.* What about the full context? How many
epic heroes even hesitate to kill their opponents? If sparing Turnus is *pietas*, so
is the obligation that Aeneas avenge the killing of Pallas. What of the Homeric
background? What of the preparation of this unsurprising final scene
throughout the second half of the epic? What of the contrast between Aeneas'
listening to Turnus' plea and Turnus' refusal to listen to Latinus' at the
beginning of Book 12?

(3) *Historical horizon.* (a) Contemporary. What were Roman attitudes
to anger? How did they deal with treaty breakers? By contrast, what is our
reaction to anger today and how did we feel, especially in the 60's, about war
and its necessities? If our attitudes are part of the interpretation, we should at
least profess this subjectivism as some of the "New Historians" have done of
late. (b) Previous interpretations, i.e. *Rezeptionsgeschichte*, the reaction to
which, whether positive or negative, influences the new interpretation. To
mention just a few: the church fathers' criticism of the end of the *Aeneid*;
conversely, the excessive tendency to make Aeneas into a proto-Christian and a
Stoic—now that he turns out not to conform to this image produced by earlier
receptions, is it not better to admit that this was simply the wrong mold to cast

---

12   Cf. W. Moskalew, *Formular Language and Poetic Design in the 'Aeneid'* (Leiden
1982).

him in rather than treat his display of human emotions as a fall from grace? Similarly, the Augustan dimension needs far greater precision. How legitimate is it to make inferences from Vergil's handling of his characters about "the grandeur for which Augustus seems to stand?" More generally, is it enough to convert previous interpretive theses (e.g., "the *Aeneid* is a glorification of Augustus") simply into antitheses instead of taking a fresh look at the text itself and proceeding from there?

As can be seen, this kind of hermeneutic does not impose unnecessary theoretical ballast nor does it predispose the reader. It takes into account the historicity of the ancient text and that of subsequent interpretations, including ours. It does not inhibit multiple interpretations and even allows for one final cause of these to which I would like to advert, i.e. multiple reader responses as part of the author's intent.[13]

It is, of course, the very characteristic of great works of literature that they generate varied and even conflicting responses. The phenomenon deserves to be defined in terms other than the convenient relic inherited from the New Criticism which Latinists have routinized, i. e. "ambiguity." It needs to be viewed in conjunction with one of the essential characteristics of Roman poetry, i.e. its constant referentiality and systemic allusion to both Greek and Roman predecessors, a subject for which Professor Conte offers some astute redefinitions. In practical terms, this factor, among others, accounts for the many layers and the sophisticated complexity especially of late Republican and Augustan poetry. Take the main characters of the *Aeneid* (cf. Griffin 193/94): Aeneas is Achilles, Hector, Hercules, Menelaus, Jason, Odysseus, and Paris, and Augustus; Dido is Nausicaa, Calypso, Medea, Cleopatra, Ariadne, and Naevius' unromantic Dido. Our responses shift and may vary from reader to reader, but the guiding intention of the poet is anything but absent. In Jasper Griffin's excellent formulation: "All this might of course be a mere chaos of contradictory directives and muddled purposes on Virgil's part. It is in reality more than that, because this complexity of response is a vital part of the poet's intention and of the greatness of his poem" (p. 195). In other words, two concepts that modern theorists have tended to wall off from one another, if not outright deny, naturally come together here: there is a strong authorial, and even moral, center *and* a constant invitation to the reader not just to respond,

---

[13]   For instance, anger, as we know from Cicero and others, was one of the most debated subjects in popular ethical philosophy at Vergil's time (cf. *AJP* 109 [1988] 321ff.); in addition, it is typical of Vergil that he ends the *Aeneid* on the note of yet another dilemma. The answers to either are not easy, but neither are they shrouded in "moral ambiguity."

but to participate in assessing the ever shifting identity of these characters (and the same could be said about the variation of recurrent themes and scenes, a process which Griffin in this volume aptly characterizes as *tema con variazioni*). It is not a deconstructionist theater, but the dynamics of the process are similar to what Paul Zanker has called "Andachtsbilder" in Augustan art, i.e. mythological figures such as Venus/Tellus/Pax on the Altar of Augustan Peace, which have a multi-referential, complex iconography whose many strands the viewer is invited to discover and reflect on. In short, we are dealing with an intentional and authorially defined polysemy.[14]

This aspect of Roman poetry also leads to the legitimate hermeneutic, exemplified by Charles Segal's essay, of expanding on an inherent characteristic of an ancient work with concepts and constructs—such as "boundary anxiety"—whose development and formulation postdate the work we are interpreting. This is a major source of "new" interpretations, but so far from being extraneously imposed on a text, they genuinely add to elucidating one of its given dimensions. The procedure accords both with progressing sensibilities and with the "original intent" of the author; I choose the phrase deliberately because similar hermeneutic questions are central to the interpretation of the U.S. Constitution and, in fact, have been put in the context of literary hermeneutics.[15] In contrast to grinding a text through the mill of a theory, it is, as Segal reminds us, "the text itself which should direct us to the method rather than the other way around." That, happily, is the kind of work we see increasingly done in the area of Roman poetry, though there could be more of it.[16] It does not satisfy Belsey's autoteleological concept of "a radical new departure," but it is governed by good sense and is essential to fulfilling the true mission of modern classicists: to interpret the ancient authors, without any lapse into anachronisms, with the sophisticated methods and resources which are available to us today. It also mediates two practices that current theory has tended to develop into a schema of irreconcilable bipolarity, i. e.

14   The term is more than appropriate: as Annabel Patterson (*Pastoral and Ideology. Virgil to Valéry* [Berkeley 1987] 30) points out, it was Servius "who introduced into European critical discourse the crucial word polysemous, as a comment on Virgil's *cano* in the opening lines of the *Aeneid*." Patterson also credits Servius, whom Latinists tend to fault for his pedantry, with "a theoretical grasp of the problem of referentiality in a 'literary' text, as well as of the critical methodology such a problem requires." Barner 506f. suggests the use of 'multifunctionality' instead of 'polysemy' because of its supposedly more objective connotations.

15   See the special issue, edited by Sanford Levinson, of the *Texas Law Review* (vol. 60.3, 1982) on "Law and Literature" with contributions by Gerald Graff and Stanley Fish.

16   Cf. the applicability of anthropologist David Gilmore's definition of manhood in terms of selfless caring (*Manhood in the Making. Cultural Concepts of Masculinity* [New Haven 1990]) to Vergil's much misunderstood Aeneas; Galinsky, Ch. 3.

past-centered historical recovery and present-centered reinterpretation (Graff, 1987, 204; cf. Section 3). This is just one of the several instances where Latinists can make a genuine contribution to the contemporary hermeneutic debate (cf. Section 6).

2. *The Legacy of the New Criticism*

"The literary criticism of Roman poetry," as Charles Segal put it politely in his introduction to Gian Biagio Conte's book (p. 8), "still remains heavily under the influence of the now aging New Criticism." As for the New Criticism, this comes close to being an understatement: six years earlier, Frank Lentricchia could justifiably say that it had been "out of fashion for the past two decades or more" (p. 320). Not so in the interpretation of Roman poetry where, as Segal notes, it still predominates. I beg the momentary indulgence, therefore, of readers other than classicists for providing an *aggiornamento* mostly for the benefit of the latter, especially as this is another example of an interpretive practice in the field of Roman poetry that is carried out without much awareness of its presuppositions, let alone reflection on them. Latinists simply adopted the major modes of New Criticism and keep on continuing them without acknowledging them as being New Critical, occasional brave souls like James Zetzel excepted.

Two principal explanations can be given for the continuing prevalence of the New Critical *modus interpretandi* of Roman poetry. One, there has been understandable reluctance to hop on the bandwagon of subsequent and especially poststructuralist theory; Ralph Johnson's essay is an articulate statement of that refusal and I will return to it later (Section 4). The retention of New Critical methods, therefore, is largely a matter of *faute de mieux* which, however, also highlights the Latinists' inertia to come up with something on their own that would be *mieux*; that is why, besides its intrinsic merit, the exception provided by Conte's hermeneutic of genre and allusiveness is so valuable and why we need similar such initiatives. Secondly, the New Criticism, in the 1940's and 50's, presented the welcome opportunity to supplement arid philological criticism with an overdue aesthetic appreciation. This coincided with the increasing need for classics departments to offer courses in civilization and literature in translation and, as time went on, with the requirement of more publication for promotion, tenure, and merit increases. The new interpretive mode was yet another gift of the American South to classics not in the least because it was and is so eminently *doable*.

The results are all around us, though few Latinists go so far as to reminisce nostalgically about the good old days with Allen Tate (and, far from being holier than thou, I speak only as active member of this particular interpretive community): from the time of a graduate student's first seminar on Roman poetry, an eager and never-ending search is on for images, motifs and motif clusters, themes, verbal links, structure in the form of Chinese boxes (although preoccupation with those schemes at last has begun to ebb away), "tensions," ironies, ambivalences and paradoxes. It is, of course, a matter of seek and ye shall find: "Given the convenient elasticity of terms such as paradox and irony, not many poems could fail to reveal these qualities somehow, under the right kind of close inspection" (Graff, 1987, 206). As for attributing significance to repetitions of words and phrases, interpreters of Roman poetry went a great deal further than their unacknowledged New Critical mentors. The frequent result has been a sort of lemon-squeezing approach to the poems that flattens poetic design into a sequence of presumably related verbal echoes.

The absorption of the New Criticism into the study of Roman poetry certainly was not all to the bad. In contrast to English departments and others, it provided for the easy integration of critic and scholar in the same person. A breath of aesthetic air was sorely overdue and some good work was done on imagery, such as the fundamental article by Bernard Knox on Book 2 of the *Aeneid*.[17] With this, however, came the drawbacks inherent in the method. Poems increasingly were treated as aesthetic monads with no frame of reference besides the poem itself (or, at most, some verbal repetitions in its adjacent sisters in a poetry book). The resulting immanentism—shared by contemporaneous art-historical criticism—detached it from the author (hence the "intentional fallacy") and any historical and social context. The final stage of this process—and I am not asserting that it was reached in each and very instance—is that characterized by Terry Eagleton: "The poem itself was as opaque to rational inquiry as the Almighty himself: it existed as a self-enclosed object, mysteriously intact in its own unique being" (p. 47). This explains that as late as 1990, there is still a great deal of resistance to rational inquiries, for instance, into the exact nature of the "voices" that govern the interpretation of the *Aeneid* in mysterious ways. We cannot blame post-New Critical theorists for making "demystification" a part of their agenda.

---

17   *AJP* 71 (1950) 379-400; reprinted in S. Commager, ed., *Virgil. A Collection of Critical Essays* (Englewood Cliffs 1966) 124-42. Knox is not primarily a Latinist.

For while literary critics of Roman poetry may be averse to the perceived trendiness of theoretical fashions, many of them share with these theorists the concern for a wider framework of reference than the poem itself. The commonality of transcending an isolationist formalism should not be overlooked even while the roads we travel may be different. Classical scholars, and Latinists in particular, tend to be eclectic in their methods and that was, after all, a good Roman virtue. While staying clear of the routinization of New Critical formalism and of its entropic tendencies, interpreters of Roman poetry may still find it a valuable tool for analysis in combination with others. Conversely, while modern theory has declared the New Criticism *passé* it actually has extended it in the worst direction: witness the "death of the author"; the transference or displacement of "power" from real life and politics to the realm of critical authority (cf. Eagleton 142ff. and Felperin 213ff.); and the resulting solipsism and anti-humanism (cf. Graff, 1987, 250ff.; Said 2ff.; Todorov 182ff.). The achievement of the posited wider framework of reference, therefore, often is defeated by such tendencies.

In contrast, it is impossible for the good scholar of Roman poetry to look even at an individual poem in total isolation given the intensity of its interaction with the previous tradition. Again, this is admirably taken into account by Professor Conte who correctly recognizes that such 'allusion' is more than an *ad hoc* relationship between a poet and his predecessor and who integrates concepts from semiotic and structural theory—such as the "competence" of the "Model Reader"—into his analysis (*The Rhetoric of Imitation*). Besides, there is, as always, the historical referent which is by no means absent from contemporary theory and to which I will turn next. In accordance with Boeckh's insight (cited by Zetzel, p. 42 below), however, that the value of theory is simply to make us conscious of what we otherwise are doing unawares, it is important especially for American-trained interpreters of Roman poetry to familiarize themselves with the genesis and stated principles of the New Criticism. We observed earlier that, like everything else, literary theories and systems of hermeneutics are the product of historical conditions, and the New Criticism is no exception. What Latinists, who are uniquely equipped to do so, will have to decide for themselves is to what extent the fact of their historicity makes New Critical methods dated and to what extent they can continue to be practicable.

3. *The role of historicism*

In his 1980 address as President of the MLA, Hillis Miller bemoaned "the turn away from theory to history." In so doing, he expressed a perceived dichotomy which is peculiar to some of the developments in current literary criticism and which, by the usual osmosis, has also rubbed off on some interpreters of ancient literature. The model of historicism that was posited as the straw man is largely the static one of 19th century *Historismus*, centered on von Ranke. Aside from, curiously enough, the current writing of new ethnic histories, this "static notion of eternal groups"[18] has been the exception rather than the rule in historiography. Goethe's observation "that world history has to be rewritten from time to time is no longer doubted by anyone" typefies it and this relativism found its most popular expression in American historiography in Carl Becker's *Everyman his own historian* (1935). Historical hermeneutic, in fact, is very similar to its literary companion: there is the constant recognition, on the part of any good historian, that there is no definitive account or interpretation. We can only approximate such a goal; to paraphrase Dryden again, no historical event is ever fully explicated just as no text ever is. Even casual acquaintance with historiography will make us aware of the fact that revisionism is endemic to the discipline. When, therefore, "textuality has become the exact antithesis and displacement of what might be called history" (Said, pp. 3f.), this is only another effect of the compartmentalization of humanistic disciplines and the solipsism of much of contemporary criticism, a solipsism that is made all the more poignant and ironic in view of the grandiose, overarching epistemological rhetoric which pretends to provide unifying concepts for experiential diversity.

A further result, as Said notes, has been that "in American literary studies there has not in the past quarter century been enough work of major historical scholarship that can be called 'revisionist'" (p. 167). Instead of providing authentic reinterpretations, the effort of modern theorists has been concentrated on redefining and repackaging an unchanged product. Often, such forms of criticism "amount to nothing more than the mere exchange of opinion," as a prescient and cantankerous Joshua Whatmough said in the preface to his Sather lectures in 1956 when he pleaded, like Ralph Johnson today, for the "enjoyment of literature as such, stripped of all unnecessary externals" (p. vii). While that includes, as Marilyn Skinner points out in her

---

[18]   Werner Sollors in S. Bercovitch, ed., *Reconstructing American Literary History* (Cambridge, MA 1986) 19.

response, intellectual enjoyment, the salient point is, in Said's words, that "for there to be effective interpretation in what is, after all is said and done, a historical discipline, there must also be effective history, effective archival work, effective involvement in the actual material of history" (p. 167). It is, without a doubt, a view that would be shared by most classicists and certainly by students of Roman poetry. The value of any literary work or, specifically, a Roman poem is not exhausted by its historical dimension. It is silly, however, to polarize interpretation into history here and aesthetics there and then go off to wallow in aporiai; the hermeneutic of Jauss, which owes everything to *praxis*, shows, just as Hirsch and Boeckh do, that these aspects need to be combined as they in fact are in many studies of Roman poetry.

That endeavor, to continue our survey of the modern scene for a moment, was also the central thesis of Wesley Morris' *Toward a New Historicism* (1972) which gave its name, though not much more, to the contemporary New Historicism whose incipient stirrings so worried Hillis Miller. Morris openly cited the parallel with literary interpretation: "There is no convincing reason given for why historical perspective and aesthetic response should be mutually exclusive. The new historicist sets as his task the resolution of literature's dual mode of existence by introducing aesthetics into history. . ."(p. 30). As an antidote to the monolithic definitions of historicism that inhabit the writings of literary theorists, Morris also usefully differentiated between several types and, by the sort of coincidence which defies hermeneutic, found as many major kinds of historicism as Empson had of ambiguity.

To jaded observers of cyclical critical fashions the "New Historicism" of the past decade may be nothing more than "history without footnotes," but its own distinctive orientation is a fitting illustration in itself of the historicity of such interpretive trends. Besides "dissolving literature back into the historical complex" without recourse to "the outmoded vocabulary of allusion, symbolism, allegory, and mimesis" and renouncing empty formalism in favor of "putting historical considerations to the center stage of literary analysis,"[19] it is a reaction against the professional compartmentalization that was exacerbated by the literary theoreticians. The New Historicism is interdisciplinary and aims at the illumination of culture (Stephen Greenblatt now prefers the term "cultural poetics") from the perspective of various

---

[19]   Veeser xii with reference to T. Hawkes, "Uses and Abuses of the Bard," *TLS* (April 10, 1987) 391-93.

relevant academic fields: literature, history, anthropology, art history, religion, etc. To a student of *Altertumswissenschaft* all this sounds strikingly familiar. Accordingly, New Historians recognize heterogeneity and the label is an umbrella rather than implying a new orthodoxy.[20]

What is new in the New Historicism and makes it a true child of its age is its congeniality to postmodern attitudes. Just as classicizing postmodern architects do not simply return to neoclassicism so New Historians eschew going back to the old school of historical determinism, to "overarching hypothetical constructs" and "causal equations." Instead, they prefer "surprising coincidences." The result is a *bricolage* not unlike that found in postmodern buildings, reflecting what Lyotard has defined as the lack of a shared spiritual center and of absolute authority in favor of the relativization of the "grand narratives" of history such as science and religion.[21] Both the architects and the New Historians had to buck an existing orthodoxy (the "Protestant Inquisition," in Jencks' apt phrase) and avoid the stigma of a full-scale return to traditionalism. Neither, therefore, dared to overthrow their immediate predecessor: hence the juxtaposition of Modernist and historizing elements in postmodern architecture[22] whereas New Historians share with the poststructuralists a preoccupation with "power" and "have substituted relationships of power for 'ideas' as fundamental units of historical analysis" (Thomas 225). Latinists will again recognize something familiar in this perspective and the New Historians' open admission that their personal attitudes (to current events, for instance) shape their writings: both, after all, were the guiding inspiration for Sir Ronald Syme's *The Roman Revolution*, still the most influential work on Augustus since it was published at the time of the autocracies of Hitler, Mussolini, and Stalin. The difference lies in the New Historians' reluctance to be systematic on a grand scale and thus commit the causality fallacy.

What can the literary critic of Roman poetry learn from all this? At least three points are worth making. One, attention to the historical aspects of literature is by no means old-fashioned but turns out to be a constituent part of the current critical scene. While there are various definitions, as there properly should be, historicism is well recognized and actively assertive.

---

20   For more detail, see the useful overview by Brook Thomas, "The New Historicism and Other Old-Fashioned Topics," in Veeser 182-203.
21   J.F. Lyotard, *The Postmodern Condition: A Report on Knowledge* (Minneapolis 1984).
22   See Jencks and my chapter on "Classicism in Postmodern American Architecture" in *Classical and Modern Interactions*.

Especially in the discipline of classics, therefore, it should not be used simply as a reductionist label. Two, there is an endeavor to combine historical and aesthetic perspectives in the writing on both literature and history. The interpretation of Roman poetry has had a distinguished tradition in this regard, from Richard Heinze to Gordon Williams (modesty prevents me from mentioning contributors to this volume). It is a good tradition that should be maintained. Three, the study of Roman poetry indeed should be a "poetics of culture" which benefits from an interdisciplinary orientation. Again, there is a good tradition to build on. Unlike the New Historicism, it does not owe its genesis to reaction formation and therefore is spared the Angst of being systematic. Eleanor Leach's recent book on literary and artistic representations of landscape in Republican and Augustan Rome is a splendid example.

There is, of course, the temptation of creative alternatives. In a recent essay on Longus' *Daphnis and Chloe* the late Jack Winkler addressed himself to the methodological issue with the kind of directness that classicists should use far more often (Winkler, 1989, 102):

> But the larger methodological issue is whether readers should simply be trying to reproduce the author's meaning (if he had one— that is, if he had *one*) as the goal. Should we concede that much authority to the writers we read? If our critical faculties are placed solely in the service of recovering and reanimating an author's meaning, then we have already committed ourselves to the premises and protocols of the past—past structures of cultural violence and their descendants in the bedrooms and mean streets of the present. This above all we must not do.

Several issues are lumped together here that need to be differentiated from one another. Recovering an author's meaning or, more broadly, the historical and social context or "horizon" is an essential task for the critic. Trying to read a work in the light of its time has nothing to do with subscribing to its values. The confusion is a common one among modern critics who "insist that interpretation is a value-making event, not a passive mimesis of values that are there" (Lentricchia 345). In fact, however, the attempt to reinterpret an Greek novel in a politically correct way, as Winkler proceeds to do in this instance, ultimately produces the ironic result of making it less objectionable to modern sensibilities. The creative ahistorical interpreter simply winds up practicing a more sophisticated kind of bowdlerization. Historicism, in short, is essential for dealing with the alterity of literature from other cultures and other times.

A final issue that needs to be taken up under the rubric of historicism is one that has produced the closest thing to a stated methodological controversy we have recently had in the scholarly criticism of Roman poetry. It centers on the degree to which the Roman poets shaped their creations on the basis of either literary precepts, rules of genre, and the preceding poetic tradition or on the basis of experience and inspiration from the social, cultural, and material world in which they lived, or both. It is not a new question because it sums up much of the aesthetic and scholarly interpretation of Roman poetry since the beginning of classical scholarship, which coincided with the Romantic period (cf. James Zetzel's essay), but it was answered concretely—and, in the view of his critics, one-sidedly—by Francis Cairns in 1972 in his *Generic Composition in Greek and Roman Poetry*. "The theory which underlies this book," Cairns wrote, "is that the whole of classical poetry is written in accordance with sets of rules of the various genres, rules which can be discovered by a study of the surviving literature itself and of the ancient rhetorical handbooks dealing with this subject," primarily Menander Rhetor and Pseudo-Menander Rhetor of the third century A.D. whose star now began to shine more brightly than ever on the interpretive horizon. Accordingly, "the poems of classical antiquity are not internally complete, but they are members of classes of literature known in antiquity as *gene* or *eide*, which will be described in this book as genres."

One of the merits of Cairns' book was to push Latinists in the direction of methodological reflection. And it may be more than a striking coincidence that it was published at the very time when literary theorists outside of classics were debating the same issue in their own way. Harold Bloom's *The Anxiety of Influence: A Theory of Poetry* appeared in the following year and its "unspoken assumption is that poetic identity is somehow a wholly intraliterary process in no contact with the larger extraliterary processes that shape human identity" (Lentricchia 326), a remarkably apt characterization for Cairns' study of poetic influence, too, despite the particular differences between his work and Bloom's. Cairns has, in the meantime, made it clear (cf. his essay in the present volume) that he is anything but blind to such extraliterary processes, but it is a matter of degree of emphasis. Responding directly to Cairns, Jasper Griffin, in several meticulously documented articles, stressed the importance of the Roman poets' contemporary milieu, to be accused, in turn, by Richard Thomas of "turning back the clock" to an uncritical romantic and biographic mode of interpretation. There are some exaggerated aspects to this discussion, as in any academic debate, in order to sharpen the point, if not the dagger; most Latinists actually are fully aware of and appreciate the complexity of the relationship between these two aspects, which is perhaps the most unique feature of Roman poetry. It appears prominently, therefore, in several of the essays in this collection and includes the attempt by Conte and Cairns to go beyond mere formalism in the definition of genre by discussing "genres of content."

4. *Resistance to theory*

The resistance of classical philology to current theory follows the same pattern that we saw in its adherence, at least in the area of Roman poetry, to the interpretive strategies of the New Criticism: it is practiced rather than articulated. Instead of being a superficial phenomenon, however, it has historical roots that connect easily with the main objections which are made by non-classicist critics to modern theory today. The subject deserves a fuller treatment than I can provide here and, in order to keep the discussion as concise and focused as possible, I will summarize it under several headings.

1) *Anti-methodism*. While classical philology may have been synonymous with hermeneutics in the early 19th century, it developed a strong anti-methodist tendency in the following decades (cf. Peradotto). Wilamowitz' disparagement, cited above (p. 6), of the "philological method" is typical and has its counterpart in Housman's pronouncement that "knowledge is good, method is good, but one thing beyond all others is necessary; and that is to have a head, not a pumpkin, on your shoulders, and brains, not a pudding, in your head."[23] It is understood, of course, that it is always the other fellow who has got the pumpkin on his shoulders and the pudding in his head. Underlying such statements is the recognition, as we saw earlier, that there is an element of subjective judgment in any critical activity, whether it involves the editing of a text or a literary interpretation. The elevation of the principle of subjectivism *über alles* on the part of the deconstructionists and pragmatists can therefore be viewed either as the triumph of utter honesty in the face of aporiai and other "undecidables" or as a *reductio ad absurdum*. While many classicists may never read the various arguments and articles supporting Knapp's and Michaels' *Against Theory*, their *anima naturaliter antimethodica* would no

---

[23] For full citation see Zetzel's essay (p. 42 below).

doubt be greatly in agreement with the sentiments expressed there. So would they with the following warning by Roland Barthes:[24]

> Some speak greedily and urgently about method. It never seems rigorous or formal enough to them. Method becomes Law, but as this Law is deprived of any effect that would be outside of itself. . . it always falls short. As a result, a work that unceasingly declares its will-to-methodology always becomes sterile in the end. Everything takes place inside the method, nothing is left to the "writing". . . the searcher repeats that his text will be methodological, but this text never arrives. There is nothing more sure to kill research and sweep it off into the leftovers of abandoned works, nothing more sure, than method. At some point, one has to turn against method, or at least to treat it without any founding privilege.

This warning against method for its own sake can easily become an excuse for evading any method altogether.

2) *The anti-humanism of modern theory.* This concern is by no means the residual defense of nostalgic, mulish classicists who are loath to be drawn into the intricacies of deep structure. Instead, it is a pervasive theme in critiques of modern theory, many of them coming from critics who are not traditionalists. Harold Bloom speaks of "the anti-humanistic plain dreariness of all these developments in European criticism" (pp. 12-13) and Tzvetan Todorov concludes his pithy travelogue through American criticism with the comment that it is "dominated by what we may as well call by its rightful name, antihumanism" (p. 190). The road that he thinks should be taken is "the one indicated by Scholes" which "might be called critical humanism" (*ibid.*).

At the center of this objection lie the scientific trappings and impenetrable lingo of much of contemporary theory.[25] If we set the clock back by a century, we find precisely those characteristics, with the concomitant professional overspecialization, applying to classical philology and, over the next few decades, vastly contributing to the reduction of the role it once held in

---

24   *Tel Quel* 47 (1971) 9f. in the translation of Harari 10.
25   Eagleton notes similar tendencies in the genesis of the New Criticism: "Its battery of critical instruments was a way of competing with the hard sciences on their own terms, in a society where such science was the dominant criterion of knowledge" (p. 50). We should be aware of this historical commonality of hard-core classical philology, the New Criticism, and modern theory.

education. As in modern theory, means became ends. The elaborate apparatuses that were designed for the study of texts became more important than the study of the texts themselves, all in an effort to be as scientific as the emerging sciences that began to claim their place in the curriculum. Roman comedy, for instance, was subjected to a rigorous scientific, line-by-line inspection in terms of "Greek" and "Roman" elements, criteria that were in themselves defined with a great deal of subjectivity. While comedy rarely becomes funnier through scholarly discussions anyway, scholars like Leo and Jachmann virtually destroyed its literary existence, something that could have been avoided if they had taken Richard Heinze's advice and looked, for instance, at its reception in the later literatures.

This self-induced narrowness, resulting from a confusion of means and ends, was one of the main contributors to a drastic diminution of the study of classics. Since then, the latter has led a tenuous existence. To risk it once more by repeating the same mistakes through modern theory that were made by autoteleological philology is obviously not a course of action many classicists would seriously contemplate. Quite on the contrary, most American classicists today see their *raison d'être*, and whatever assurance there is of the continued viability of the discipline, precisely in raising "questions of more general significance about literature" which their 19th century predecessors did not do (Graff, 1987, 35). The harmful experience with solipsistic philology has taught us not to retreat again, to use Said's words, from our "constituency, the citizens of modern society," which is what entropic modern criticism has done (Said 4). Humanistic outreach, and not theory, is the road to survival (see, however, Marilyn Skinner's remarks for a somewhat different perspective). The result is that most American classicists, just like postmodern classicizing architects, are idiosyncratic practitioners, a characteristic that reinforces the tendency toward empiricism and free-style eclecticism in preference to any theory.

This is related to the strongest sociological determinant of American classics departments. Most departments are small—three to eight faculty members—and therefore cannot afford a theorist, especially one who teaches only theory as their counterparts in English departments have become accustomed to doing. Critics like Graff and have correctly equated the growth of the theory industry with the triumph of excessive professionalization that is endemic to American academic bureaucracies. In contrast, the tendency of some of the larger classics programs in the U.S. has been to put Humpty Dumpty together again and make classics an integrated study of literature, language, history, art, archaeology, philosophy, law, linguistics, and religion and to encourage their faculty to teach across these lines. The late Bartlett Giamatti held such classics programs up as a model for the humanities in general.[26] Whereas such models fill an intrinsic need and are the organic result of academic content, the establishment of autonomous theory programs is increasingly perceived as the result of artifical academic job creation, leading only to further fragmentation of a discipline. It is ironic, in view of the Marxist orientation of so many of these theoreticians, that they are conforming to Walter Benjamin's observation "that in capitalist culture, the desire for novelty becomes recurrent in both senses of the word: 'Fashion is the eternal return of the new'."[27] More fundamentally, the interdisciplinary orientation of modern American classicists stands in stark contrast with the hermeticism of many modern American theoreticians. Under these circumstances, calls to broaden the classical discipline and revitalize it by engaging in a dialogue with modern literary theory can take on all of the force of an oxymoron (I need to reemphasize that not all these views coincide with my own: I am simply trying to explain why the classical *résistance*, and especially that of Latinists, is not merely capricious).

3) *Respect for text and author*. Modern American theorists are products of the U.S. educational system: rarely do they master a foreign language. Perhaps that is why they have invented their own. By contrast, not in the least by virtue of having to be expert in two demanding foreign languages, classicists come from a tradition which is attentive to language and the way authors use it. Even the aberrations of this tradition, such as the "scientific" philology of the late 19th and early 20th centuries, are excesses of this concern rather than invalidations of it. While believing in interpretive freedom, classicists will be wary of the free-for-all of *langue* and *parole* and side with the truisms of Scholes that "this freedom . . . is most certainly constrained by language" (p. 154) and Eagleton that "it is an academicist delusion to see the literary work as an arena of infinite possibility which escapes it" (pp. 87f.). Or, to give another example, the following critique of *interpretationes modernae* might easily have been written by a classicist:

---

[26]　　*The University and the Public Interest* (New York 1981) 58. For further context, cf. my remarks on "Rome, America, and the American Classics Profession Today" in *Classical and Modern Interactions*, ch. 6.
[27]　　Brook Thomas (note 20, above) 187 with reference to W. Benjamin, *Gesammelte Schriften* 1.2 (Frankfurt 1972) 677.

Interpretation in our time, however, is even more complex. For the contemporary zeal for the project of interpretation is often prompted not by piety toward the troublesome text (which may conceal an aggression), but by an open aggressiveness, an overt contempt for appearances. The old style of interpretation was insistent, but respectful; it erected another meaning on top of the literal one. The modern style of interpretation excavates, and as it excavates, destroys; it digs "behind" the text, to find a sub-text which is the true one.

Instead, these observations are those of Susan Sontag (p. 6). In due course, there came the empowerment of the critic at the expense of the author—a displacement, as we noted earlier, into the realm of theory, of the power academics could not attain in the real world. Besides the more clamorous assertions of Stanley Fish to which I already have adverted, Harold Bloom's concept of a poet's relation to his precursor as "the anxiety of influence" provides an interesting illustration. Arguing that one way for the later poets —all of whom Bloom makes out to be fairly neurotic about this—to cope with this burden of the past is to engage in a deliberate misreading or even misprision of their predecessors' work, Bloom then demands at least equal status for the interpreter: "Your work as an event is no more or less privileged than the later poet's event of misprision in regard to the earlier poet. Therefore the relation of the earlier poet to the later poet is exactly analogous to the relation of the later poet to yourself" (Bloom, 1975, 58). It is anything but that, of course (see Lentricchia 338f.). The different perspective of scholars of Roman poetry on the issue of poetic influence and Roman attitudes (cf. Section 5) to it has by and large protected them from such misconceptions.

Then again, in some cases it may just be a matter of not thinking things through. With respect for language, its manipulation and its nuances comes respect for the author. It leads, confusedly enough, to an identification with authorial intent of even the most (*de facto*) deconstructionist readings of Roman poetry, especially Vergil's *oeuvre*. Literary critics, and not just classicists, are fortunate to deal mostly with the works of authors who are long deceased. Living specimens, alas, speak a highly unambiguous language: "It is in the nature of deconstruction" writes John Updike, "to rob literary works of

26   *Karl Galinsky*

their intended content, substituting instead subliminal messages the author did not intend."[28] The process certainly has been observable in the interpretation of authors such as Catullus and Vergil, but, both naively and implicitly, it is still always equated with the poet's intent. The upside has been an absence of authoritarian tendencies such as those exhibited by Barthes (cf. Felperin 203)— with all its conservatism, classics actually has held to attitudes that are far more liberal and tolerant than those of its feuding siblings. The reason is a mix of inertia, laissez-faire, and the genuine flexibility and tolerance that Robert Stern has rightly singled out in his assessment of the classical tradition in architecture.[29] We have avoided, for instance, applying a double standard to our writings and the dead poets': while the recognition that poetry is a special kind of discourse is anything but a new insight (cf. Whatmough), a poem does not simply mean whatever anyone but its author wants it to mean—a standard to which deconstructionists in particular are not known to hold their own pronouncements (cf. Felperin 34f.). The inconsistency, nay, hypocrisy of such an attitude was all too well summed up by Derrida's reproach to John Searle of misconstruing what Derrida meant.

    4) *Enjoy! Enjoy!* Much of what I have outlined in this section is the natural background to Ralph Johnson's "jeremiad" wherein he is asking for a return to the simple joy of reading for pleasure. Readers will determine for themselves, as Marilyn Skinner does, the degree of affinity between his arguments and Barthes' *jouissance*, the "*nouvelle cuisine* of the pleasure of the text," in the ironic definition of a recent critic (Huyssens 38). It is actually a time-honored repast, though Professor Johnson certainly is not lacking for fellow banqueters on the contemporary critical scene.

    They include Susan Sontag who, more than ten years before Barthes formulated his idea of *jouissance* with its sensual connotations, postulated that "in place of a hermeneutics we need an erotics of art" (p. 13). The mimicking of science on the part of modern theorists has met with frequent disapproval because it is inadequate to the task (cf. Crews 1040f.). Todorov expresses his hope "that this forgettable episode of contemporary criticism might be quickly forgotten" and asks for a return of the critic to his proper function, "that of a

28   *New York Times Book Review* (June 10, 1990) 40. Cf., with a great sense of humor, Levin, esp. 500f.

29   *Modern Classicism* (New York 1988) 283: "Classicism offers the architect a canon as a guide, but what a liberal and tolerant canon it is. It proposes models of excellence in composition and detail. It does not set out on a singular route but points out various ways . . . Classicism has flexibility and built-in tolerance." The debate about the classical "canon" in literature should be informed by similar perspectives.

participant in a double dialogue: as a reader, with his author; as author, with his own readers—who in the process might even become somewhat more numerous" (p. 191); Todorov, like Johnson, does not address himself to feminism, something for which Marilyn Skinner's response vigorously tries to make up. At the very least, there is the general realization that the "great classic texts, which continue to repay so richly each historical construction and deconstruction they attract" (Felperin 223) will remain at the center of the changing critical discourse and, for that matter, enjoyment without the paraphernalia and cant of an overprofessionalized, self-serving interpretation industry. The latter also became a focal point of the systematic attack on theory by Stephen Knapp and Walter Benn Michaels in *Critical Inquiry* and in the ensuing, lively discussion which went on for three years (1982-85). Much of this echoes the similar sentiments of classicists as diverse as Joshua Whatmough and the editors of *Arion* against the intrusion of excessive philological method into the enjoyment and understanding of classical literature. The point is not a return to innocence, but this kind of aesthetic reading, as emphasized by Jauss, is a necessary first reading. Sometimes, we may just want to stop there, and at other times, that may not be enough. The answer to this question, too, is a matter of reader response.

5. *Convergences*

The foregoing discussion illustrates, as could expected, that there are indeed "significant common investments" in the interpretation of Roman poetry and modern literary criticism and theory. The answers and methods may be different, but, unsurprisingly, many of the central questions and concerns are the same. They include the range of possible meanings, the search for a greater referentiality than the monadism of poems, the more than positivistic role of historicism, the balance between historical and aesthetic response, and the concern for a humanistic criticism that transcends excessive professionalization. In addition, we have observed some strikingly traditional notions underneath even the most modern garb, such as de Man's affirmation of the "critical reader who . . . takes us closer to the original insight." We can add to it, for instance, Jane Tompkins' statement that a literary text provides "men and women with a means of ordering the world they inhabit"[30] and compare it with C. M. Bowra's dictum that the *Aeneid* "has succeeded in doing something that no epic has done before and since, and helped many generations

[30]   *Sensational Designs: The Cultural Work of American Fiction* (New York 1985) xiii.

of men to formulate their views on the chief problems of existence."[31] I hope
to have made clear, at the same time, that such convergences should not foster
complacency among Latinists that what goes around comes around and that we
can practice our craft by the mere imbibing or osmosis of suitable exemplars
without critical reflection.

Two final, specific examples may illustrate that classicists can usefully
sharpen their reflection on even some of the most traditional topics of Roman
poetry while, conversely, modern literary critics can gain a valuable
perspective from a proper understanding of the special nature, such as it has
been elucidated by Latinists, of these issues as they apply to Roman poets. The
first, to use the well-known phrases of Bate and Bloom, is the burden of the
past or the anxiety of influence.

"Why the Romans," as one modern scholar has remarked so aptly,
"threw themselves into the difficult business of aborbing the culture of one
foreign nation just when they were involved in exhausting wars with another
foreign nation (i.e. Carthage in the 3rd cent. B.C.), remains one of those
puzzles which characterize nations in their most inscrutable and decisive hours
. . . The assimilation of Greek language, manners and beliefs is
indistinguishable from the creation of a national literature which, with all the
imitation of alien models, was immediately original, self-assured and
aggressive."[32] From its beginnings, then, Roman literature, and poetry in
particular, was characterized by the deliberate *imitatio* of Greek models. That
relationship has been studied exhaustively by Latinists in a positivistic way.
Beyond that, however, there is the clear recognition that the Roman poets did
not consider the past literary tradition as a burden but rather as a challenge to
their creativity. The convenient label of *aemulatio* includes some, though by
no means all aspects of this creative concept, which amply merits further
investigation (cf. Woodman and West). Bloom's studies in the English poets
are, at least, a useful foil. Latinists will be intrigued by the classicaly inspired
definitions—such as *clinamen*, *tessera*, and *apophrades*—he uses for various
categories of poetic influence and by his attempts to categorize the
phenomenon, much as some of us do, in terms other than the mere individual
relationship of one poet to the other. In this context, interpreters of Roman
poetry often resort to the notion of genre, which is a prominent topic in
several essays in this volume and a recourse that is not used by Bloom. As will

31   *From Virgil to Milton* (London 1945) 34. That is true from Dante to Joe Paterno; see
Paterno: by the book (New York 1989) 40-46.
32   A. Momigliano, *Alien Wisdom. The Limits of Hellenization* (Cambridge 1975) 17.

be seen, genre has both an inherent elasticity and an even greater one of modern definition, but it usefully mediates between the extremes of framing the question of the poetical tradition in either completely individual or rigorously totalizing terms. That, ultimately, is the road taken by Bloom who defines the relationship in terms of the victimization of the later poet by his predecessors. Poets are "condemned to tradition" and respond with attitudes of hatred and bitterness. The most they can struggle for is "the illusion of a fresh priority." Bloom then proceeds to categorize, with six idiosyncratic classical terms, their attempts to make themselves discontinuous with their predecessors.

Bloom's focus is on the romantic poets—not an inappropriate point of reference, as James Zetzel's essay suggests—and even if his assessment needs to be qualified for the romantic tradition itself, it helps us appreciate yet more the achievements of the Latin poets which we often take for granted. Even though we cannot look into their souls, they dealt with the anxiety of influence successfully in their poetic works. Ovid, for instance, ostensibly did so by ignoring it; instead of anxiety, he displays a playfulness about the poetic tradition which, however, he understands all too well. Not surprisingly, therefore, some of his poetry has been read as poetology (cf. the discussions of von Albrecht and Fantham). That is precisely the kind of reading Bloom uses especially for Satan in *Paradise Lost*. Or, to give another parallel: while Horace is unanxious vis-à-vis his Greek predecessors and urges the Romans to write in that tradition in the *Ars Poetica* and elsewhere,[33] he is quite depressed, in the *Letter to Augustus*, about the Romans' obsessive preference for his Roman precursors. Their appreciation of a poet's merit is proportionate to the length of time he has been dead. New poets like Horace are, in fact, victimized by such attitudes. This is not quite the same intra-poetic problem as discussed by Bloom, but an interesting variant: the burden of the past is inflicted on the poet by his audience. It is another salutary reminder that such an audience exists and needs to be taken into account by literary historians and critics. More generally, scholars of Roman poetry should be cheered by Lentricchia's pronouncement that "Bloom has put forth bold and important ideas which threaten to make the moribund subject of influence the pivot of the most satisfying historicism to appear in modern criticism . . . The ultimate impact of his four books will be to take the subject of influence away

---

[33] See especially *A.P.* 268f.: *vos exemplaria Graeca/nocturna versate manu, versate diurna* and his boast in *C.* 3.30.13f.: *princeps Aeolium carmen ad Italos/deduxisse modos.* For his attitude in *Epist.* 2.1, cf. my extensive discussion in *Atti del Convegno mondiale scientifico su Virgilio* 1 (Milan 1984) 245-49.

from the source-hunters and echo-recorders" and potentially "to reinforce our
most traditional of approaches to literary study" (pp. 325f.). All this is very
apropos for Latinists.

A second topic which is reappearing in modern literary criticism and has
some obvious relevance to Roman poetry is the notion of the moral dimension
of literature. Given the latitude of definition of both morality and its opposite,
a mutual awareness by Latinists and modern critics of their discussions of the
applicability of the concept can only be beneficial for refining it. Conforming
to its construct of the poem as an autonomous entity, the New Criticism
considered the moral dimension as being inherent in the poem itself instead of
depending on either the poet or the reader: "Neither the quality of an author's
mind nor the effect of a poem on the reader's mind should be confused with
the moral quality of the meaning expressed by the poem itself" (Wimsatt 87).
Scholes (p. 14), citing Ricoeur and Fredric Jameson, argues that to find such
meanings is the essential task of the critical reader: ". . . we will have to
restore the judgmental dimension to criticism, not in the trivial sense
(discredited by Frye and others) of ranking literary texts, but in the most
serious sense of questioning the values proffered by the texts we study."
Todorov extends this notion by setting it in contrast with a value-free
empiricism and emphatically concludes his discussion of "Pseudo-Issues and
Real Issues" on this note: "Criticism needs to become aware of the ethical
dimension from which it is inseparable: not to the detriment of empirical
knowledge of facts, but by freeing itself from the illusions of another
empiricism, whatever its nature, that would suffice unto itself. Here, for me,
is where the real issue lies" (p. 181). Accordingly, Conte, in the words of
Charles Segal, "does not empty character or other narrative elements of their
human significance. He is always concerned to bring the semiotic analysis of
literary structure back to the moral significance of the action: the questions of
ideology, values, suffering, and history" (p. 15).

This is all the more appropriate as the moral aspect is central to much of
Roman poetry. The time-honored view in Rome of poetry in particular was
that it existed to inculcate morality. We find a succinct expression of it in
Horace's *Art of Poetry* where the specific area of morals is that of marriage
and marital conduct.[34] Song and poetry, according to Horace, first taught men
"the wisdom to distinguish public from private property, to forbid random

---

[34]   See Griffin 204 and, for the Augustan context and other Horatian poems, my article on
"Augustus' Legislation on Morals and Marriage," *Philologus* 125 (1981) 126-44.

sexual intercourse and impose the laws of marriage" (*A.P.* 396-98). The moral purpose of poetry was recognized as perfectly legitimate in Greece and Rome, although the result did not have to be overt moralizing. The basic fact is that "the Augustan poets found a source of inspiration in reflection on moral ideals, and some of their greatest poetry takes its origin from it" (Williams 578). I am not contending that their idea of morality in poetry is identical to that of the modern critics, but there is a great deal of common ground we can explore fruitfully.

6. *Some conclusions and challenges*

Several conclusions have emerged in the course of this survey concerning the desiderata and *agenda* for the literary criticism of Roman poetry today especially in America. For the sake of avoiding the genre of overt didacticism, a brief summary of the main issues will suffice.

1) While, as Thomas Habinek points out in his essay, Latinists may have been the stepchildren of the American classics profession, that situation makes it all the more imperative that they clearly state their methodological principles and procedures. What LaCapra says about historiography (p. 12) is applicable to the interpretation of Roman poetry, too: "Historiography that turns away from critical reflection . . . is not a craft. It is little more than a pampered profession." It is also an intellectually lazy one. Misguided and excessive as it often may be, the current intellectual debate about theory has raised fundamental issues that beg for the responsible and distinctive participation of classicists.

2) That does not mean that theory has to be embraced for the sake of theory and means should be converted into ends. Latinists need not follow the poststructuralists in particular on the road to inconsequentiality, trivialization of both research and criticism, and hermeticism. The very fact that ancient poets, and especially Roman poets deliberately reworking Greek models, are meticulously attentive to language flies in the face of current critical pronouncements about poetic language, the limits of its intentionality and meaning, and such voices need to be heard.

3) Interpreters of Roman poetry, while being able to learn much from the current discussion, are excellently equipped to overcome some of the major shortcomings of the current practice of literary theory and criticism. Again, I can limit myself to just a few illustrations.

First, classics in the U.S. increasingly is regaining its interdisciplinary orientation and with it the basis for the kind of dialogue some modern theorists had in mind at least initially. The search for this wider referentiality, as we have seen, was a reaction against the purely intraliterary tendencies of the New Criticism, but the reaction often ended up with even greater isolationism or meaningless, totalitarian theorizing. In contrast, on the current scene of self-imposed and bureaucratic compartmentalization in the humanities, classics departments provide a more congenial context than many others for cultural poetics and criticism. They can do a great deal, for instance, to break down the false dichotomy between aesthetic and historical criticism.

Second, as Said, Graff, Eagleton, and a host of others have noted, the current practice of theory has little to do with the study of literature, but is primarily a sociological phenomenon in the American context. It is yet another dubious triumph of academe's endemic tendency to professionalization and, for that matter, solipsism to whose pursuit some of its denizens have been known to devote a lifetime. Said's acute comments (p. 4) in particular deserve to quoted in full because they also are a suitable backdrop for Ralph Johnson's spirited plea:

> But it is no accident that the emergence of so narrowly defined a philosophy of pure textuality and critical noninterference has coincided with the ascent of Reaganism, or for that matter with a new cold war, increased militarism and defense spending, and a massive turn to the right on matters touching the economy, social services, and organized labor. In having given up the world entirely for the aporias and unthinkable paradoxes of a text, contemporary criticism has retreated from its constituency, the citizens of modern society, who have been left to the hands of the "free" market forces, multinational corporations, the manipulation of consumer appetites. A precious jargon has grown up, and its formidable complexities obscure the social realities that, strange as it may seem, encourage a scholarship of "modes of excellence" very far from daily life in the age of declining American power.

In contrast, the damage suffered by the interpretation of Roman poetry has consisted largely of the matrix of the Vietnam war being imposed on the wars of Aeneas in Italy. All these, however, are salutary reminders of the historicity of literary theory and interpretation, much as modern theorists have been trying to escape it.

Thirdly, therefore, Latinists and classicists have a splendid opportunity to transcend such entropy and write for an audience other than themselves and professional theoreticians, i.e. precisely for "the citizens of modern society." In so doing, they need not lapse into anachronisms and make the ancient world over in our image (cf. Habinek's comments on such tendencies in the 19th century). Writing about Roman poetry with modern sensibilities requires a clear definition and awareness of various "horizons of expectation" as Charles Segal well demonstrates in his paper and the ensuing discussion. For classics, this outreach function is a matter of survival. The good news is that the demand for it certainly is there and is likely to increase if English departments become mere theoretical affiliates and the students who want to learn about authors, read literature, study and enjoy texts will turn elsewhere. Again, this should be an occasion not for complacency but for practicing our craft as responsibly and creatively as we can.

7. The contributions to this volume

I have already referred, at appropriate junctures in this introductory overview, to the various essays in this collection and therefore can limit myself to outlining their central arguments. In their diversity of perspectives and pluralism of method they are typical of current interpretive work on Roman poetry. They are atypical, however, in their reflection on method and, for the most part, in their concomitant familiarity with modern theoretical movements.[35] Some are more specific than others about textual application. Overall, they are a representative example of where the interpretation of Roman poetry is at today, and many of the contributors suggest some desirable directions for future work.

In his opening essay, James Zetzel raises several hermeneutic issues, such as the avoidance of "the high priori road" (following R.S. Crane). He speaks for most Latinists when he stresses that "theory must arise from the text, not be imposed on it," and he proceeds to discuss extra- and intraliterary considerations—a complex of critical issues that has been with us since the Romantic period or, more correctly, the literary criticism of the Romantic period which Zetzel uses as a point of reference throughout, just as many contemporary critics do. He also comments on the role of historical

[35] The contrast is instructive with a fine collection of essays on Roman poetry that appeared only sixteen years ago (T. Woodman and D. West, eds., *Quality and Pleasure in Latin Poetry* [Cambridge 1974]) and affirmed "no specific knowledge in the recent history of literary criticism" (p. 129).

understanding, poetological readings, und he uses Catullus' poem 34 as a specific illustration.

In his animated repartee, Peter Wiseman plays the historian, returns to a discussion of Catullus 34, and refines the relationship between "romantic," biographical and historical aspects on the one hand and intrinsically "literary" ones on the other. The question ultimately turns, as is is so often the case in literary criticism, on the privileging of one hypothesis over the other, although we are not left with a sense of aporia.

With Francis Cairns' essay on Propertius 4.9 we enter into the current controversy over genre, its definition, and boundaries. Written by the leading exponent of the generic approach to Roman poetry, his paper is an erudite tour de force. The underlying question is to what extent the multiplicity of associations and inspirations, which is so typical of much of Roman poetry, can be accommodated to such generic definitions. In his response, therefore, William Anderson accentuates the problematic nature of the concept of "genre of content." Given the phenomenon of a thousand points of contact and the varying degrees to which they are compelling, how many topoi does it take to make a genre? Anderson also discusses the interaction between extraliterary factors, such as Roman cult and topography, and the poetic tradition that is being utilized.

The discussion of genre is further refined by Gian Biagio Conte and set in the context of empiricism, hermeneutics, and semiotic theory. Conte emphasizes that genres are more than a taxonomical convenience. Instead, consciousness of genre informs the horizon of expectations of both author and reader. Conte's discussion is refreshing for its lack of dogmatism and his incorporation of the requisite historical perspective as he seeks out "the cultural project of the author and at the same time the expectations of his addressees." Jasper Griffin in his reply differentiates between stylistic levels and genres. He cautions against overemphasis on genre in current criticism; I might add that its definitions are rather broad even in ancient literary criticism. The strict definition of epic, for instance, operates in purely formal terms, i.e. any hexametric poetry is epic, including the *Idylls* of Theocritus and Vergil's *Eclogues*. Content is wide open: "Epic," writes Theophrastus, "is the encompassment of divine, heroic, and human affairs."[36] Even Callimachus' famed *Aitia* prologue most likely does not define epic, but elegy, as Alan

[36] Theophrastus as cited by Diomedes grammaticus I.483, 27ff.; see the detailed discussion by Koster 86ff. Hirsch, 1967, 68-126 also has a useful discussion of "The Concept of Genre."

Cameron makes plausible in a forthcoming book. Another important consideration is that genres were not static but evolved.

I cited Charles Segal's essay earlier as a paradigm of the successful application of modern concepts to an ancient poem. His judicious employment of the notion of "boundary anxiety" to Lucretius illuminates many important aspects of the text and does not stumble into anachronisms. In fact, Frederick Ahl in his response extends the range of legitimate applications to other poets and correctly perceives this characteristic to be one of the major reasons for their richness and polyphony (a term used already in ancient Homeric criticism). Accordingly, the resulting discussion was extraordinarily productive and methodologically focused and most of it is therefore included in a slightly edited version.

Ovidian criticism, especially as it pertains to the *Metamorphoses*, has freed itself in recent years of previous, more schematic modes of interpretation and therefore is a particularly good example of the current pluralism and diversity. Michael von Albrecht presents a critical survey of the major scholarly and interpretive trends and outlines some desiderata. Ovidian criticism can still be enriched by a great range of procedures, including "traditional" studies of style and the composition of individual books. The impulse for the latter, as von Albrecht points out, comes from a development in the history of the reception of the *Metamorphoses* in illustrated editions. With its authorially intentional polyphonality the poem also is eminently suitable for reader response criticism and Iser's concept of "the implied reader." Elaine Fantham extends the argument by referring to narratology and scrutinizing the validity of poetological readings especially with regard to Ovid's rendition of the myth of the poet-singer Orpheus.

The last three contributions enlarge the critical panorama and address themselves to some larger issues rather than specific Latin poets or texts. As we have seen, Ralph Johnson's lively plea for an enjoyment of poetry that is unencumbered by theory lacks neither a considerable tradition nor contemporary analogues. Marilyn Skinner responds by emphasizing the role of theory as an ontological commitment, in this case feminism. She relates this to some concerns about the American classics profession in general,[37] a perspective which recurs, with a stricter Latinist focus, in Thomas Habinek's analysis of the role of Latin (as opposed to Greek) studies from the time of the

---

[37]   For a somewhat different perspective see my article "Classics beyond Crisis" in *CW* 84 (1991) 441-53 and *Classical and Modern Interactions,* ch. 6.

founding father of academic classics in the U.S., Basil Gildersleeve. Habinek concludes that, for a variety of historical and sociological reasons, the study of Roman literature has been considered inferior to that of Greek and has never been as pronounced. I would add that this very fact, in view of our increasing awareness of the historicity of interpretive trends, presents literary critics of Roman poetry with more genuine opportunities, choices, and challenges than exist for our counterparts in many other literatures. There is still incomparably much to be done, and the vitality of the study of Roman poetry will depend solely on our response.

BIBLIOGRAPHY

Abrams, M.H., "How to Do Things with Texts," *Partisan Review* 46 (1979) 566-86

_____, *Theories of Criticism: Essays in Literature and Art* (Washington 1984)

_____, "Audience-Oriented Criticism," *Arethusa* 19.2 (1986)

Barner, W., "Neuphilologische Rezeptionsforschung und die Möglichkeiten der Klassischen Philologie," *Poetica* 9 (1977) 499-521

Barthes, R., *The Pleasure of the Text* (New York 1975)

Bate, W.J., *The Burden of the Past and the English Poet* (Cambridge, MA 1970)

Belsey, C., *Critical Practice* (London 1980)

Bloom, H., *The Anxiety of Influence: A Theory of Poetry* (New York 1973)

_____, *Kabbalah and Criticism* (New York 1975)

Boeckh, A., *Encyklopädie und Methodologie der Philologischen Wissenschaften*, ed. by E. Bratuschek, 2nd ed. by R. Klussmann (Leipzig 1886)

Booth, W.C., *Critical Understanding. The Powers and Limits of Pluralism* (Chicago 1979)

Cairns, F., *Generic Composition in Greek and Roman Poetry* (Edinburgh 1972)

Conte, G.B., *The Rhetoric of Imitation. Genre and Poetic Memory in Virgil and Other Latin Poets*, ed. by C. Segal (Ithaca 1986)

Crane, R.S., *The Idea of the Humanities and Other Essays Critical and Historical* 2 (Chicago 1967)

Crews, F., "Literary Criticism," *Encyclopedia Britannica*, 15th ed. (1978), vol. 10.1037-1041

de Man, P., *Blindness and Insight: Essays in the Rhetoric of Contemporary Criticism* (New York 1971)

Eagleton, T., *Literary Theory* (Minneapolis 1983)

Felperin, H., *Beyond Deconstruction. The Uses and Abuses of Literary Theory* (Oxford 1985)

Fish, S., "Literature in the Reader: Affective Stylistics," in *Self-Consuming Artifacts* (Berkeley 1972)

___, *Is There a Text in this Class?* (Cambridge, MA 1980)

Galinsky, K., *Classical and Modern Interactions* (Austin and London 1992)

Gentili, B., *Poetry and its Public in Ancient Greece* (Baltimore 1988)

Graff, G., "Fear and Trembling at Yale," *The American Scholar* 46 (1977) 467-78

_____, *Professing Literature. An Institutional History* (Chicago 1987)

Green, P., *Classical Bearings* (London 1989)

Griffin, J., *Latin Poets and Roman Life* (London 1985)

Harari, J.V., ed., *Textual Strategies. Perspectives in Post-Structuralist Criticism* (Ithaca 1979)

Harvey, D., *The Condition of Postmodernity* (Oxford 1989)

Heinze, R., "Die gegenwärtigen Aufgaben der römischen Literaturgeschichte," *Neue Jahrbücher für Antike und Deutsche Bildung* 19 (1907) 161-75

Hirsch, E.D., *Validity in Interpretation* (New Haven 1967)

_____, *The Aims of Interpretation* (Chicago 1976)

Huyssens, A., "Mapping the Post-Modern," *New German Critique* 33 (1984) 5-52.

Iser, W., *The Implied Reader* (Baltimore 1974)

Jauss, H.R., *Literaturgeschichte als Provokation* (Frankfurt 1970)

_____, "Zur Abgrenzung und Bestimmung einer literarischen Hermeneutik," in M. Fuhrmann, H.R. Jauss, and W. Pannenberg, eds., *Text und Applikation. Theologie, Jurisprudenz und Literaturwissenschaft im hermeneutischen Gespräch* (Munich 1981) 459-81

Jencks, C., *Post-Modernism. The New Classicism in Art and Architecture* (New York 1987)

Konstan, D., "What is New in the New Approaches to Classical Literature?," in P. Culham and L. Edmunds, eds., *Classics. A Discipline and Profession in Crisis?* (Lanham, MD 1989) 45-49

Koster, S., *Antike Epostheorien* (Wiesbaden 1970)

Kresic, S., ed., *Contemporary Literary Hermeneutics and Interpretation of Classical Texts* (Ottawa 1981)

LaCapra, D., *History and Criticism* (Ithaca 1985)

Leach, E.W., *The Rhetoric of Space. Literary and Artistic Representations of Landscape in Republican and Augustan Rome* (Princeton 1988)

Lentricchia, F., *After the New Criticism* (Chicago 1980)

Levin, R., "The Poetics and Politics of Bardicide," *PMLA* 109 (1990) 491-504

Lobsien, E., "Die rezeptionsgeschichtliche These von der Entfaltung des Sinnpotentials (Am Beispiel der Interpretationsgeschichte von James Joyces 'Ulysses')," in H.-D. Weber, ed., *Rezeptionsgeschichte oder Wirkungsästhetik* (Stuttgart 1978) 11-28

Mitchell, W.J.T., ed., *Against Theory. Literary Studies and the New Pragmatism* (Chicago 1985)

Morris, W., *Toward a New Historicism* (Princeton 1972)

Olsen, S.H., *The End of Literary Theory* (Cambridge 1987)

Peradotto, J., "Texts and Unrefracted Facts: Philology, Hermeneutics and Semiotics," *Arethusa* 16 (1983) 15-33

Putnam, M.C.J., *The Poetry of the Aeneid* (Cambridge, MA 1965)

Rosenmeyer, T.G., "Ancient Literary Genres: A Mirage?," *Yearbook of Comparative and General Literature* 34 (1985) 74-84

Said, E.W., *The World, the Text, and the Critic* (Cambridge, MA 1983)

Schmidt, E.A., review of M.C.J. Putnam, *Artifices of Eternity. Horace's Fourth Book of Odes* (Ithaca 1986), in *Gnomon* 60 (1988) 501-505

Schmidt, P.L., "Reception Theory and Classical Scholarship: A Plea for Convergence," in W.M. Calder III *et al.*, eds., *Hypatia. Essays Presented to Hazel E. Barnes* (Boulder 1985) 67-77

Scholes, R., *Textual Power. Literary Theory and the Teaching of English* (New Haven 1985)

Selden, D., "Classics and Contemporary Criticism," *Arion* 3rd ser. 1 (1990) 155-178

Sontag, S., *Against Interpretation and Other Essays* (New York 1961)

Sullivan, J.P., "Synchronic and Diachronic Aspects of Some Related Poems of Martial," in S. Kresic, *Contemporary Literary Hermeneutics* (Ottawa 1981) 215-26

Szondi, P., *Einführung in die literarische Hermeneutik* (Frankfurt 1975)

Thomas, B., "The New Historicism and Other Old-Fashioned Topics," in H.E. Veeser, *The New Historicism* (London 1989) 182-203

Thomas, R.F., "Turning Back the Clock," *Classical Philology* 83 (1988) 54-69

Todorov, T., *Literature and Its Theorists. A Personal View of Twentieth-Century Criticism* (Ithaca 1987)

Tompkins, J.P., ed., *Reader Response Criticism from Formalism to Poststructuralism* (Baltimore 1980)

Veeser, H.E., ed., *The New Historicism* (London 1989)

Whatmough, J., *Poetic, Scientific and Other Forms of Discourse. A New Approach to Greek and Latin Literature* (Berkeley 1956)

Williams, G., *Tradition and Originality in Roman Poetry* (Oxford 1968)

Wimsatt, W.K. and Beardsley, M., *The Verbal Icon* (New York 1958)

Winkler, J.J., *Auctor&Actor. A Narratological Reading of Apuleius' Golden Ass* (Berkeley 1985)

40   *Karl Galinsky*

———, "The Education of Chloe: Hidden Injuries of Sex," in J. Winkler, ed., *Constraints of Desire* : *The Anthropology of Sex and Gender in Ancient Greece* (New York 1989) 101-26

West, D., and Woodman, T., eds., *Creative Imitation and Latin Literature* (Cambridge 1979)

ROMAN ROMANTICISM AND OTHER FABLES

> "Come," said I to my friend, starting
> from a deep reverie,— "let us hasten
> home, or I shall be tempted to make a
> theory—after which there is little hope
> of any man."
>
> Nathaniel Hawthorne, "The Hall of
> Fantasy"

The topic of this volume urges us to consider the dichotomy between hermeneutics and empiricism, or between literary theory and positivism, in the study of Latin poetry. These subjects are problematic, and they demand at the outset some brief acknowledgment of the difficulties posed by the question, before I even attempt to give an answer. It is, in fact, necessary to recognize that the antithesis between theory and positivism is a false one: any decision to avoid theory is itself based on a theoretical stance, namely that the interpretation of a text is somehow self-evident and requires no prior theoretical orientation. Self-evidence, however, is (to me, at any rate) not itself self-evident; and a survey of the interpretations of any text will show that what seems obvious to me now was not self-evident to critics a generation ago, and vice versa. But further qualification is needed: the position that I am now taking—against self-evidence—is itself a theoretical stance, and may not be self-evident to others. In short, the problem of establishing a theoretical basis for theory itself leads to an infinite regression; and that way lies madness or deconstruction. At the very least, it tends to a skeptical crisis with no Cartesian *cogito* to resolve it.[1]

I will not pursue this philosophical question here, as I obviously have no solution. The basic problem, as it relates to the use of theory in literary criticism, was recognized and formulated very clearly more than thirty years ago by a critic to whom I am greatly indebted here, R.S. Crane of the University of Chicago. To put it simply: honesty in literary interpretation

[1]   In keeping with its origins as a lecture, I have kept annotations to a reasonable minimum. I am grateful to Susanna Zetzel for commenting on several drafts of this paper, and for assisting me in problems of eighteenth- and nineteenth-century literature.

requires avoiding aprioristic arguments, what Crane called "the high priori road."[2] This is itself, of course, an *a priori* positivist approach—the *a priori* belief that there is no *a priori* method for choosing or applying literary theory. There is no master algorithm, no meta-theory or hermeneutic rule that solves the problem of theory. I must therefore state now that, in strict logic, everything that I will say here violates the approach I will advocate. This is a paradox familiar to all classicists: all Cretans are liars, saith the Cretan.

Nevertheless, it is worth emphasizing at the outset the fallaciousness of denying theory, and of assuming that positivism or empiricism are themselves somehow value-free. The most memorable statement of this view by a classicist that I know is Housman's, at the end of the lecture on "The Application of Thought to Textual Criticism": "Knowledge is good, method is good, but one thing beyond all others is necessary; and that is to have a head, not a pumpkin, on your shoulders, and brains, not pudding, in your head."[3] But any reader of Housman will realize that he uses trenchancy and vitriol, combined with a specious appeal to common sense, as a disingenuous method for masking his own biases. Far better, I think, is the approach of Boeckh:[4]

Durch die Theorie wird Niemand ein guter Exeget und Kritiker werden, so wenig als man durch die Kenntniss der Logik ein philosophischer Denker wird. Der Werth der Theorie besteht darin, dass sie das, was man sonst bewusstlos treibt, zum Bewusstsein bringt. Das Ziel, wohin Auslegung und Kritik streben, und die Gesichtspunkte, nach welcher sie geleitet werden müssen, schweben demjenigen, welcher die philologische Thätigkeit rein empirisch betreibt, nur dunkel und unvollkommen vor und werden allein durch die Theorie zu wissenschaftlicher Klarheit erhoben. Daher regelt die Theorie die Ausübung der philologischen Thätigkeit; sie schärft den Blick und bewahrt vor Verirrungen, indem sie die Ursachen derselben und die Grenzen der Gewissheit aufzeigt. Durch die Theorie wird also die Philologie erst wirklich zur Kunst, obgleich viele Philologen die blosse empirische Fertigkeit in der Auslegung und Kritik schon als Kunst betrachten; denn auch hier heisst es: πολλοὶ μὲν ναρθηκοφόροι, Βάκχοι δέ γε παῦροι.

---

2   R.S. Crane, "Criticism as Inquiry; or, The Perils of the 'High Priori Road,'" *op. cit.* (in bibliography to Introduction) 25-44. On Crane, see also the discussion of Gerald Graff (cited *ibid.*) 233-40.
3   A.E. Housman, *Selected Prose*, ed. John Carter (Cambridge 1961) 150.
4   *Op. cit.* (in bibliography to Introduction) 76-77.

In general terms, I have very little to add to Boeckh's dictum or to Crane's discussion of the limits of theory: what they say still seems to me valid and to the point. My purpose here is to consider some specific problems within this framework. I will concentrate on Roman poetry of the late Republic and Augustan periods, and try to suggest some grounds for the choice of theoretical approaches to these texts. What particularly interests me here is the applicability of the concept of Romanticism to this poetry; by which I mean, roughly, the idea that the poet is an isolated individual, relying on personal experience and immediate inspiration, whose imagination separates him on the one hand from the constraints of the poetic tradition, and on the other hand casts him in the role of an outcast from, or rebel against, history and society.[5]

The Romantic Fallacy

In a previous discussion of literary patronage, I suggested that what Roman poets in the latter part of the first century B.C. said about patronage in their poems had no necessary relationship to their actual need for, or involvement in, patronage relationships: as they were in fact reasonably well-to-do *equites*, they may have used patronage as a trope for speaking of the literary independence of poets from the social and financial relationships in which they may or may not have had a part.[6] This view has recently been criticized by William Fitzgerald, who believes that I have "elided all the complexities of this gesture in a leap to the modern conception of the autonomy of art."[7] I may then have been unconsciously reflecting Romantic attitudes; but I still believe that, within the context of the poems themselves, these poets do in fact talk about, and even proclaim, the autonomy of art; such an attitude

[5] The description of English Romanticism given here is superficial but not, I hope, wrong in its general outlines. Romanticism is notoriously difficult to define; for a recent discussion, see the introduction to Kenneth R. Johnston et al., *Romantic Revolutions: Criticism and Theory* (Bloomington 1990). I am particularly indebted to three recent works, the use of which should be assumed even when a specific reference is lacking: Marilyn Butler, *Romantics, Rebels and Reactionaries* (Oxford 1981); Stuart Curran, *Poetic Form and British Romanticism* (New York 1986); and Alvin Kernan, *Samuel Johnson and the Impact of Print* (Princeton 1989 [originally published as *Printing Technology, Letters, and Samuel Johnson* (Princeton 1987)]).

[6] James. E. Zetzel, "The Poetics of Patronage in the Late First Century B.C.," *Literary and Artistic Patronage in Ancient Rome,* ed. Barbara K. Gold (Austin 1982) 87-102. For detailed discussion of Horace's equestrian status and its role in his poetry, see David Armstrong, "*Horatius Eques et Scriba*: Satires 1.6 and 2.7," *TAPA* 116 (1986) 255-88.

[7] William Fitzgerald, "Horace, Pleasure and the Text," *Arethusa* 22 (1989) 90-91, note 18.

is to be found in Catullus, in Horace, in Propertius, in Ovid. Given all the differences between English poetry between 1780 and 1850 and Latin poetry between 60 B.C. and A.D. 20—in literary traditions, in social context, in technological circumstances of writing—it is only fair to ask, therefore, in what sense it is legitimate to speak of Roman poets as Romantics.

"Romanticism" is not an uncommon accusation to level against other classical scholars. I did so myself in reviewing Professor Wiseman's *Catullus and his World*,[8] and Professor Cairns did so in *Generic Composition in Greek and Roman Poetry* to criticize those who reject a generic approach to Roman poetry:[9]

> Incredible as it may seem to scholars working in other literatures, there is continued, wide acceptance among persons interested in ancient literature of "Romantic" ideas about poetry; to such persons generic studies are a desecration of their ideas about poetry. Poetry, according to them, should be the beautiful, simple product of individual writers of deep feeling. Generic studies with their emphasis on what is commonplace, sophisticated and intellectual therefore seem to be almost sacrilegious.

I am left with the feeling that we (and I include myself) use "Romantic" without much accuracy, as a rhetorical gesture of dismissal without any very precise definition in mind. Indeed, the oversimplification of Romanticism in such accusations (and I refer exclusively to English Romanticism in this paper) involves an understanding of Romantic poetry that is itself not shared by many of the Romantic poets themselves, but is a product of late Romantic reinterpretations of the 1830s and later. The term was not used in its modern sense until most of the Romantics themselves were dead, and they would not, as recent criticism has shown, have accepted such a label with any degree of comfort.[10] In this context, it might be recalled that "hermeneutics" too is a term which has changed its meaning drastically over the past century or so, and

---

8   T.P. Wiseman, *Catullus and His World* (Cambridge 1985); James E.G. Zetzel, *CP* 83 (1988) 80.
9   Francis Cairns, *Generic Composition in Greek and Roman Poetry* (Edinburgh 1972) 32-33.
10   For the development of modern views of Romanticism in the 1830s, notably through the writings of J.S. Mill and John Keble, see Butler, *Romantics, Rebels and Reactionaries* 7-9, 183-87; Curran, *Poetic Form* 204-9. For a discussion of Wordsworth's *Prelude* as the paradigmatic High Romantic text, see Kernan, *Samuel Johnson* 287-97.

what is now implied or advocated by that term is very different from what it meant to August Boeckh in his lectures in the 1860's.[11]

I will not attempt to define Romanticism precisely here; I use it to refer to a complex of attitudes summarized above, about individual genius and isolation, the poetry of personal experience, and the autonomy of poetic art. And, as I suggested above, the problem with the rejection of a Romantic interpretation of Roman poetry from Catullus to Ovid is that there is a genuinely romantic element in the pose that some of the Roman poets themselves employ. An obvious example is the opening poem of Propertius' *Monobiblos*: here we have a poet stating at the outset of his work that it is Cynthia and passion that govern his every thought, and that they are the origins of his poetry: his elegies are presented as dramatic moments arising from immediate inspiration. So too in the opening poem of his next book, where he says as much in so many words:

Non mihi Calliope, non haec mihi cantat Apollo.
    ingenium nobis ipsa puella facit. (2.1.3-4)

Here, indeed, he goes so far as to reject the traditional divinities attached to the Alexandrian poetic tradition of which he partook.[12] The most famous such poem of passion and personal expression is Catullus 85, "Odi et amo," a poem designed to present the poet as a romantic. So too with the rejection of politics and public life in Catullus and in the elegists. The poet, in all these cases, takes a stance which enhances his own isolation and inspiration; the same is true, I believe, of the language of patronage which I discussed here in 1979. I am not suggesting that the romantic attitude of these texts is to be taken as literal truth, any more than it is in the case of the English Romantics; but it is none the less the case that these poets deliberately choose to refer to themselves in such terms. These texts are, quite clearly, an artful representation of the lack of art, a socially conditioned rejection of society. In terms of the familiar contrast between tradition and originality, or between generic constraint and individual genius, it is worth remembering that one of the most familiar mannerisms of neoteric and Augustan poetry is the proclamation of poetic originality in words and images borrowed from earlier poets. But even if the romanticism of the

---

[11]   For Boeckh's discussion of the term, see *Encyklopädie* 79-93.
[12]   For a fuller discussion of Propertius 2.1, see Zetzel, "Re-creating the Canon: Augustan Poetry and the Alexandrian Past," *Critical Inquiry* 10 (1983) 83-105. Curran in *Poetic Form* offers a similar interpretation of the mixing of genres in Romantic poetry.

poetic rhetoric is not an accurate reflection of the true methods of poetic composition, the dissonance between the surface and the technique ought itself to be significant: we need to ask why the poet *chose* to represent himself in this fashion. It is clearly not enough to look at these poems in purely generic or formal terms, or to concentrate entirely, as some critics of Propertius do, on Alexandrian or Gallan precedents for the first poem of the *Monobiblos*: such an approach is as naive and limiting as taking the surface Romanticism for the whole. It is the relationship between the two that is interesting. A parallel which reveals both the artificiality of the stance of immediate passion and inspiration and its rhetorical power may be found in the work of William Bowles, a poet of the late eighteenth century whose sonnets were praised by Coleridge for their spontaneous expression of emotion. His sequence of sonnets "written chiefly on Picturesque Spots during a Tour" commemorated, according to his own later explanation, his grief at the untimely death of a woman with whom he had been in love. Bowles, a vicar who was to become canon of Salisbury Cathedral, had indeed been in love—but the object of his passion had not died; she had merely rejected him for another man. The goal of the poems is not the expression of grief and mourning; it instead represents a state of mind. As Stuart Curran puts it, "It is not just that his mental reaction to the scenes through which he travels is our focus throughout these poems, but that mental reaction is their only point."[13] If the parallel between Catullus and Propertius on the one hand and Bowles and the younger Coleridge on the other has any validity, it would enable us to find a more precise definition for the attitude embodied in the Roman poets: not romanticism but sensibility. And to that characteristic of this period of Roman poetry I will return later.

If one turns from Catullus and early Propertius to later Augustan texts, the problem is more complex, and I will give only one illustration. Ovid, *Amores* 1.14, proclaims itself as an address to his mistress, simultaneously consoling her for the fact that her hair has fallen out from the excessive application of dye, and gloating because he had in fact warned her of the dangers. He praises at great length her ex-hair, remembers his previous warnings, says that she has only herself to blame, and advises her to buy a German wig. Barsby takes the poem literally, and calls it "heartless";[14] and its surface text is certainly that. The incident is presumably as fictitious as the rest of the *Amores*, but it represents vividly a realistic (if slightly grotesque) scene.

13   Curran, *Poetic Form* 33; see his discussion of Bowles, *ibid.* 32-35. On Bowles as a representative of sensibility, see Butler, *Romantics, Rebels and Reactionaries* 34.
14   J.A. Barsby, *Ovid: Amores Book I* (Oxford 1973) 157.

If one concentrates on literary antecedents and imitations, however, one can construct a completely different reading: the attributes of the hair (*tenuis, doctus*, like a spider web) are those of neoteric/Alexandrian poetry; and when the color of the missing hair is described as that of a cedar tree the bark of which has been peeled off, it may not be too far-fetched to see allusions to the unecological habit of Callimachus' Acontius and his literary epigoni of writing poetry on the bark of trees, and to the cedar as a preservative of books. Seen in this light, the poem is an ironic history of and obituary for neoteric poetics, and a carefully constructed reply to, and parody of, Propertius 1.2 on Cynthia's desire for expensive cosmetics and jewelry.[15] It has nothing at all to do with Corinna or hair. For myself, I am inclined to give more emphasis to reading of Ovid's poem in terms of poetics and Alexandrianism, less to its surface rhetoric; but that choice depends on my sense of Augustan, and particularly of Ovidian, understanding of what the goals and methods of poetry are. The important point, however, is that Ovid accepts the combination of sensibility and *doctrina* in the poetry of the previous generation, and parodies both at the same time. The sensibility sonnets of Bowles and others received precisely the same response from the gothic novelist William Beckford, who pseudonymously published an "Elegiac Sonnet to a Mopstick" which both echoed the traditional form and mocked the emotional subjectivity of his models.[16] In speaking of Ovid's poem, the question of interpretative method is not to decide what theoretical approach or critical attitude should be employed in reading the poem, but rather to consider what theories and attitudes the poet employed in constructing it. As so often, Ovid is one of the best commentators on his predecessors, and his parodies reveal what is only implicit in the objects of his wit. The romantic pose, as he reveals throughout the *Amores* and *Ars*, was an essential element of neoteric and post-neoteric poetry; but one can no more take that as the basis for interpretation than one can be satisfied with sticking on a generic label or simply murmuring *poeta doctus* in a reverent tone. The theory must arise from the text, and not be imposed upon it.

Pick a Theory, Any Theory

How is one to find a proper ground for the interpretation of a given text? The question can not be answered abstractly (at least not by me), and so I

---

15   Neither the metaphorical poetics of *Amores* 1.14 nor its relationship to Propertius 1.2 appears to have been noticed. I hope to discuss this poem in detail elsewhere.
16   See Curran, *Poetic Form* 225-26, note 8.

want to turn to a poem that Professor Wiseman discussed in *Catullus and His World*, and which I discussed in my review of his book, Catullus 34, the hymn to Diana.[17] Professor Wiseman—and I hope that I do not misrepresent him—placed great emphasis on the mention of Delos and on the attribution to Diana of responsibility for crops, and argued that poem 34 was in fact a hymn written for performance at a festival on Delos. I relied on literary and generic arguments, as set out by Norden, to argue that poem 34 is a literary exercise, rather than a genuine hymn, and that no Delian connection can be inferred from the reference to the goddess's birthplace.[18] Since writing that review, I have found in R.S. Crane a lucid statement of the approach I took:[19]

> It would seem therefore that the first business of practical criticism, in dealing with a given work, must be to ask what were the *literary* problems the writer was faced with, why these were problems for him in relation to his overall *literary* task, and what *literary* reasons or justifications may be found for what he actually did in solving them. We can then go on to look for reasons or causes beyond the literary, and we obviously need to do this. But there is always a danger that in concentrating on these without first considering the specifically literary rationale of a literary work, we may come out with explanations or judgments either wholly or partly beside the point . . .

This is, in some ways, an *a priori* judgment, but it is based on what I think is a legitimate recognition that a poem is a different type of utterance from a conversation or an inscription, and that the internal rules of a literary form play an important role in governing its contents and presentation. But I should in fairness point out that Crane himself gives some very strong arguments against criticism which begins from an *a priori* definition of what poetry is or does, and some of his own most valuable work was historical and philological. Crane was a strong advocate of the New Criticism, who became increasingly unhappy with new-critical disregard of historical criticism; neither he nor I would deny the necessity for thorough consideration of historical context in the interpretation of a poetic text.

---

17   Wiseman, *Catullus and His World* 96-99; Zetzel, review 81-82.
18   Eduard Norden, *Agnostos Theos* (4th ed., Darmstadt 1956) 148-50.
19   Crane, *Idea of the Humanities* 2:209.

But even if, to be purely hypothetical about it, Catullus 34 offered explicit reference to performance on Delos; if Catullus had said not that Diana was born at Delos, but was born *here* at Delos, one must ask whether or not there would be grounds for taking Delian performance as the sole or primary basis of interpretation of a literary text in a collection of poems. Does this mean the same thing as "Catullus 34," as it would if it were found on a stone on Mt. Cynthus? In that case it would, of course, tell us something about the society of the *negotiatores* at Delos and about Roman social history and religion; it might give us ideas about the intellectual background or aspirations of Romans in the Greek east; but it would tell us much more about the audience than about the poet or the poem. My own belief, in any case, is that the assumption of immediacy is very questionable, and is essentially a form of Romantic fallacy. It assumes that what looks like a hymn was written as a hymn, that a local setting within the poem must provide the external context for the poem itself; and it disregards both the formal characteristics and the actual context of the poem that we have. There is also a second-order question for texts which combine obvious stylization and formality with particular people, places, and events, a question which Professor Wiseman posed to me, and on the answers to which I think we disagree: why did the poet choose to write it; what are the conditions leading to the existence of *this* hymn, at *this* point, by *this* author? In the case of Catullus 34 (the real, not the hypothetical Delian poem that I have been imagining), I think that the first features that one should notice are the generic conventions, the use of Greek manner and meter—all the material that Norden discussed—and only then should one consider the features that do not fit that analysis. The Delian connection clearly can be explained generically, and I have given arguments in my review for understanding the picture of Diana as grain-goddess in the context of poetic technique. The features, to my mind, that do not fit are not the ones that Professor Wiseman emphasizes, but the more particularly Roman elements: the use of Roman archaisms—perhaps appropriate even in a prayer of Greek form—and the prayer for the salvation of the race of Romulus. Gordon Williams singles out this last element as particularly surprising, and suggests (like Professor Wiseman) that it is a real hymn—but this time part of the aftermath of the disaster at Carrhae.[20] But if the recognition of formal and generic elements, as a first step, leads to seeing the Roman elements as marked, I would still not look for a specific political or historical context in the real

[20]   G.W. Williams, *Figures of Thought in Roman Poetry* (New Haven 1980) 209.

world of Rome; rather, I think that it belongs in the context of other Roman archaisms and references to Romulus in Catullus, the context of Catullus' awareness of a moral and political crisis in his own time, and his frequent transmutation of Alexandrian techniques to fit his own particular poetic goals. Professor Wiseman sees poem 34 as the work of a Roman in Greece; I see it as the importation of Greece into Rome. Where I think that we would agree (at least I hope so) is in seeing the poet as an active agent in transforming whatever he saw and experienced in the world around him, and whatever he read of previous poetry.

As parallel rather than as argument, let me turn again to English poetry. The Romantics too wrote hymns: Canon Bowles the sonneteer wrote a Hymn to Woden, and Southey wrote a hymn to the Penates; and yet the former was not a devotee of Norse gods, nor the latter of Roman.[21] Wordsworth's hymns, as those of other Romantics, tend not to emphasize the religious elements that might be expected in a genuine hymn, but concentrate on the psychological state of the worshiper rather than piety towards the divinity. And the single most famous Romantic hymn, Blake's "Jerusalem," did not actually become a hymn until it was set to music as an anthem for a feminist conference in 1918.[22] Even if Catullus 34 were found in an ancient equivalent of "Hymns Ancient and Modern" that would not mean that its religious aspect was primary in its author's intention.

I realize that I am here committing the intentional fallacy, and I am doing so intentionally, because I do not believe that it is a serious critical problem. In any case, given the assumption—and it is an assumption—of poetic intelligence and control of the text, and given the assumption that we are ultimately interested in the poetry and its composition rather than in using it as evidence for something else, a critic must deal not only with what the historical circumstances are, but how the poet uses them; not with the reconstruction of the psychology and emotions of the poet, but with the depiction of them in the poem; not with what the generic conventions are, but how the poet manipulates them. I quoted Crane on the problem of historical as against literary interpretations, and on the problem of genre I can do no better than to quote Tzvetan Todorov: "The major work creates, in a sense, a new genre and at the same time transgresses the previously valid rules of the genre. . . One might say that every great book establishes the existence of two genres, the reality of

21   See Curran, *Poetic Form* 58-60.
22   Curran, *Poetic Form* 58.

two norms: that of the genre it transgresses, which dominated the preceding literature, and that of the genre it creates."[23] Historical criticism, psychological, and generic criticism have all to focus on the poem as created, not with its preconditions, no matter how important they may be to our ultimate interpretations.

None of these questions is particularly novel; the point is, rather, that they are still questions, and some means of resolving them would be desirable. And yet there is no simple answer. Let me take two more poems of Catullus which are even more familiar than the hymn to Diana. Poem 101, "Multas per gentes . . . ," positively cries out for a romantic interpretation: the bereft poet, at long last at his brother's grave, pours out his spontaneous pain and grief in simple and memorable verses. And yet, as Professor Wiseman suggests in *Catullan Questions*, there is no reason to believe that Catullus ever went there, and there is no clear connection with the Bithynian sojourn of 57.[24] And as Professor Conte has shown in an article to which I am greatly indebted, Catullus' opening lines are drawn from the opening verses of the *Odyssey*.[25] Both historical circumstance and literary model thus alter the grounds of interpretation; one is forced to look at the poem in the context of Catullus' other allusions to Troy and the Trojan War rather than giving primacy to a Romantic reading. And there is yet another layer of allusion in this text, which is revealed by a fragment of Parthenius (SH 626), probably from the elegy for Timander, in which there are references to tears, to being far from home, and to the rocks of Achilles; all of which suggests that Catullus not only made use of Homeric allusions in his poem, but in fact may have modelled it on a particular Hellenistic poem.[26] A thoroughgoing interpretation of Catullus 101 along these lines would require reading it as a pure fiction, a vehicle for the display of allusive learning, but there are no more logical grounds for that than for taking the surface meaning as primary. Just as historical circumstance is used by the poet, so are *doctrina* and genre. Aprioristic theoretical approaches

---

[23] Tzvetan Todorov, *The Poetics of Prose*, tr. R. Howard (Ithaca 1987) 43. I note the similarity of this opinion to that of Samuel Johnson in *Rambler* 125 (quoted by Kernan, *Samuel Johnson* 247): "There is therefore scarcely any species of writing, of which we can tell what is its essence, and what are its constituents; every new genius produces some innovation, which, when invented and approved, subverts the rules which the practice of foregoing authors had established."

[24] T.P. Wiseman, *Catullan Questions* (Leicester 1969) 37.

[25] Gian Biagio Conte, "Memoria dei poeti e arte allusiva," *Strumenti Critici* 16 (1971) 325-33; now in English translation in Conte, *The Rhetoric of Imitation* (Ithaca 1986) 32-39.

[26] On this, see Zetzel, "Fragmentary Pleasures," *CP* 82 (1987) 357.

to Catullus or other poets can supply useful materials for an interpretation; they can not supply that interpretation.

Finally, let me say a few words about Catullus 51, the translation of Sappho. Here too Romantic interpretations have proliferated: Catullus is said to have chosen Sappho's poem as a vehicle for the expression of his own feelings about Lesbia/Clodia; this has led to the absurd rejection of the final stanza on *otium*, as well as to the reconstruction of biographical circumstances for which there is no evidence at all.[27]   But interpretation purely through poetics or Alexandrianism can lead to equal absurdity, emphasizing the postponement of a conjunction, or pointing out that the Sappho poem must have been a standard school text, or dwelling on the Hellenistic antecedents of *otium* in *truphe*, with no consideration of the possible poetic reasons for Catullus' modifications of Sappho. But, to the familiar Alexandrian elements of the poem, one might add another possible allusion: in the phrase *gemina teguntur lumina nocte*, not only the hypallage but the use of *lumina* for "eyes" and *nox* for blindness are unusual in both Latin and (with the equivalents *phaos* and *nyx*) Greek poetry; in fact, the two appear together in only one text, Callimachus' Fifth Hymn, in which they refer to the blinding of Teiresias.[28] One of the most notable features of that scene is that Teiresias, like Catullus in poem 51 (and, of course, Sappho), remains completely silent: "He stood there, unable to speak, for anguish stuck fast his limbs, and helplessness took his voice" (*H.* 5.83f., tr. Bulloch). I need not dwell on the possible ramifications of this allusion, if it is indeed a genuine allusion—that Teiresias gains prophetic power and inner vision in recompense for his blindness, while Catullus, at least in the fictional narrative implicit in his collection, gains poetic power; that Teiresias' sexual transformations, in the more familiar versions of the story if not in Callimachus, have a peculiar relevance to Catullus' translation of Sappho and his general use of sexual imagery. As with poem 101, I suspect, the use of *arte allusiva* as an interpretative device makes sense only if it is subordinated to

---

27   It should be clear that I do not mean to offer here any interpretation of Sappho's own poem, merely of Catullus' reading of the poem.
28   I have found no example earlier than Catullus of *nox* = blindness; for *lumina* = *oculi* (described by W. Ferrari, "Catulls carmen 51," *Catull*, ed. R. Heine, *Wege der Forschung* 308 [Darmstadt 1975] 250 as a "gewählten Ausdruck"). There are only six earlier instances in poetry (Cic., *Arat.* 313; Lucr. 3.364-65; 410; 4.721; 5.778; 6.1211), frequently involving play on words (*lumina luminibus*, Lucr. 3.364) or explanatory glosses. It appears twice in Cicero's speeches (*Dom.* 105, *Har. Resp.* 38), in both cases referring to the blindness of Appius Claudius Caecus and suggesting a context of blindness resulting from profanation of a ritual. For *phaos* and *nyx*, see Callimachus *Hymn* 5.82, 92, with Bulloch's notes (A.W. Bulloch, *Callimachus: The Fifth Hymn* [Cambridge 1985]).

a quasi-Romantic interpretation: that Catullus chooses to represent the development of his poetic passion through the use of learning; that he uses the literary circumstances in which he worked as a method (at one remove) for exploring very personal ideas. In short, I would understand Catullus 51 as the dramatic presentation of what I have called the Romantic reading of the poem, making use of the current theories of Callimachean poetics to create a portrait of a learned poet in the throes of unfamiliar passion. The Romantic reading is there; the Alexandrian reading is there; but both are techniques, they are means rather than ends. The poem itself (and here my own new-critical and formalist bias comes out) is the end.

Intrinsic and Extrinsic Theory

None of what I have said about the interpretation of Catullus, I should imagine, is unfamiliar: the problems posed are standard examination questions and fill innumerable articles. And yet that, precisely, is the point, and it is also the reason that some attention to theory is necessary, even if it does not point the way to a particular theory. Any *a priori* acceptance of a particular approach is inappropriate; no blanket hermeneutic theory is automatically correct; it is merely a hypothesis, of greater or lesser plausibility, and cannot be assumed to be a valid method of interpretation in any specific instance. R.S. Crane—and he is the only critic I know who has done so—quite correctly adduces Sir Karl Popper's theory of the falsifiability of hypotheses as the only reasonable way to deal with theoretical approaches to interpretation: that a privileged hypothesis automatically predetermines the facts by which the hypothesis itself is to be judged, and that unless there is possible evidence that could refute a hypothesis, it has no validity.[29] If we approach a text assuming that there is one key to interpretation, we will ignore or distort any evidence to the contrary, and end in a circular argument. Those who look for "anti-Augustanism" in Augustan poetry sometimes provide illustrations of this kind of reasoning: if a poet is critical of the emperor, then the text is to be taken at its surface value; if he is flattering, then he must be concealing his antipathy. Such readings *may* be true or false—and I think that they are sometimes true; but better arguments are needed to prove them.

Despite this objection, however, it is clear to Crane and to everyone else that one must start with some hypothesis, and the starting-point of criticism, or in training our students, must be not only to recognize the logical problems,

---

[29] Crane, *Idea of the Humanities* 2:245-46; see also Graff, *Professing Literature* 234-36.

but to arrive at some means of finding useful theoretical hypotheses to test in any given situation. And in this endeavor, it is clear to me that historical understanding of what theories are appropriate is necessary; in other words, the theories of literature that are intrinsic to the text, or at least not anachronistic and irrelevant to Rome, should have some bearing on the extrinsic theories that we bring to reading them. Thus, it seems to me that Professor Cairns's emphasis on formal and generic characteristics is a very reasonable one, although I would disagree with him on the extent of its applicability. It is clear that consciousness of poetic form and tradition, and generic considerations in general, were far more important in antiquity than they have been in the past century. Even in Romanticism, as Stuart Curran has shown, considerations of genre are extremely important in understanding poetic practice. And yet, even though I believe that generic criticism is historically the most likely approach to much of Latin poetry, it is not always: and I think that Professor Cairns might agree that he was selective in his choice of texts in *Generic Composition* not only because of the limits of space. Poets decide to use formal categories or not, to follow them closely or not; Catullus in particular experiments with new forms and new relationships, and in a poem (or poems) like 68, with its constant changes of perspective, tone, and even diction, a deconstructionist approach like that of Thomas Hubbard makes more sense than it does for many Latin poems.[30]

My own approach, clearly, is less empiricist (or new-critical) than it is eclectic; and it is also obviously the case that more than one theoretical approach can ask and answer interesting questions about a given text. But I do think that no theory can be employed without also accepting the falsifiability rule of Popper and Crane, and indeed without extending its application somewhat. If our goal is to understand the composition and meaning of a poem, then we must not only show that our interpretation is the least unlikely of possible hypotheses, we must also show that it is one that corresponds to the intrinsic theories of the poets themselves. The poets of the later first century, it is abundantly clear, were as deeply concerned as the Romantics with the process of poetic composition, and with the tension between personal expression and generic and social constraints. This leads, in both cases, to self-conscious meditations on the nature and purpose of poetry, even if it does not mean that such meditations are an end rather than a means. But if one assumes,

---

30   Thomas Hubbard, "Catullus 68: The Text as Self-Demystification," *Arethusa* 17 (1984) 29-49.

as I do, that these poets at any rate knew what they were doing and were in control of their art, then it is the dissonance between circumstance, or genre, or style, and the actual poem that provides the means of interpretation. One needs to find not where a theory is correct, but where it is not: where generic expectations are not fulfilled, where historical circumstance is refracted through the poetic medium, where the poet is Alexandrian in Roman contexts, or simple in learned ones. It might perhaps even be said that in a period such as this—like the later eighteenth century—any poem that does not display theoretical concerns of this type is an anomaly which itself deserves explanation. Aprioristic approaches lead us to explain such things away, but they can also provide the signpost off the high priori road onto the narrow path of criticism. It would be impossible to overestimate either the theoretical problems posed by Alexandrianism in the mid-first century B.C. or the effect of the political and social problems of that period on anyone living in Rome; and it is the conflicts among these areas, and the different resolutions adopted by different poets, that most deserve our attention.

There are a number of features of neoteric poetry that seem new and important. A domestication of subject matter and a taste for natural and homely scenes; a refusal to validate the contemporary social world, and a concomitant search for purity through the evocation of the distant past; a revulsion against sophisticated urban life; the choice of an emotive style; an interest in death. These are by no means the only aspects of neotericism, and they apply equally well to Alexandrian poetry and, perhaps to a lesser degree, to other literature of the 50s—Cicero's major dialogues and Lucretius. What is notable about these descriptions, however, is that I have taken them not from an account of Catullus, but from Marilyn Butler's characterization of English literature in the latter half of the eighteenth century, from Walpole and Ossian to the *Lyrical Ballads*.[31] One could also add to them other features of pre- and early-Romantic English literature: a revived interest, both antiquarian and poetic, in earlier poetic forms and in the elevation of sub-literary genres to literary levels; blending of genres; the conscious manipulation of levels of diction. And, of course, both periods share a concern with the social context of literary production—not least its changing audience—and with its political ramifications.[32]

---

[31] Butler, *Romantics, Rebels and Reactionaries* 16-31.
[32] On genre, see Curran, *Poetic Form*. Kernan, *Samuel Johnson*, provides a detailed and convincing analysis of the effects of print technology on letters in the eighteenth century, leading, as he shows, to many of the developments associated with Romanticism; although

James E.G. Zetzel

This is not to say that the parallel is exact, or that we should interpret the development of Roman poetry in the light of the history of English poetry. Typology is an argument of dubious validity, and yet it has its uses. In particular, like literary theory, typological comparison may perform its greatest service in leading us to ask why, and where, it is not valid. While comparison of the generation of Catullus to the sentimental poets of the pre-Romantic period is often, to my mind, striking, and while one might consider parallels between the political aspects of high Romantic poetry and high Augustan poetry, it might be even more interesting to study the obvious divergences: why neoteric poetics leads toward classicism, while Romantic poetry seems to lead away from it; why Romantic poetry develops continuously, while Roman poetry, apparently silent for a time after the death of Ovid, takes very new directions in the later first century A.D. But to elaborate on this would go beyond both my time-limit and my knowledge.

What I am suggesting here is, I repeat firmly, very tentative and based on very limited knowledge. But the larger point that I want to make on the topic of hermeneutics in the interpretation of Roman poetry has, I think, a validity independent of the merit of this peculiar parallel. Much modern literary criticism is, as recent works have shown, deeply indebted to its Romantic origins; indeed, the teaching of literature in the American university begins in the period of late Romanticism, and has obvious connections with it. From that legacy, which extends at least as far as the recent Cornell-Yale critics, we need to escape.[33] But if we should not impose extrinsic theories on

there is no comparable technological revolution in first-century Rome, it is possible that the expanding audience for literature and the beginnings of both public libraries and a retail market for books may have had somewhat similar effects. It is also relevant that the relative wealth and independence of the Roman poets allowed them to adopt a position that was possible for English poets only as a result of the changing economics of publication in the eighteenth century. Marilyn Butler, writing about the conditions of early Romanticism, offers a description that is surely relevant to Roman poets from the 50s to the 30s B.C.: "For the existing British constitutional arrangements debarred most members of the literary community, whether readers or writers, from a role in the state, yet the unprecedented size and coherence of the market for books gave writers a voice in the national community, in the public sphere, that they had never enjoyed on their own account before. At once endowed with influence and denied power, English writers around 1800 are preoccupied with the topic of external authority and its corruptions" (M. Butler, "Plotting the Revolution: The Political Narratives of Romantic Poetry and Criticism," *Romantic Revolutions*, ed. Johnston et al., 134). It would also be worth considering the parallel between the provincial origins of most Roman writers in this period— on which see Wiseman's discussion of the values of the Transpadani, *Catullus and His World*, 107-15—and the role of the English provinces in the literary revival of the later eighteenth century: see Butler, *Romantics, Rebels and Reactionaries* 31-38.

33   The political tendencies—derived from later Romanticism—of post-war criticism of literature are analyzed by Butler, "Plotting the Revolution," *Romantic Revolutions*, ed. Johnston et al., 133-57; for other analyses of the origins of modern criticism from various

the texts we read, that does not mean that we should not read them with an eye to theory. If it is a mistake in one direction to interpret the Romantic poets Romantically, it is equally wrong to exclude the genuine elements of Romanticism in Rome. We should not be Romantics in reading Roman poets, but we should not exclude the possibility that they were.

points of view, see Graff, *Professing Literature*; Jonathan Arac, *Critical Genealogies* (New York 1987) 11-113; Edward Said, *the World, the Text, and the Critic* (Cambridge, Mass. 1983), particularly 1-30, 158-77. I hope that the emphasis on intrinsic qualities of Roman literature in this paper will not be confused with the new-critical and deconstructionist formalism (itself Romantic in origins) attacked in particular by Butler and Said. By "intrinsic" I mean to suggest theories appropriate to the author and text, including both social and literary contexts of interpretation.

ERRIDGE'S ANSWER
Response to James Zetzel

We must address ourselves first to the question of genre. A colloquium in Texas on hermeneutics and empiricism has got to be a David Lodge screenplay; and since I come on before Jasper Griffin, it is clear that I have the role of Philip Swallow—ingenuously defending traditional praxis to the indulgent amusement and politely concealed contempt of an audience of hard-nosed theorists.

But what is this? Professor Zetzel, whose job it was to play Maurice Zapp, has stolen all the Swallovian lines himself and used them in his own performance—referring to his own theoretical naiveté; claiming not to understand the meaning of critical terms; committing the intentional fallacy and boasting of it; even asking, as no true theorist could ever ask, how one is to find "a proper ground for the interpretation of a given text;" as if there could be a *proper* ground in an infinite plurality of meanings!

This treachery has forced me back to a position that I had hoped to be able to avoid occupying, since it involves me in a somewhat humiliating confession. The truth is that I have always found abstract nouns difficult; and since the discourse of critical theory consists very largely of abstraction and metaphor, much of it is simply impenetrable to me. I have tried. As a historian, I have done my best to come to terms with the different strategies of narrative, to explore the common ground of fiction and historiography, and that has involved me in reading a certain amount of advanced critical theory. And I have to report that some of the authorities who are most highly regarded have proved, for me, the least intelligible.[1] I infer, without irony, that the

---

[1]   I am thinking of Hayden White, *The Content of the Form: Narrative Discourse and Historical Representation* (Baltimore 1987), and to a lesser extent Dominick LaCapra, *History and Criticism* (Ithaca 1985). But my favorite examples come from other authors: (1) Albert Cook, *History/Writing* (Cambridge 1988) 7: "The algorithm of the slash in my title, *History/Writing*, is open to several interpretations, but the activity upon which it is meant to converge is not, or not finally, to be replotted. The term "event" has been based on an assumption that this is the case, in old-fashioned relativism on the "history" side, and in new-style semi-structuralism on the side of "writing." Mediately it would be so, and the *Dinge an sich* of "events" cannot be separated from the act of writing, or fused with it either. "Events" and "writing" would both, and paradoxically, have to engage the attention before the two could be provisionally rejoined." (2) Barbara Foley, *Telling the Truth: the Theory and Practice of Documentary Fiction* (Ithaca 1986) 227f: "In one sense, of course, the modernist text's empyrean positioning of a transcendental subject simply signifies an increased implication in the

fault is mine: these authors are evidently saying something important which I cannot pick up.

Faced with the competing "isms" of modern critical theory,[2] I drop the role of Philip Swallow and assume for a moment that of Lord Erridge, in Anthony Powell's *Dance to the Music of Time*. Erridge is an English peer of vaguely left-wing sympathies who goes to do his bit in the Spanish civil war and returns ingloriously, having narrowly escaped being arrested by his own side. The narrator discusses him with a Marxist friend, J.G. Quiggin.[3] Quiggin speaks first:

"If you can't tell the difference between a Trotskyite-Communist, an Anarcho-Syndicalist and a properly paid-up Party Member, you had better keep away from the barricades."

"You had, indeed."

"It's not fair on the workers."

"Certainly not."

Perhaps I had better keep away from colloquia, in case I get arrested.

Approaching the subject through the works of novelists—even comic novelists—is not wholly inappropriate. After all, critical theory, when it is not merely self-reflexive, is largely devoted to the interpretation of fiction. I found it very striking that Professor Zetzel did not find it necessary to excuse, or explain, his reference to "the fictional narrative implicit in (Catullus') collection;" and I wonder a little whether modern critical techniques do not tend to make all genres, ancient and modern, approximate to the condition of the novel. That could be a source of confusion when we try to explore the presence or absence of the author in his own creation.

fetishistic epistemological paradigms that had been fostered by capitalist production in its early phases. In the modernist novel, however, the transcendental subject is fully transcendentalized, for the *res extensa* cannot provide a locus of significance or value in which the *ego cogitans* may meaningfully define itself." (I love the "of course.")

2   Cf. Marjorie Levinson, in Levinson, Butler, McGain and Hamilton, *Rethinking Historicism: Critical Reading in Romantic History* (Oxford 1990), whose approach "sandwiches Romanticism and historicism, conceived as comparable functional responses, between Enlightenment materialism on the one side, and Marx's dialectically historical materialism on the other."

3   Anthony Powell, *Casanova's Chinese Restaurant* (London 1960) 197.

Philip Swallow holds a post (Professor of English at "Brummidge") which is David Lodge's own position, under the thinnest of disguises. Lord Erridge bears exactly the same family relationship to Nick Jenkins, Anthony Powell's narrator, as Lord Longford—a very real English peer with left-wing sympathies—does to Powell himself. Of course it would be absurd to suppose that Philip Swallow just *is* David Lodge, that Nick Jenkins just *is* Anthony Powell. But would it be equally absurd—or would it be absurd in the same way—to suppose that the character whom Catullus the author calls "Catullus" just *is* Catullus the author? The parallel may be too inexact to be helpful; so at this point I drop the novelists and concentrate on Catullus.

When I said at the beginning that I was a historian, I was not making any special point. We are all historians, in that our subject matter consists of survivals from the past. All we have is evidence and argument. The evidence is the survivals—texts and other artefacts—and the argument is the way we make the survivals *mean* something.

Theory, as in Boeckh's definition of hermeneutics that Professor Zetzel quoted, is intended to improve the quality of the argument—and when it does so we must be glad of it, because the evidence is always so fragmentary and intractable. No historical account can ever be more than a provisional hypothesis, and that goes as much for the interpretation of texts as for the interpretation of any other piece of the surviving past.

So I wonder whether it is any less "high priori" to assume that Catullus' implied narrative is fictional than to assume that it is autobiographical. What is the evidence? Well, poem 16 presents Aurelius and Furius evidently assuming that the kiss poems told them something not about an implied narrator but about the author himself.[4] And Ovid, making a serious case to exculpate himself in *Tristia* 2, evidently assumed that his readers understood Catullus' love poetry as a confession of the author's adulteries.[5] St. Augustine wasn't sure whether Apuleius' *Metamorphoses* were a true record or an invention;[6] that should warn us not to be too confident about ancient readers' sophistication when the narrator or the protagonist bears the author's name.

Even sophisticated moderns can shoot themselves in the foot on this question, as Edmund Wilson did when he assumed that Henry Miller's narrator in *Tropic of Cancer* and *Tropic of Capricorn* was an ironic portrait. Miller replied: "The theme is myself . . . if he means the narrator, then it is me . . . I

---

4   Wiseman, *Roman Studies Literary and Historical* (Liverpool 1987) 222-24, cf. 382.
5   *Tristia* 2.427-30: "in quibus ipse suum fassus adulterium est."
6   *Civitas Dei* 18.18: "aut indicavit aut finxit."

am the hero, the book is myself."[7] In the ancient world the concept of fiction was still very little explored, as may be seen from a comment in Lucian's *How to Write History* (ch. 40):

> Homer indeed in general tended towards the mythical in his account of Achilles, yet some nowadays are inclined to believe him; they cite as important evidence of his truthfulness the single fact that he did not write about him during his lifetime: they cannot find any motive for lying.

It seems to me very unlikely that a reading like Edmund Wilson's was even possible. As for Catullus, I still believe what I wrote in 1979:[8]

> The fact that he refers to and addresses by name identifiable historical personages means that, other things being equal, the "Catullus" he refers to and addresses by name should be no less real a figure. Not that we have to believe everything he says about him, but we are not automatically prevented from believing anything at all.

Take poem 101. It may, or it may not, record a real visit by the author to his brother's grave; without external evidence, there is no way of telling. But it surely has the aim of making the reader believe in, or imagine, such a visit. And what difference does the allusion to the *Odyssey* make? The literary model alters the grounds of interpretation, says Professor Zetzel; "one is forced to look at the poem in the context of Catullus' other allusions to Troy rather than giving primacy to a Romantic reading." But perhaps Troy was important to Catullus in this and other poems *because* his brother died there? I do not, of course, assert that as a fact; but I would resist any reading that *forbade* me to believe it.

I come at last to *Catullus and his World*. It is, very conspicuously, a historian's book. I set out to get at Catullus' poetry from the angle of social history—a procedure that was characterized by one American lady

---

[7]   Quoted, with another example from Mary McCarthy, in Wayne Booth, *The Rhetoric of Fiction* (2nd ed., Harmondsworth 1987) 367f.
[8]   *JRS* 69 (1979) 161.

(anonymous, alas) as the approach *a tergo*.[9] The point of entry, as it were (*pace tua fari liceat, dea Cynthia*), is the hymn to Diana, poem 34, the very item on which Professor Zetzel concentrates his fire. I notice that both in his review of the book and in his paper just now he attributes to me the view "that poem 34 was *in fact* (my emphasis) written for performance at a festival on Delos."[10] But I did not say "in fact": my proposal was couched in rather careful language; I refer back to the phrase "poem 34 may well be a real choral ode."[11] These niceties do matter.

It is a hypothesis—a suggested reading, if you prefer that idiom—and I try to justify it by the presentation of evidence and argument. As always, the evidence is fragmentary and haphazard, but what there is of it is enough to show (a) that Delos was a bilingual and bicultural milieu much frequented by Romans of what seems to be Catullus' social background, and (b) that the gods of the island were celebrated in choric competitions, for which hymns were composed by authors whose names sometimes survive on inscriptions—just as Horace's name survives on the inscription recording the *ludi saeculares* of 17 B.C. (*ILS* 5050).

As for the argument, no doubt I was too dense and elliptical (failings into which I know I sometimes fall), so let me make it explicit. We know there were occasions for which choral hymns were composed; we have texts—like Catullus 34—which are *prima facie* choral hymns; so in my view the onus of proof lies with those who say that the texts *cannot* be what they purport to be.

Professor Zetzel cites Ronald Crane on the necessity to consider first "the specifically literary rationale of a literary work;" but why should writing a hymn for a Delos festival not be a "literary task" in Crane's sense? A poem, Professor Zetzel goes on, "is a different type of utterance from a conversation"—that is true enough—"or an inscription." Then what sort of an utterance is a Simonidean epitaph? Does it mean something different when transcribed into a "collected Simonides?" Professor Zetzel poses that very question: since Catullus 34 is a literary text in a collection of poems, does it "mean the same thing . . . as it would if it were found on a stone on Mt. Cynthus?" He doesn't offer an answer, but he clearly means *no*.

My answer would be "not quite, but almost." The very fact that a poem is used, or re-used, in a collection does add another dimension to it, as I tried

---

9   The comment was reported to me at second hand; I thought it was Marilyn Skinner's, but she disclaims it.
10   *CP* 83 (1988) 81.
11   *Catullus and his World* (Cambridge 1985) 96-99, 199.

to illustrate in *Catullus and his World* (though Professor Zetzel rightly complained in his review that on poem 60, at least, I was culpably inexplicit).[12] But how much cross-reference to other themes and ideas in the collection does poem 34 offer? Some, certainly, but not so much as to make one suppose that it was written, or re-written, to *be* part of the collection.

Here again the onus of proof must be properly assigned. In a collection of 116 poems, most of them short, the presumption must be that some (many? most?) had an independent existence before being collected. I see no reason to think that poem 34 is an exception; so yes, with a minor reservation about cross-reference, it *does* mean the same as if it had been found as an inscription on Mt. Cynthus.

Professor Zetzel then goes on to declare that "the assumption of immediacy is very questionable, and is essentially a form of Romantic fallacy . . . it disregards both the formal characteristics and the actual context of the poem that we have." Let me offer a few, brief comments by way of clarification.

First: I do not *assume* immediacy, or anything else; I offer a hypothesis, and I hope there is no Romantic fallacy about that.

Second: the assumption that the poem is a literary exercise is equally "questionable," and I see no *a priori* reason to privilege one hypothesis over the other.

Third: yes indeed, in the collection one does have to take the context into account, and that is what I tried to do in *Catullus and his World*.[13]

Fourth: if the poem had been preserved only on stone, one would equally have to take account of formal characteristics.

And fifth: to call it a "poem" proves nothing either way; a real hymn can be a poem in a collection. There is nothing *special* about literary texts; they just need more careful arguments than most artefacts do if they are to be made sense of.

I have been so eager to take up Professor Zetzel's invitation to discuss poem 34 that I have hardly touched on most of his paper. A great deal of it I agree with; and I entirely share his rejection of Romanticism, if that troublesome abstract noun does indeed denote "the idea that the poet is an isolated individual whose imagination on the one hand separates him from the constraints of poetic tradition, and on the other hand casts him in the role of an

[12] *CP* 83 (1988) 82. I should have made it clear that I think poem 60 was probably written for the collection, in order to provide an allusive closure to the polymetric "Book I."
[13] At p. 148; cf. *Catullan Questions* (Leicester 1969) 13-15 on poems 28-47.

outcast from, or a rebel against, history and society"—or again, "the autonomous artist, the poet independent of the world of time and politics, who creates from his own mind a world of his own." I hope I have never said, or written, anything that suggests such a notion.

If that is Romanticism, Professor Zetzel is right to call it a fable. I must say I find it alarming that the Catullus I tried to recreate in *Catullus and his World* could be mistaken for that fabulous monster. But I think I see how it happens. Professor Zetzel speaks of "the poet who relies on personal experience and immediate inspiration"—as if those two things were indissoluble. But you can use personal experience in your work without necessarily having it pour out in profuse strains of unpremeditated art. And contrariwise, a poet who is a careful and conscious artist in the Callimachean tradition can still be exercising that art on material which has been lived and not just imagined. I repeat: if he uses his own name for the protagonist in the drama, and if his readers—innocent of our type of theory—take it as the report of his own experience, then I think the onus of proof is on those who say it can't be.

That conclusion no doubt makes me an empirico-positivist.[14] So be it, but it is no help to me: like Erridge, I would not know one of those from an anarcho-syndicalist.

---

14   Cf. C. Robert Phillips III, *AJP* 110 (1989) 637 on "the empirico-positivist interpretative strategy which informs much of contemporary classical scholarship" (compared unfavorably with *Wissenschaftsgeschichte*).

PROPERTIUS 4.9: *"HERCULES EXCLUSUS"* AND THE DIMENSIONS OF GENRE

I. *Introduction*

Scholarly treatments of Propertius 4.9 prior to W.S. Anderson's article *"Hercules Exclusus:* Propertius IV, 9" in 1964 were comparatively limited in scope: the elegy was discussed in the main as post-Callimachean aetiology, incorporating and reflecting Augustan literary and political interest in Hercules' mythical visit to Rome.[1] Anderson then highlighted at least two important "generic" dimensions of 4.9, showing: 1) that, in terms of genres of form,[2] Propertius had blended with his epic theme the colors, tones, and concerns of the elegiac genre, principally by assimilating Hercules to the excluded lover of elegy, and 2) that, in doing so, Propertius had exploited a genre of content with strong elegiac and epigrammatic links, the *kômos* (*"paraclausithyron"*).[3] Most later treatments of Propertius 4.9 have been influenced heavily by this approach.[4] The present paper will not be challenging Anderson. Rather it will (after some methodological remarks and a brief interpretative summary of the elegy) set out from a remote starting point to traverse rapidly terrain (mythico-religious as well as literary) which,

[1]   Some early papers along these lines, esp. Winter and Sbordone, contain valuable information and observations. Alfonsi is similarly useful.
[2]   I use the term "genres of form," as at Cairns (1972) 6, of such classifications as "epic, lyric, elegy or epistle."
[3]   The statement by Copley 145 n. 6 that "the word used by the ancients to designate it (i.e., the *paraclausithyron*) was not παρακλαυσίθυρον, but κῶμος etc.," and the evidence he adduces still (cf. Cairns [1972] 6) seems to me compelling. The question of what the lover's "song at the door" was called is a separate one. That it had a name or names in antiquity is unquestionable. But Yardley, esp. 19 (apparently received favorably by Fedeli 1899f.), attempting to revive the use of "paraclausithyron" for this song (as opposed to the overall activity, i.e. *kômos*) does not establish the utility, let alone the historical validity, of this term.
[4]   Cf. esp. Pillinger; Galinsky 153-6; Pinotti. McParland saw Prop. 4.9 as more than humorous, but her specific proposals met with criticism from Warden, who concentrated on the epic/elegy interface, and argued for imitation with variation of Virg., *Aen.* 8 (a disputed topic for long: cf. Sbordone 163-5 with accounts of earlier debates). The "wild cards" in the recent bibliography are Holleman, who interprets the myths of Prop. 4.9 as reflecting "the history of Roman religion up to his time" (92), and Piccaluga. The latter's title does not reveal it as (in part) about Prop. 4.9; it is not cited in Harrauer and has remained unknown to Propertian scholarship. It clearly appeared shortly after Anderson, which it dismisses summarily (196f. n. 1), arguing that Prop. 4.9 can be used to reconstruct Roman cult and that it belongs "integralmente al patrimonio tradizionale romano" (197): cf. also below, nn.7, 9, 10. Although the conclusions of Piccaluga about Prop. 4.9 are mainly rejected below, his study is not without interest for the elegy.

it seems, has remained unexplored in relation to Propertius 4.9. The paper
aims to expand the generic dimensions of the elegy—not, however,
exhaustively, since that would be a very lengthy process, and so to help
reconcile some of the polarities found in earlier scholarly attitudes to it. A
preliminary *caveat* may anticipate needless skepticism: the connections
between the new material adduced and Propertius 4.9 will not be claimed as
direct, or even for the most part indirect, but mainly as "generic."

That term, which is also part of the paper's title, is employed in both its
traditional sense, i.e., of genres of form, as well as of genres of content. Late
nineteenth- and early twentieth-century classical scholarship provided the
foundations for more recent advances in generic studies. But much remains to
be done in this field: in particular there is a need to integrate our concepts of
the different types of ancient genres[5] (genres as defined by metre, or length,
or performance, and so forth, as well as genres of content and form), and to
harmonize the generic aspects of ancient literature with its social roles in its
contemporary real-life environments. The as yet unresolved status of the latter
question is well illustrated, for example, by the diametrically opposed views of
Jasper Griffin and Richard Thomas.[6] Propertius 4.9 may prove to be useful as
a source of data towards such an eventual enterprise, always provided that the
limits of its usefulness are recognized.

The main such limitation might be thought too obvious to be worth
noting:[7] although it deals with myth and cult, Propertius 4.9 is an elegy
composed within a complex literary tradition, not a piece of scholarship.
There is no reason, then, to think that before writing it Propertius assiduously
visited the Roman temples of the Bona Dea and Hercules, attended the worship
of Hercules and enquired of women who took part in the Bona Dea cult, talked
to contemporaries learned in myth and religion, researched widely in serious
prose works of reference on these topics, or attempted to go beyond common
Roman knowledge of the Roman aspects of his subject.   After all, if the
"historian" Livy could be so cavalier about the "sources" for the *spolia opima*

---

5   The multiplicity of possible types of "genres" in European literatures of all periods is
well illustrated and discussed by Fowler esp. Ch. 3, which raises many of the pertinent
questions about their definitions and relationships.
6   Cf. Griffin esp. Ch. 3; Thomas (1988).
7   Piccaluga, however, argues that Propertius did have the attitude and knowledge rejected
for him below, and even (226) that information about the archaic ritual of the Bona Dea can be
recovered from Prop. 4.9. Cf. below, n. 9.

and the temple of Jupiter Feretrius,[8] why should the poet Propertius have been any more scholarly? That he was not is amply demonstrated by the relative uninformativeness of 4.9 about the myths and cults of the Bona Dea and Hercules at Rome in Propertius' day.[9] Propertius probably did know a Varronian account of the establishment of the Ara Maxima and of the reason why women were excluded from the cult there (Section V); but the "learning" of Propertius 4.9 lies mainly in what it drew from Gallus and from the same hellenistic Greek poetic sources as were used by Gallus, and in the "emulative" adaptation and incorporation of these sources into Propertius' Roman context. It has long been observed that the Augustan poets' lack of pure intellectual curiosity, together with their literary inventiveness and their desire to emulate predecessors, led them, even when they probably knew Augustan Roman rituals and so forth first hand, to write not factual accounts of these events, but fantasy descriptions which are blends of the true facts and of Greek analogues and other models.[10] Even the Varronian material may have been mediated by Gallus (Section VI), and if Propertius perhaps knew more about the cults of Hercules than those of the Bona Dea (Section VI), his knowledge probably came from poetic reading. In practical terms, then, Propertius 4.9 may help only indirectly with the problem of integrating different types of genre; but it *will* help only indirectly with the broader cultural aspects of the genre/life question, especially since its mythico-religious aspects and its literary antecedents cannot be discussed in mutual isolation because the analogues for its myth and cult are mostly themselves literary. Yet even indirect assistance may be welcome if it contributes towards eliminating conceptual strait-jacketing. The antithesis life/literature, if accepted naively, makes no sense, particularly in classical antiquity. Literature is everywhere and at all times an integral part of life; this fact is especially clear in ancient societies, where literature was essentially oral and for performance, however varied the modes of orality and

---

[8]   Ogilvie 5-7 (general discussion of Livy as a "historian"), 70-3, 563-7 (on Jupiter Feretrius and the *spolia opima*); for the latter, cf. most recently Harrison.
[9]   Even Piccaluga (cf. above, nn. 4, 7, and below, n. 10) admits (236 n. 166): "è certamente eccessivo sperare in una ricostruzione del racconto leggendario" [i.e., of the Bona Dea], and (197 n. 5): "non si sa niente di preciso sul rito [i.e. of the Bona Dea] che aveva luogo in maggio." Surmises (e.g., "presumibilmente solo etc.," 197f.) about her cult add nothing. Not only the details of the myths and worship of the Bona Dea but even the precise location of her places of worship remain obscure. Prop. 4.9 offers scant help with these matters, and conversely the exhaustive detailing of evidence about the Bona Dea in Brouwer throws little direct light on Prop. 4.9.
[10]   Cf. e.g., Cairns (1979) 133f., with n. 45. Studies of Prop. 4.9 aiming to reconstruct from it particulars of myth of cult (esp. Piccaluga; Holleman) seriously underestimate its debts to earlier literature.

performance could be. Again the fact that ancient "poetry" was often in origin and function part of ancient religious and social ritual makes a literature/life dichotomy doubly unsustainable. Propertius 4.9 demonstrates all this and more: fictionality of content cannot be taken to imply fictionality of context, as becomes clear once the apparent obstacle presented by its genre of content (*kômos/paraclausithyron*) is turned instead to advantage.

So much for methodology. The summary of the elegy, written with an eye to the discussion which follows, is the last preliminary required. Propertius 4.9 is a bipartite elegy, narrating two episodes from Hercules' mythical visit to Rome. Both are aetiological, and, as Anderson has shown, they have many correspondences of detail as well as an overall parallelism of subject matter. This binary aspect of the elegy not only provides it with its thematic structure, but will turn out to be important also for 4.9's relations with some of its mythical and literary antecedents. Each episode relates how Hercules was deprived of something; each then tells how he punished a wrongdoer. In the first episode (1-20) the robber Cacus steals Hercules' cattle and is killed by him as punishment. This briefer narrative provides continuity with, and the pretext for, the second, more extensive, tale. Hercules is parched with thirst as a result of his battle with Cacus, and there is no water at hand (21f.). Hercules hears the laughter of girls enclosed within a shady grove where there is a spring; this is the sacred precinct of the Bona Dea forbidden to men (23-9). Like the standard ancient excluded lover Hercules begs to be admitted (30ff.), but unlike the lover he wants admission not for erotic purposes but to drink. Hercules reveals his identity (37ff.) and—ostensibly in order to reduce the girls' alarm at his appearance, but on another level to meet the objection that, being male, he cannot enter the grove—he narrates how he carried out female tasks and wore woman's dress as a slave of Omphale (45ff.). But the elderly priestess of the Bona Dea refuses him entrance (51ff.): so he breaks down the gates, satisfies his thirst, and as a punishment prohibits girls from worshipping at the Ara Maxima (61ff.), which he had already set up to commemorate his victory over Cacus (16ff.). The explicit mention of the Ara Maxima is postponed to a late, effective point (67ff.). But its actual establishment has taken place earlier,[11] as is clear from the perfect tenses of *devota est* (67) and *facta* (68):

---

11   The *communis opinio* (e.g. Anderson 4; Galinsky 154; Pinotti 51f., 58; Coli 298-305, 300) places the foundation of the Ara Maxima after the exclusion of Hercules from the shrine of the Bona Dea, and offers various interpretations of this "fact." It regards Prop. 4.9.16-20 as signalling only the establishment of the Forum Boarium. The alternate view offered here brings

'Maxima quae gregibus devota est Ara repertis,
    ara per has' inquit 'maxima facta manus,
haec nullis umquam pateat veneranda puellis,
    +Hercle exterminium nescit+ inulta sitis.'

                                        (67-70)

The Greatest Altar, which was vowed after I had recovered my
herds," he said, "the altar that became the greatest by my hands,
let it not ever be open to worship to any women;" (text
corruption) . . ."unavenged thirst."

The Ara Maxima was sited in the Forum Boarium, not in the precinct of the
Bona Dea; so lines 16-20 must contain the oblique record of its foundation:

    . . . Alcides sic ait: 'Ite boves,
Herculis ite boves, nostrae labor ultime clavae,
    bis mihi quaesitae, bis mea praeda, boves,
arvaque mugitu sancite Bovaria longo:
    nobile erit Romae pascua vestra Forum.'

                                        (16-20)

Hercules said: "Go cattle, go cattle of Hercules! This is the last
labor of my club, cattle that I sought and took as booty twice.
Consecrate with your drawn-out lowing these pasture-grounds:
your pasture will be a renowned forum at Rome."

Presumably *sancite* (19), linked by its standard ancient etymology with the
blood of sacrificial victims,[12] will have been sufficient to convey this
information to Propertius' contemporary readers, accustomed as they were to a
wide range of hellenistic foundation literature and to hellenistic *arte allusiva*.
The sacrifice by Hercules of some of his cattle appears explicitly in the account
of these same events given in a text from late antiquity which drew on earlier

---

Propertius' account into harmony with all other known versions of the foundation of the Ara
Maxima (cf. Pinotti 51f.). The existence of an "orthodox" account would of course have made
it even easier for Propertius' original readers to grasp his allusion to it.
[12]   Cf. Maltby *s.v. sancio*, esp. Serv. *ad Aen.* 12.200 *sancire . . . proprie est sancum
aliquid, id est consecratum, facere fuso sanguine hostiae: et dictum sanctum, quasi sanguine
consecratum;* Isid., *Etym.* 15.4.2.

sources, *Origo Gentis Romanae* 6.7 (Richard): *aram dedicavit appellavitque Maximam et apud eam decimam sui pecoris profanavit.* Sancire is of course a key word in Propertius 4.9; cf. also:

> hunc quoniam manibus purgatum *sanxerat* orbem
> sic *Sanctum* Tatiae composuere Cures (73f.)

with the additional emphasis on *Sancte* or *Sance* in lines 71f. These other appearances give further weight to the etymological implications of *sancire* at the earlier point. *Sancire* may also belong to the traditional vocabulary of accounts of Hercules' visit to Rome, since it recurs (in a different context) in *Origo Gentis Romanae* 6.7 (Richard): *sanxit ne cui feminae fas esset vesci ex eo quod eidem arae sacratum esset.*

II. *Pindar Paean 6 and the Kômos*

These preliminaries over, the remote starting point for this paper can be introduced. It is the initial portion of Pindar's sixth *Paean*, which has so much in common with Propertius 4.9.21ff. that coincidence cannot easily be invoked as a full explanation. To begin with, *Paean* 6 is, like Propertius 4.9.21ff., a *kômos*, in the broader ancient sense in which "*kômos*" could refer to a range of religious and secular activities involving a processional element (see also below).[13]   Again, as will emerge, *Paean* 6 even has, *qua kômos*, erotic overtones.   In its opening lines (1-6) its speaker, a performing chorus of νέοι,[14] having come to Delphi, uses the technical language of the komast to beg Delphi for admission:

> Πρὸς 'Ολυμπίου Διός σε, χρυ[σέ]α
>   κλυτόμαντι Πυθοῖ,
> λίσσομαι Χαρίτεσ ⁻
>   σὶν τε καὶ σὺν 'Αφροδίτᾳ,
> ἐν ζαθέῳ με δέξαι χρόνῳ
> ἀοίδιμον Πιερίδων προφάταν·

---

13   Cf. *RE s.vv.* Komos, Comissatio. *Paean* 6 is cited from the Teubner text of Snell-Maehler (1975).
14   The chorus of νέοι would have been visible to the first audience of *Pae.* 6; the modern reader meets them in their self-injunctions to sing the paean (121f.).

Golden Pytho, famous for your oracles, I entreat you, by the
Olympian Zeus, with the Graces and and Aphrodite, to welcome
me in this sacred season as a prophet, famous in song, of the
Muses.

Already Radke *ad loc.* had observed that there is a close parallel for this
request in the earliest surviving extract from an ancient erotic[15] *kômos*,
Alcaeus *fr.* 374 LP:

δέξαι με κωμάσδοντα, δέξαι, λίσσομαί σε, λίσσομαι

In *Paean* 6 λίσσομαι (3) and δέξαι (5)—cf. also the allusive ἔλαβες (130)—
are as strong signals that a komast is speaking and is requesting admission as
could be wished; *precor* at Propertius 4.9.33 and *accipit* at 4.9.42 and 66 may
be compared.[16] These initial komastic signals are reinforced by the strong
emphasis Pindar gives throughout *Paean* 6 to the processional element, this
being (as noted above) the lowest common denominator of *kômoi* of all types
in antiquity: cf. ἦλθον (9), κατέβαν (13), and καταβάντ ᾽(60).

Lines 1-6 of *Paean* 6 contain then an indubitable komastic announcement;
and they exploit it to introduce slim hints of other topoi, less clearly or
uniquely komastic, but recognizable as such in context. Thus they follow the
ancient practice whereby clear generic signals introduce less explicit or more
sophisticated topical allusions.[17] In particular the phrase Χαρίτεσ- / σίν τε
καὶ σὺν ᾽Αφροδίτᾳ (3f.), whatever its precise syntactical role or roles in the
sentence,[18] and the phrase ἀοίδιμον Πιερίδων προφάταν (6), may carry
further komastic implications,[19] by hinting at the music and singing which was

---

15 Heath 182 questions whether this fragment is erotic rather than komastic in a more
general sense. However the repeated δέξαι and λίσσομαι suggest strong emotion, and the
overall tone makes anything but an erotic context most improbable; in any case the assumptions
about the priority of the non-erotic *kômos* which underlie Heath 181f. are suspect.
16 For the repetition of this line in the MSS and the solutions which editors have adopted,
cf. the standard commentaries on Propertius, and Fedeli in his Teubner text (1984) *ad loc.*
17 Cf. Cairns (1972) e.g. 25, 120ff., 204ff.
18 Cf. Radt 103-8.
19 These motifs recur in Pindar (Graces: *O.* 4.9, 9.27; Aphrodite and the Graces: *P.* 6.1f.)
so that the allusiveness claimed for them here is secondary. The νέοι of *Paean* 6 are a typical
choric ἐγώ - figure speaker: cf. Slater (1969) 86-94 (formulating earlier perceptions). Hence
they embody a number of voices, among them the poet's voice. This, and the fact that the
poet's voice tends to be strong at the beginning and end of choric odes explain why there is a
fair presence of Pindar in the first lines of *Paean* 6, he being, equally with the chorus, the

a constant concomitant of all *kômoi*, and notably of erotic *kômoi*.[20] The first may also point to the erotic interest which the performing chorus of νέοι would have aroused in the original spectators;[21] and it might additionally suggest the companions, human and/or divine, who often accompany the komastic lover.[22] The plausibility of such allusiveness is enhanced if it is remembered that erotic and non-erotic *kômoi* were not seen as distinct in antiquity but as part of a continuum (see Section VI).[23]

Other, and certainly significant, material in common with Propertius 4.9.21ff., which is also not specifically komastic, appears in the next lines of *Paean* 6:

> ὕδατι γὰρ ἐπὶ χαλκοπύλῳ
> ψόφον ἀϊὼν Κασταλίας
> ὀρφανὸν ἀνδρῶν χορεύσιος ἦλθον
> ἔταις ἀμαχανίαν ἀλέξων
> τεοῖσιν ἐμαῖς τε τιμ[α]ῖς·
>
>   (7-11)

For beside the water from Castalia, which issues from bronze spouts, I have heard the sound (of water) bereft of the dancing of men and have come to turn aside the helplessness of your citizens and my own honors.

ἀοίδιμον Πιερίδων προφάταν (6). But to limit the sense of these two phrases to poetic inspiration would be over-restrictive.

20   Cf. Copley 5f., 145 nn. 7-10.

21   Cf. above, n. 14.

22   Cf. e.g. Xen., *Symp* 2.1; *p.Teb.* 2(d); Headlam-Knox on Herodas 2.34-7; *Collectanea Alexandrina* ed. Powell 181f.; Plaut., *Curc.* 1ff.; Tib., 1.2.1ff.; Prop., 1.3.10; Plut., *Mor.* 772F-773A; Aristaen. *Ep.* 2.19. The topos is pointedly negated at e.g. Alexis *fr.* 224.5ff. K; Prop. 2.29.2. Zeus is mentioned in *Paean* 6.1, while Zeus/Jupiter is sometimes invoked or mentioned in *kômoi*: e.g. Posidippus, *AP* 5.213.2; Asclepiades *AP* 5.167.5f.; Hor., *Od.* 3.10.8; Tib. 1.2.8. But Zeus appears in *kômoi* as part of the "bad weather topos" (on which, cf. Pinotti 66 n. 64), and so the link is fortuitous.

23   The fact that Pindar's ornate phrase addressed to Delphi: χρυ[σέ]α / κλυτόμαντι Πυθοῖ (1f.) "Golden Pytho famed for your prophetess" alludes to the Pythia, the (usually) elderly priestess of the mantic shrine of Apollo, while the elderly priestess of the Bona Dea plays a crucial role in Prop. 4.9 is a further coincidence. The latter does, however, reflect the elderly *lena* who often features in erotic poetry, including *kômoi* (e.g. Cairns [1972] 173f.; [1979] index *s.v. lena*), and may act as the *custos* who excludes the lover, e.g. in Tib. 1.5.48ff. (cf. Anderson 9).

Radt's cautious interpretations *ad loc.* of lines 7-9,[24] based on close study of the Pindaric parallels, reveal at least the primary significance of the lines: he takes ψόφον ἀϊὼν Κασταλίας as one word-group, and ὀρφανὸν ἀνδρῶν χορεύσιος as another. On this basis, *Paean* 6.7-9 has the following relevant content: water, its sound, the hearing of that sound, and the statement that the sound of water is "bereft of the dancing of men" (9). This last phrase is explained in what follows:

ἤτορι δὲ φίλῳ παῖς ἅτε ματέρι κεδνᾷ
πειθόμενος κατέβαν στεφανῶν
καὶ θαλιᾶν τροφὸν ἄλσος ᾽Α-
πόλλωνος, τόθι Λατοίδαν
θαμινὰ Δελφῶν κόραι
χθονὸς ὀμφαλὸν παρὰ σκιάεντα μελπ[ό]μεναι
ποδὶ κροτέο[ντι γᾶν θο]ῷ

(12-18)

I have obeyed my dear heart, as a son obeys his dear mother, and have come down to Apollo's grove, the nourisher of garlands and banquets, where, beside the shadowy center of the earth, the maidens of Delphi often beat the ground while they celebrate the son of Leto with song and dance.

Here a context with, as will be seen, much further material in common with Propertius 4.9, treats (15-18) of the singing and dancing of κόραι (16) by the shady navel of the earth in the sacred grove of Apollo to which the chorus has come, a grove which "nurtures crowns and feasts" (13f.). The singing and dancing of the girls stands in implied contrast with the singing and dancing of the chorus of (male) νέοι (122) which performs *Paean* 6, and which the grove is "bereft of," i.e., "is waiting for." This implication is confirmed when Pindar states that the songs and dances of the girls are the frequent (θαμινά, 16), and so the normal, practice there, which explains further why the water of Castalia is "bereft of the dancing of men" (9) until Pindar's νέοι come to dance and sing the paean there.

---

[24] Cf. Radt 108-13. The lines have been much disputed. When controversial phrases in Pindar seem to make sense when taken in two different syntactical relationships, this raises a suspicion of double reference.

In this way, as well as being, like Propertius' *Hercules Exclusus*, komastic, the initial portion of *Paean* 6 presents a scenario close to that of Propertius 4.9.21ff. There too a grove, that of the Bona Dea, is described, and there too girls are inside it (23-6, 33f.); there Hercules "hears" (*audit*, 23, cf. ἀϊὼν, *Paean* 6.8) their laughter. A festival of the Bona Dea is in progress in Propertius 4.9.21ff.: this might in any case have been presumed, but it is made certain at line 43, where Hercules says: "If you were celebrating the feast of harsh Juno" i.e., as opposed to "the feast of the Bona Dea," which they are celebrating. It was also already implicit in line 26: *nullis sacra retecta viris*; and a passage from Macrobius treated below provides further confirmation. The point is worth stressing, not only because it links Pindar *Paean* 6 and Propertius 4.9.21f. further in that both describe a sacred festival as in progress, but because it also confirms another specific detail in common between the two texts, namely that both involve the dances of girls. For *luditis* (33), addressed by Hercules to the girls, means "<you who> are dancing," and not, as the commentators have taken it, "<you who> are sporting." The specialized meaning of *ludo*, "dance," which is found here, is well enough attested at *TLL s.v.* 1772.45ff., where the dancers are often, but not always, female; and the plausibility of this rendering is increased by the pseudo-solemn and possibly pseudo-etymological language[25] of line 33:

Vos precor, o luci *sacro quae* luditis *antro.*

This combination outweighs any possible implication in *ridere* (23) that the girls were just amusing themselves.[26] There are further such details in common between the two texts: the *sacra* of the Bona Dea's grove and the grove itself are forbidden to men (26, 55f.), while the grove at Delphi was "bereft of the dancing of men;" the Bona Dea's grove has its singing birds (30), whereas the Delphic grove had its singing νέοι and κόραι. Like its Delphic equivalent, the Roman grove has springs (25, 59f.), is full of the sound of water (35), and offers shade (24, 29f.). It contains a white poplar (29), the tree sacred to Hercules, from which crowns were made for victors at Olympia

---

25   Maltby *s.vv. lucus, ludo*, etc. evidences no connection made between the two words by "professional" ancient etymologists. But given the "creative etymologizing" practiced by Roman poets (cf. Cairns [1979] Ch. 4, esp. 95ff.) Propertius may well be suggesting an etymology here.
26   Piccaluga 199f. with n. 16, 222f. with n. 121, had already perceived that *luditis* referred (on her account *inter alia*) to dancing, and had linked this perception with evidence about dance in the cult of the Bona Dea.

and other games,[27] just as the crowns which the Delphic grove "nurtures" (*Paean* 6.13f.) were made at Delphi from Apollo's sacred bays as prizes for victors.[28] The poplar may have featured in the rites at the Ara Maxima.[29]

After *Paean* 6.18, its papyrus is defective for some thirty lines, after which it resumes (50ff.) with an invocation of the Muses, followed by a brief account of the Delphic festival being celebrated, before moving to Apollo's achievements at Troy, with their consequences. Since lines 1-18 of *Paean* 6 are the main, although not exclusive, location of material shared by *Paean* 6 and Propertius 4.9.21ff., and since they have now been surveyed, the vital question can be asked: given the many points in common between them, is there a connection between the two texts, and if so, what is its nature? At first sight, nothing might seem further removed from an elegy of Propertius, written for a sophisticated Augustan readership in the years 22-16 B.C., than a Pindaric paean composed for performance by a chorus of νέοι at a Delphic sacred festival around four hundred and fifty years earlier.[30] But there would in fact be no implausibility in hypothesizing a link, particularly an indirect link, between Pindar and Propertius: it is now fully established that Propertius' master Callimachus is indebted to Pindar for many of his themes and for most of the symbolism of his poetics.[31] There is also growing evidence for interest in Pindar among Augustan poets[32] above and beyond the well-known influence of Pindar on Horatian lyric, an interest usually regarded as mediated through Callimachus.[33] So if it were necessary to offer a hypothesis of indirect influence, with Callimachus standing somewhere between the two texts, and if

---

[27] On the white poplar in antiquity, including its links with Hercules and the Ara Maxima, and its role as a victory garland, cf. Boetticher 441-4; by a coincidence a komast at Theocr. *Id.* 2.121f., wears (in his imagination) a white poplar garland, which he identifies as "Ἡρακλέος ἱερὸν ἔρνος" (121). But he wears it *qua* athlete, not *qua* komast.

[28] On the worship of Hercules as *Invictus*, cf. Wissowa 272ff.; Nock 599.

[29] Cf. Virg., *Aen.* 8.276f. where Evander is crowned with poplar while celebrating rites at the Ara Maxima, and Wissowa 275. But there is better evidence for the use of laurel crowns there (cf. Wissowa 274).

[30] On the suggested dates for *Paean* 6, i.e., 487 B.C., or more likely 467 B.C., cf. Kirkwood 257.

[31] Cf. e.g., Poliakoff; Newman (1967) 45ff.; (1985); Richardson.

[32] Cf. e.g., Thomas (1983a); Thomas on Virg., *Georg.* 3.7-8, 13; Cairns (1989) 217f.

[33] Propertius' own reference to Pindar at 3.17.40: *qualis Pindarico spiritus ore tonat* (cf. Fedeli *ad loc.* and 538f., again pointing out Callimachean intermediacy), is of particular importance. The heavy apparent input from the archaic Greek period into the *Aeneid* (cf. Cairns [1989] Chs. 7, 9) may, however, indicate that first-hand knowledge on the part of more Augustan poets than Horace is an additional possibility. On Virgil and Pindar, cf. most recently *Enciclopedia virgiliana s.v.* Pindaro (A. Setaioli).

the details of the correspondences between Pindar *Paean* 6.1ff. and Propertius 4.9.21ff. supported such a hypothesis, it would not be intrinsically absurd. But it is neither necessary, nor perhaps prudent, to go as far as this. To begin with, *Paean* 6 is not unique in the Pindaric corpus in containing komastic topoi shared with Propertius 4.9.21ff. Heath 188-91 assembles, along with much other relevant data, a group of examples of the "reception motif." Among these *Olympian* 8.9f. is the most obviously relevant parallel:

ἀλλ' ὦ Πίσας εὔδενδρον ἐπ' ᾿Αλφεῷ ἄλσος,
τόνδε κῶμον καὶ στεφαναφορίαν δέξαι.

O grove of Pisa abounding in trees beside the Alpheus, give welcome to this *kômos* and this crowning of the victor.

Here the similar context, along with εὔδενδρον ἄλσος, τόνδε κῶμον, and δέξαι[34] all signal beyond question a *kômos* similar to that of *Paean* 6. The other examples show many of the same features. Thus the komastic topoi in common between Propertius 4.9.21ff. and *Paean* 6 could be thought to show the indirect influence of a wider range of Pindaric material upon Propertius than *Paean* 6 (i.e., Pindaric paeans and epinicia in general). But even this may be too "ungeneric" an approach, since, as has been noted, the ancient *kômos* was a broad institution and genre, of which the erotic *kômos* was only one subclass. The word *kômos* could designate first many religious and secular activities with a processional element, ranging from rituals of gods to celebrations in honour of heroes and men. Again *kômos* could refer in a more specialized sense to the komastic activities of the lover (or party-goer), and of groups of such erotic or symposiastic komasts, activities which led to their admission, or exclusion, as Copley has described so well. Finally of course a group, including a choric group, participating in komastic activities, religious or secular, might itself be described as a *kômos*, i.e., a group of komasts.[35] It is then primarily as an aspect of their membership of the genre (or "typical scene") *kômos* that the common ground between *Paean* 6 and Propertius

34   Heath 190 notes that E. Bundy, following W. Schadewaldt, interpreted the "δέξαι motif" in epinicia as "purely hymnal," but himself rightly sees it as also komastic.
35   Cf. *RE s.vv.* Komos, Comissatio. Recent scholarly controversies over the choric versus the monodic performance of archaic and fifth-century epinicia (e.g. Heath) have no bearing on the hellenistic and Roman periods, or upon hymnic archaic poetry like *Pae.* 6, where a choric speaker is unquestionable.

4.9.21ff. should be viewed. More will be said about komastic matters later; but in the meantime two further "typical scenes," both with cultic associations, will be introduced which underlie some of the other resemblances observed between the two poems.

III. *Locus Amoenus and Theoxenia*

The first, and more obvious, "typical scene" underlying portions of *Paean* 6 and Propertius 4.9.21ff. is the *locus amoenus*, and specifically among *loci amoeni* the *ekphrasis* of a god's sacred grove (which in the archaic period could signify "temple"). Both *ekphrasis*[36] and *locus amoenus*[37] have been the subject of much scholarly investigation, so that a cursory reference to another well-known archaic Greek poem containing a description of a sacred grove, where many of the same topoi recur,[38] i.e., Sappho *fr.* 2.1-16 LP (= *Lyrica Graeca Selecta* 192 Page), may suffice to illustrate the point.

δεῦρύ μ᾽ ἐκ Κρήτας ἐ[πὶ τόνδ]ε ναῦον
ἄγνον, ὄππ[αι τοι] χάριεν μὲν ἄλσος
μαλί[αν], βῶμοι δὲ τεθυμιάμε-
νοι [λι]βανώτῳ

5   ἐν δ᾽ ὕδωρ ψῦχρον κελάδει δι᾽ ὔσδων
μαλίνων, βρόδοισι δὲ παῖς ὁ χῶρος
ἐσκίαστ᾽, αἰθυσσομένων δὲ φύλλων
κῶμα κατέρρει,

ἐν δὲ λείμων ἱππόβοτος τέθαλεν
10   ἠρίνοισιν ἄνθεσιν, αἱ δ᾽ ἄηται
μέλλιχα πνέοισιν [   ]
[   ]

ἔνθα δὴ σὺ στέμματ᾽› ἔλοισα Κύπρι
χρυσίαισιν ἐν κυλίκεσσιν ἄβρως
15   ὀμ‹με›μείχμενον θαλίαισι νέκταρ

---

[36] Cf. esp. Palm with older bibliography; also Cairns (1979) 134 with n. 48; Ravenna (1974); (1980); (1980a); Shapiro; Thomas (1983).
[37] Cf. esp. Schönbeck with earlier bibliography; and, for useful remarks in relation to Prop. 4.9, Pinotti 63.
[38] I.e., the most common elements: *grove* 2f.; *altar(s)* 3; *water* 5; *shade* 6f.; *foliage* 6-8.

οἰνοχόαισον.

Come to me from Crete to this holy temple,
Aphrodite. Here is a grove of apple
trees for your delight, and the smoking altars
    fragrant with incense.

Here cold water rustles down through the apple
branches; all the lawn is beset and darkened
under roses, and from the leaves that tremble,
    sleep of enchantment

comes descending. Here is a meadow pasture
where the horses graze and with flowers of springtime
now in blossom, here where the light winds passing
    blow in their freshness.

Here in this place, lady of Cyprus, lightly
lifting, lightly pour in the golden goblets
as for those who keep a festival, nectar:
    wine for our drinking.

                         (transl. R. Lattimore)

As well as explaining the presence in Pindar and Propertius of springs, shade, trees, and so forth, the *locus amoenus* may lie behind such verbal and onomatopoeic resemblances such as ὕδατι . . . ψόφον (*Paean* 6.7f.) and *sonantia lymphis* (Propertius 4.9.35), and the more remote ζαθέῳ . . . χρόνῳ (*Paean* 6.5) and *sacro . . . . antro* (Propertius 4.9.33).

    If *locus amoenus* and *ekphrasis* and the illumination they bring to Propertius 4.9.21ff., and its links with *Paean* 6, are obvious and limited, the second typical scene underlying both texts is less well-known and more illuminating. It manifests itself explicitly in *Paean* 6 after the gap in the papyrus:

        . . . . ἔρα[ται] δέ μο[ι]
        γλῶσσα μέλιτος ἄωτον γλυκὺν [
60   ἀγῶνα Λοξία‹ι› καταβάντ᾽ εὐρὺν

ἐν θεῶν ξενίᾳ.

θύεται γὰρ ἀγλαᾶς ὑπὲρ Πανελ-
λάδος, ἅν τε Δελφῶν
ἔθ[ν]ος εὔξατο λι-
65   μοῦ θ[

(58-65)

My tongue loves (to pour forth) the choicest and sweetest bloom of
song when, at the festival of the gods, I have entered the broad
lists of Loxias. The sacrifice is being offered on behalf of the
splendid panhellenic feast which the people of Delphi vowed (to
avert) the famine.

Here the festival at which *Paean* 6 is being performed is revealed as the
Delphic Theoxenia. The indications come especially in line 61, along with line
131: τὰν θεμίξενον ἀρετ[άν, and in the allusive ἄδορπον of line 128,[39]
taken together with lines 63-5. Theoxenia were held in many cities of Greece
and Italy at different times, and they have been the subject of a number of
specialist studies, concentrating on the festival as a whole or on its central
element, the Roman *lectisternium* and its Greek equivalent, the "hero (or god)
on the couch."[40] The concept behind the Theoxenia was always that gods (or
heroes) were guests at a banquet, as the worshippers might also be. A god
could also be host at the banquet, as at Delphi Apollo was host and entertained
a number of other gods. The *kômos* of νέοι which asks for admission to the
grove in *Paean* 6 is therefore asking for admission to the banquet of the
Theoxenia, something which brings its komastic activities closer to those of
everyday symposiastic *kômoi*. The νέοι then will dance and sing the paean at a
feast given primarily by a god for gods.

In Propertius 4.9 Hercules, like the chorus of *Paean* 6, asks to be
admitted to a sacred grove where the cult celebration of the Bona Dea and the
dancing of maidens are in progress. There is no explicit statement that feasting

---

[39]   Cf. Radt 83f.; 131-4.
[40]   As well as *RE s.v.* Theoxenien, cf. Deneken; Mischkowski; Weniger; Eitrem; Amandry;
Nock (very important); Meuli; Neutsch; Thönges-Stringaris; Gill; Milani; and Flückiger-
Guggenheim, citing much additional material.

is going on,[41] but since a meal was almost universally part of *sacra* and sacrifices in antiquity, it may be presumed that it is. Now Hercules is not a mere mortal, or even a hero, asking admission to the grove; he is also a god to be. This dual status of Hercules is driven home by Propertius in typical hellenistic manner through the counterpointing in *viris* (34) of the closely preceding *verba minora deo* (32). So Hercules asks hospitality of the Bona Dea as a fellow god, as well as *qua* mortal hero. The ambiguous address to Hercules by the priestess at line 53 as *hospes* ("stranger" and "guest"), which picks up the theme of violated hospitality already prominent in the Cacus episode,[42] is intended partially as a reminder that Hercules is a divine as well as a heroic ξένος"[43] coming, he might hope, to a Theoxenia. Hercules does not even ask for food (as one might expect even a less excessive hero/god than the typical gluttonous Hercules to do), but only for water, the *vilissima rerum*, and the most basic demand of hospitality in the ancient world. He is flatly refused, and this refusal triggers off his justifiable violence and his sanction against the women who refused him. The sequence—thirst/Theoxenia—in Propertius 4.9.21ff. recalls the fact that the Delphic Theoxenia commemorated a famine which had afflicted Greece and which had been ended by the prayer of the Delphians,[44] and suggests that hunger and thirst may have been a typical motif in aetiologies of Theoxenia in the ancient world.

The scene of Hercules' arrival at the Bona Dea's grove is then reminiscent of some aspects of Theoxenia. This raises the question whether Propertius could have had this institution in mind in 4.9. Apart from the points already made, it should be emphasized that *lectisternium* (the central

---

[41]   I.e., unless *luditis* means "<you who> banquet." On a purely linguistic level, this is possible (cf. *TLL s.v. ludo* 1770), but contextually it is much less likely; cf. above, Section II.
[42]   Cf. 7f.: *sed non infido manserunt hospite Caco / incolumis: furto polluit ille Iovem;* 13: *non sine teste deo;* 34: *pandite defessis hospita fana viris.* The discussion of the *ius hospitii* in primitive Rome at Serv. *ad Aen.* 8.269 suggests that hospitality/inhospitality was a traditional motif in accounts of Hercules' visit to Rome.
[43]   The duality of Hercules cults (i.e. as hero and god) is already remarked on by Hdt. 2.44.5 as something familiar in Greek cities. Cf. also Nock 576ff.; Nilsson 449ff. That there is a "learned" antiquarian point in the god/hero antithesis in Prop. 4.9 is assured by Steph. Byz. *s.v.* κυνόσαργες: Δίομος γὰρ ʹΗρακλεῖ ὡς θεῷ θύων τὰ †ξενώσων† ἱερὰ ʹΗρακλεῖ ἥρῳ ἔδειξε . . . where the text, although corrupt, points to Theoxenia (cf. Deneken 27). The point may relate to Evander's having been the first to recognize Hercules as a god to be, and to this being the aetion of his worship and festival at Rome: cf. Dion. Hal., *Ant. Rom.* 1.40. Hercules was in fact a frequent guest at Theoxenia (cf. Deneken 12f., 25-9), which might have increased the expectation that he would be entertained by the Bona Dea. His reception by others at Rome certainly fulfilled that expectation: cf. Dionys. Halic., *Ant. Rom.* 1.40; Diod. Sic. 4.21.2.
[44]   Cf. *Paean* 6.64f. λιμοῦ, 128 ἄ[δ]ορπον; Radt 131-4.

element of Theoxenia) was a characteristic Roman institution. Many different gods were honored with *lectisternia* at Rome, including, interestingly, the Bona Dea, in whose cult they formed a significant element.[45] The notion that Hercules might be coming to be the guest of the Bona Dea at the Roman equivalent of Theoxenia was therefore a natural one for a Roman poet to conceive. A further curious oblique confirmation that Theoxenia was in Propertius' mind comes from certain known features of the worship of Hercules at Rome, particularly at the Ara Maxima, which suggest that such a concept had a broader circulation. The first is that, although Hercules was included in the first *lectisternium* held at Rome in 399 B.C., and featured in many other such celebrations later, *lectisternia*, that key element in Theoxenia, were specifically prohibited at the Ara Maxima. Cf.:

> et Cornelius Balbus' Ἐξηγητικῶν libro octavo decimo ait apud
> Aram Maximam observatum, ne lectisternium fiat.
> (Macrobius *Saturnalia* 3.6.16)[46]

So just as the prohibition of women worshippers from the Ara Maxima[47] was explained by their exclusion of Hercules from the Bona Dea's grove, so the prohibition of *lectisternia* at the Ara might have been regarded as a commemoration of the women's refusal of Theoxenia to Hercules. Other oddities of the proceedings at the Ara Maxima may have had similar traditional explanations at Rome: the fact that none of the food offered might be carried away, and the invocation of no other god except Hercules,[48] may also reflect a link between the establishment of the Ara Maxima and the notion that Hercules had been treated inhospitably by a fellow god and had been excluded from Theoxenia.

---

[45] In general, cf. Wissowa, Namen- und Sachregister *s.v.* Lectisternium. On the Bona Dea, cf. Brouwer 366, 369, 379.

[46] Cf. also Serv. *ad Aen.* 8.176.

[47] On prohibitions of women from cult in antiquity, cf. Wächter 125-9; for the cult of Hercules, cf. *id.* 128 n. 2; Lawler 262; Piccaluga discusses this and other prohibitions (esp. of wine).

[48] On the cult, cf. Wissowa 274ff.; Nock Appendix 2. The non-covering of the head by worshippers may be another such feature, although it may simply relate to the fact that worship there was *Graeco ritu*.

IV. *Divine 'Adventus' and Conflicts with Monsters and Fellow Gods*

The genres and typical scenes so far examined do not exhaust the traditional material which lies behind Propertius 4.9. Other major influences on the elegy derive from two areas of myth, for which again the surviving evidence is mainly literary. These are the *adventus* of gods and heroes in general, and the legendary conflicts of gods and heroes with monsters and of gods among themselves.

"Götteradvente" are a frequent phenomenon in ancient religion, and one in which myth and cult go hand-in-hand.[49] Often the arrival of the god (or hero) was welcome, and indeed prayed for. Arriving gods were usually received hospitably, and this might be reflected in a regular cult of ἐπιδημία. But with heroes the *adventus* was not always welcome, and this too could have cultic repercussions. The most notorious case is Dionysus' arrival at Thebes, his reception there by Pentheus, and its destructive results.[50] Similarly Triptolemus and Ikarios were killed when they brought men corn and wine respectively.[51] Among the heroes, Heracles seems to have been particularly prone to a poor reception or to ill-treatment after his arrival. At Oichalia Eurytus tried to deprive him of his daughter Iole, even though Heracles had won her from Eurytus in an archery contest. The outcome was violent.[52] The various mythical refusals of water (or wine) to Hercules by Italian women fall into this category.[53] Finally the myth of Heracles' arrival and poor welcome on Cos has several features of interest for Propertius 4.9.[54] The hero was shipwrecked there and asked a shepherd for a ram. The shepherd, however, wanted to wrestle with Heracles, and this led to a conflict between Heracles' followers and the Meropes, the inhabitants of Cos. Heracles eventually won, but initially his side had the worse of the conflict, and he himself was forced to disguise himself in female garb and take refuge with a Thracian woman. This change of clothing was commemorated in cult there (see below, Section VI).

Numerous texts could be cited to illustrate both "Götteradvente" and divine and heroic battles with monsters and gods. But for brevity's sake discussion will be confined to two: in Section V, a hellenistic literary analogue containing both themes will be treated, and in this Section a particularly

---

49   Cf. esp. Weniger; Flückiger-Guggenheim.
50   Cf. Flückiger-Guggenheim 101ff.
51   Cf. Flückiger-Guggenheim 109f.
52   Cf. Flückiger-Guggenheim 75f.
53   Cf. below, n. 60.
54   Cf. Nilsson 451f. and his remarks on the double aetion involved.

interesting archaic text will be noted which combines the *adventus* of a god with a (first) conflict with a monster, and which then introduces a second conflict—between the god and a fellow divine being. This binary structure gives it some similarity to Propertius 4.9 in its entirety, i.e., to its two episodes, not just to *Hercules Exclusus*; and even more interesting, the linkage between its two parts to some extent echoes the relationship of the two episodes of Propertius 4.9. The parallel text, like *Paean* 6, involves Delphic Apollo. This is probably coincidence, although it should perhaps be remembered that according to one myth Apollo and Hercules conflicted for the Delphic tripod.[55]

The passage in question comes from the third *Homeric Hymn* (to Pythian Apollo), which relates how Apollo went about the earth looking for a place to establish his oracular shrine. He came eventually to the (female) spring Telphousa, and proposed to her that he should build his oracular temple there (241-53). Telphousa deceitfully dissuaded him and suggested that instead Apollo should go on to Crisa (255-76); this he did, and built his temple at Crisa (294-99). At this point there begins an episode parallel to the Cacus episode of Propertius 4.9: near the temple flowed another spring (300), and there Apollo killed a monstrous (female) snake (300ff.), whose subsequent rotting away gave the place its name Pytho (372). The monster had been a bane to men and their sheep (302-4); having killed her, Apollo boasted over her (363ff.), referring *inter alia* to the offerings that men would bring to his shrine, i.e., there is a reference to cult. At this point (375) the second episode begins, although in another sense it had already begun before Apollo met Pytho. Apollo now realizes that Telphousa had deceived him in directing him to Crisa (375-8). He tells her that he will enjoy renown at her site as well as she; and he then covers her with rocks and builds himself an altar in a tree-filled grove nearby (379-87). The drastic treatment of Telphousa may be compared with Hercules' drinking dry of the Bona Dea's spring at 4.9.63.

Homeric Hymn 3 therefore also contains dual offences and punishments: a monster who had caused problems with livestock is slaughtered; and a divine being who has attempted to exclude another god from an area is worsted, in that the attempt fails and retribution is exacted. The interesting point that Apollo's altar is established right at the end of the narrative parallels the withholding of explicit mention of the Ara Maxima until after the end of the second episode in Propertius 4.9 (even though it was built earlier). Both texts

[55]   Cf. Bowra 55f.

may then reflect a tradition of climaxing such compound narratives with the building of the god's altar. *Homeric Hymn* 3 is not remote from Propertius 4.9, since in overall generic terms Propertius 4.9 is a hymn, and specifically (in Menander's terminology) a μυθικὸς ὕμνος,[56] recounting the achievements of the god, and having at (or near) its end a specifically hymnic envoi typical of the homeric hymns and their hellenistic imitations.[57]

V. Hellenistic and Later Literary Analogues?

What has been seen so far in the background to Propertius 4.9— *kômos, locus amoenus*, Theoxenia, divine *adventus*, and the destructions and punishments of monsters etc. which are aetiologies of temple and altar foundations—all these point, not surprisingly, to the explicitly acknowledged literary dependence of Propertius' fourth book on Callimachus' *Aetia*.[58] This is where all these strands, more visible to us in Callimachus' archaic models, which have survived better than the *Aetia*, will have come together. Pillinger 186 noted in this connection various aetia based on Hercules' gluttony, viz. the Lindian sacrifices (*frr*. 22f. Pf.) and the Theiodamas story (*frr*. 24f. Pf.). Pillinger also, after mentioning some details in common with Callimachus *Hymn* 3, pointed (188) to *Hymn* 5, to which Propertius alludes at 4.9.57f., as Callimachus' sole elegiac hymn and so as a possible literary predecessor.

Another trace of a marginally analogous aetion is *Aetia fr*. 187 Pf., a testimonium from Clement of Alexandria confirmed by a passage of Pausanias.[59] It is the aetiology of how the cult-title of Artemis worshipped at an ἄλσος καὶ ναός in Arcadia changed. The story is very different from either episode of Propertius 4.9; points in common are limited to binary structure, a trespass on a ἱερόν, and a punishment inflicted on women. *Fr*. 187

---

[56]   Like e.g. Prop. 3.17 (cf. Cairns [1972] 97 and 4.6 and [1984], esp. 137-48). On the hymnic envoi, cf. also Pillinger 183, comparing *inter alia Aen*. 8.301f., "the concluding prayer of the hymn of the Salii." For ancient theoretical material on hymns in general and on specialized varieties of hymn, cf. Färber, *Abhdlg*. 28ff., *Texte* 26ff.; for the most substantial ancient discussion of hymns, cf. Russell-Wilson 2-29; for the "mythical hymn," cf. *id*. 15-19, together with some aspects of the *Sminthiakos* (207ff.). *Qua* mythical hymn Prop. 4.9 possesses yet another generic dimension, and one in which genre of form and genre of content overlap to an interesting extent.

[57]   Pinotti 52f., rejecting the transposition of lines 73f. to before lines 71f., compares the end of 4.9 with that of 4.4 (92-4); but placing the envoi at the very end of the hymn remains attractive, in the absence of a specifically hymnic counter-example: cf. Fedeli in his Teubner text (1984) *ad loc.*

[58]   Cf. esp. *Umbria Romani patria Callimachi* (Prop.. 4.1.66) with *sacra diesque canam et cognomina prisca locorum* (Prop. 4.1.69) and below, n. 63.

[59]   Clem. Alex. *Protr*. 2.38.3; Paus. 8.23.6.7. The story includes at least two major alien elements, the "hanging" of the deity and child-killing.

Pf. then does no more than strengthen the already considerable likelihood that Callimachus in the *Aetia* treated aetiologies of the same general type as those of Propertius 4.9. Far closer to the Bona Dea story of Propertius 4.9.21ff. is the myth derived from Varro retold at Macrobius *Saturnalia* 1.12.27-9 in explanation of why women were excluded from the cult of Hercules in Italy. This myth relates their exclusion to a refusal of water to Hercules at an unspecified place in Italy by an unidentified *mulier* who said: *aquam se non posse praestare, quod feminarum deae celebraretur dies, nec ex eo apparatu viris gustare fas esset* (28). This version has often been noted as pointing to Varro as a possible source for Propertius' *Hercules Exclusus* episode. Varro is likely to have contributed, perhaps through Gallus. Little, however, can be deduced from Macrobius' account,[60] although it is useful in one respect, whatever its status: it tends to confirm in the words *quod feminarum deae celebraretur dies* that a festival was going on in the grove of the Bona Dea when Hercules arrived there. But it does not help with the question of Propertius' originality in 4.9.[61]

A last, hellenistic, literary analogue of considerable interest is *Argonautica* 4.1394-1460. There the Argonauts are in the Libyan desert at the Garden of the Hesperides. They are parched with thirst (with ξηρὴ . . . . / δίψα, 4.1394f., cf. **sicco** *torquet* **sitis** *ora palato*, Propertius 4.9.21) and looking for a spring (πίδακα μαστεύεσκον, 4.1394—cf. ὕδωρ ἐξερέων of Heracles at 4.1443—and πλαζόμενοι, 4.1396 = *fontis egens erro*, Propertius 4.9.35). They come to the sacred plain where up to the day before Ladon, the monstrous serpent of the Hesperides, had guarded their golden apples while the nymphs sang their lovely songs. Now Ladon lies dead, killed by Heracles when he had arrived there (part of the episode alluded to by Hercules at Propertius 4.9.37f.), so that the nymphs are now lamenting his death. They turn to dust as the Argonauts approach, but when Orpheus prays to them λισσόμενος (1422) to show the Argonauts water (cf. Hercules' "prayer" to the girls at Propertius 4.9.33ff.), the nymphs transform themselves into trees and narrate how Heracles took their apples and killed their serpent (1432ff.). It seems that

---

60   It is generally assumed that Propertius and Macrobius got the same story independently from Varro, cf. e.g., Anderson 5; Brouwer 237. Piccaluga 197 n. 2 refers to two variant legends: on the first (*ORG* 6.5f. Richard) cf. below, n. 64. The second derived from Alcimos (5th cent. B.C.) as reported by Athen., *Deipn.* 10.441, has an Italian woman trying to persuade her husband to give the thirsty Heracles water, not wine, which leads to a ban on wine drinking by all Italian women. This points to a broader tradition which Propertius may well have known. Cf. also Lawler 262.

61   Of course reconstructions like that of Anderson 5 are tempting but inevitably cannot be compelling.

Heracles too was on that occasion, after this feat, parched with thirst (δίψη καρχαλέος, 1442, cf. above), and could find no water. Striking a rock with his foot, he caused a spring to gush out and drained a huge draught from it (1446ff.). The Argonauts now benefit from Heracles' spring. There are many obvious points of contact with Propertius 4.9 here. In addition the *Argonautica* passage is binary in two senses. The Argonauts in general duplicate part of Heracles' experience; and the story of Heracles' arrival also contains a binary myth about Heracles. He kills a monster, which causes him great thirst; then he procures water. The Hesperides' descriptions at 4.1436-40 of Heracles' rough appearance, lionskin, club and bow, of course cover standard features, but they are close to the portrait of Hercules at Propertius 4.9.14, 31f., 39 and 45f.; and the enormous draught of water which Hercules drinks at 4.1447-9 parallels Propertius 4.9.63f. There are, however, no grounds for arguing that Apollonius was Propertius' model in 4.9. But if Propertius' indirect model was, as seems likely, a now lost passage of Callimachus, Apollonius probably drew on that same Callimachean text.

VI. *Questions and Conclusions*

The background to Propertius 4.9 could be amplified further;[62] but sufficient new material has been brought to bear to allow further questions to be asked and some conclusions, albeit tentative, to be reached. The questions concern the tone and intent of Propertius 4.9. Is it, especially in the second episode, the story of *Hercules Exclusus*, a hyper-grotesque Augustan reworking of a tale told originally in the context of divine/heroic *adventus* and Theoxenia, one which Propertius (or Gallus) will most probably have found in Callimachus? In this case the Callimachean model will have told how a god or hero (possibly but not necessarily Hercules[63]) arrived somewhere (most probably not Rome), killed a monster, felt thirst, obtained water by some extraordinary means, and established a temple and/or altar. Or/and is Propertius retelling in Callimachean terms a story which he (or Gallus) had found in a Roman author, perhaps Varro, again involving, originally or by

---

62   Winter and Sbordone provide possible starting points; but the suggestion of Piccaluga 226 that Propertius' inclusion of girls in the grove of the Bona Dea reflects primitive female initiation rites at Rome seems most implausible.

63   Cf. *fr.* 698Pf. with Pfeiffer's final comment: "*Herculis fabulae in omnibus Aetiorum libris;*" and, among secure *Aetia* fragments, *frr.* 7.20f., 22-25, 32(?), 54-59, 76-77, 101, 114.18ff.(?), among those of uncertain location 515, 551, 617, 692 Pf. Unfortunately, *Fr.* 804 Pf. (from Tertullian *De Corona* 7, dealing with victory crowns—on which topic, see above Section II), is classed by Pfeiffer among the *Fragmenta incerti auctoris.*

importation, *adventus* and Theoxenia?[64] In either event Propertius (or again perhaps Gallus) will have contributed such novel touches as the *exclusus amator* motifs and the self-representation of Hercules, possibly remembering the Bona Dea incident involving Clodius in 62 B.C., although that incident probably looms larger with us than it did with Romans of 22 B.C. on.[65] Or, although this is not necessarily an alternative to the other possibilities suggested, should a more socially integrative interpretation of the elegy be sought in the light of the complex cultic and mythical background which has emerged?

One or more of the three scenarios outlined above seems almost mandatory as an explanation of the poem's genesis, and many of the perceptions of Anderson could be harmonized with any of them. But that is not necessarily the whole story: the complex background to Propertius 4.9, especially its mythical and cultic elements, wherever they derive from, suggest that the elegy is handling religious and social interests which go beyond the merely humorous. Saying this does not imply a belief that the ancients regarded such categories as "serious" and "unserious," "solemn" and "humorous" as mutually exclusive, in the way moderns tend to do, or that they thought of such pairs of opposites as together covering the whole field.[66] This can be seen in the very genre from which Propertius 4.9 draws so much: the apparent presence within the introductory religious *kômos* of *Paean* 6 of allusions to the erotic *kômos* would itself indicate that the boundaries were not rigid; and if such erotic elements could already be part of a religious *kômos* in Pindar's day, then Propertius' use of the *exclusus amator* theme in 4.9 may be more than humorous.

Hercules is a hero and/or a god, and the attitudes of ancient polytheism were manifestly more relaxed than those of modern monotheism.[67] Deriving amusement from the gods and their antics was not necessarily seen as

---

[64]   The Macrobius version, derived from Varro, (cf. above and n. 60), would not in itself speak strongly for this possibility, although it is strengthened by the *Origo Gentis Romanae* 6f. Richard (on which, cf. Alfonsi). Like Prop. 4.9, *ORG* combines both aetia, that of the foundation of the Ara Maxima in two accounts, and that of the exclusion of women from it. Although the *ORG*'s version of the latter aetion differs from that of Prop. 4.9, the combination for the two, along with some verbal links between *ORG* and Prop. 4.9 noted by Alfonsi suggest the dependence of both on the same sources, one of them probably being Varro. But Propertius' sources for the incidents seem to go beyond Varro.

[65]   For a full discussion of this event cf. Brouwer 363-70.

[66]   For another case where such considerations seemed relevant, cf. Cairns (1975), esp. 134-7.

[67]   For a recent acute treatment of some aspects of classical polytheism, cf. Howie.

blasphemous in antiquity, any more than, when Epicureans met to γελᾶν ἅμα
. . . καὶ φιλοσοφεῖν,[68] they saw themselves as rejecting or ridiculing
philosophy. In this context the view sometimes expressed that archaic (and
even classical) Greek literature handles the gods in a serious manner, while
Hellenistic and Roman literature does so in an irreverent and unserious way, is
certainly an oversimplification.[69] For while it is true that Hellenistic and
Roman poetry has overall a less reverent attitude, a greater degree of
flippancy, and a greater emphasis on grotesquerie and humor in its treatment
of religion than earlier literature, the differences are quantitative, not
qualitative,[70] and they do not imply that the writers and readers of hellenistic
Greece and Rome were atheists or despisers of the gods, any more than their
archaic and classical forebears were. Religious and philosophical attitudes
changed and became more sophisticated from around 330 B.C. on, but a glance
at the monumental and epigraphic remains of later periods proves beyond
doubt that worship of the gods was alive among all classes in all periods down
to late antiquity. Conversely, a glance at early Greek poetry reveals that it is
far from unhumorous in its treatment of the gods. Can anyone believe that
Sappho *fr.* 1 LP is a serious and reverent hymnic prayer to Aphrodite? Or
was the ancient reader of *Homeric Hymn* 4 (to Hermes) to see no humor in the
infant Hermes' thefts, let alone in his forensic speech to Apollo denying them
(261-277). At one point (273) Hermes actually says "I was born yesterday!"
Even the treatment of the gods in the *Iliad* is frequently humorous. Not only
their domestic confrontations on Olympus, but also their internecine battles,
especially in Book 21, are often more or less unserious. But no one would
assert that the poets of archaic Greece were atheists or mockers of the gods.

     It was possible for ancient writers to be humorous at the expense of the
gods without impiety because antiquity's attitudes to the divine were in general
more sophisticated than those of later cultures. Ancient gods are neither all-
virtuous nor all-powerful; hence a wider range of attitudes to them was not just
permissible but inevitable. The flogging of a statue of Pan by his worshippers
in Theocritus *Idyll* 7.106-8, the sacrifices in *Aetia fr.* 7.19-21 Pf. of the
peoples of Anaphe to Apollo and of Lindos to Heracles, accompanied by
obscenity in one case and ill-omened words in the other, the aetiology of the
ban on women at the Ara Maxima—notions such as these were not necessarily

---

68   Cf. Festugière 23 with n. 22.
69   Dover, *Introd.* p. lxvii characterizes such attitudes in the words: "'Humanisation' of the
gods and a flippant attitude to mythology" before correcting it succinctly.
70   For the principles involved, cf. Cairns (1979) 7ff.

in themselves impious or indicative of contempt for, or disbelief in, the gods. In any case explanations of these odd religious events or activities in the form of μυστικοὶ λόγοι were often available to give spiritual or philosophical meaning to them. Even more, when oddities were incorporated in cult, they became an accepted part of the worshippers' religious lives. When therefore the activities themselves, and not just the poets' perceptions of them, are primarily and intrinsically grotesque, particularly if they actually formed part of ancient life and cult, their grotesqueness may have been less apparent to contemporaries, or seemed quaint rather than ludicrous.

This approach has a direct application to what might seem the most ridiculous portion of Propertius 4.9, i.e., lines 47-50. There Hercules' pleas to be admitted into the female sanctum of the Bona Dea's grove modulate into an account of how he performed female tasks and wore female dress as a slave of Omphale. At first sight Hercules wearing a brassiere might seem pure absurdity—and of course in one dimension it must be humorous. But it was also a widespread feature of ancient *kômoi*, both religious and secular, for the komasts to wear female dress. A number of surviving vases, some contemporary, show Anacreon and other komastic males so dressed. The matter has been treated and copious evidence adduced by W.J. Slater.[71] Slater also assembles many other examples, literary, real, epigraphic, and from vase-painting, illustrating transvestism in association with *kômoi* of different types from many different periods. Of course transvestism was even more common in ancient religious cult, as Slater again demonstrates. At Theoxenia in particular the worshippers might dress as the host and guest gods; and males could sometimes dress as female gods.[72] This fact alone without other evidence would prove that some elements of the light-hearted were in place even in religious Theoxenia and *kômoi*—and such events were not remote in time from Augustan literature. In 40 B.C. the young Octavianus held a "Theoxenia" at which he dressed as Apollo;[73] later Caligula at such banquets played the part of goddesses.[74] Real *kômoi* (*comissationes*) and literary examples of the genre were of course commonplaces of Augustan experience. Slater has some words about religious tranvestism which may have a further

71   Cf. Eitrem, who discusses the practice at length and refers to earlier treatments.
72   The value of Slater (1978) as a collection of material illustrating komastic practices etc. is independent of his main thesis (about Anacreon *fr.* 82 Gentili) which has not won general approval. Most recently Hoffman discusses a number of aspects of Dionysiac cult, including cross-dressing.
73   Cf. Suet., *Aug.* 70; Eitrem 42f.
74   Cf. Eitrem 49ff.

bearing on Propertius 4.9: "Wherever we hear of transvestite heroes, we may suspect rites involving transvestism, especially with Heracles, Achilles, Leucippus, and Hymenaeus" (190). Slater illustrates this remark about Heracles with reference to the cult of Heracles at Tlos in Asia Minor: this involved a ritual based on his exchange of clothes with Omphale. Hercules' emphasis at Propertius 4.9.47ff. on the *fascia* (brassiere) which he wore in Lydia (49) may thus relate both to ritual and to private *kômoi* involving transvestism, as well as being humorous. The μίτρα is the garment which was most clearly distinctive of cross-dressing in religion and komastic contexts: in cult the transvestite priest of Heracles at Cos wore a μίτρα to commemorate the arrival there of Heracles, his poor reception, and his hiding in female disguise (see above, Section IV).[75] Most often the μίτρα was a female "headband" or "turban," but the word does sometimes refer to a "waistband," just as *fascia* seems sometimes, though not at Propertius 4.9.49, to refer to "headgear."[76] A final observation to end this topic: the reference to Tiresias at Propertius 4.9.57f. may do more than allude to Callimachus *Hymn* 5, since Tiresias was both man and woman.[77]

Propertius 4.9 emerges from this discussion as a multi-dimensional elegy. Its generic dimensions have been discussed at various points. But its multi-dimensionality goes beyond the generic, extending to the literary, cultural, social, and political fields. For Propertius 4.9 is both serious and humorous, both elegant hellenistic wit and Roman politico-religious poetry. In this way it was able both to cater to the literary sophisticates of contemporary Rome and to satisfy the emblematic expectations which surrounded the figure of Hercules in the Augustan age, particularly after the publication of the *Aeneid*. The elegy still, however, eludes final judgement. Some of the reasons for its complexity must lie in its presumed Callimachean background.[78] Again, if the *Amores* of Gallus had survived, more would doubtless be clear.

---

75   Cf. Slater (1978) 189ff. with the bibliography cited there.
76   Cf. Slater (1978) 188 n. 13; LSJ s.v. μίτρα; TLL *s.vv. mitra, fascia* IAc: "brassiere;" IAe (Sen., *Ep.* 80.10 and Curt. 3.3.19): "headgear."
77   Piccaluga 200 n. 21 links the Bona Dea with cures for blindness, and with punishing violators of her rites with blindness, and at 236f. n. 166 notes that Appius Claudius was struck by blindness for admitting women to the rites of Hercules (Serv. *ad Aen.* 8.269). Cf. also Brouwer 260f., 366, 400. Blindness is thus another possible strand.
78   Pillinger 183ff. usefully compares the combination of irony, wit and "aura of simple faith" in Prop. 4.9 with Callimachus' *Hymns*. The relevance of the comparison goes beyond Callimachus' literary influence: social and political conditions in Augustan Rome were in many respects the continuation of those found in the capital cities of the hellenistic kingdoms, especially Alexandria.

Some use by Propertius of a Gallan intermediary between himself and Callimachus is virtually certain: the appearance of the *schema Cornelianum* in line 3 (*venit ad invictor pecorosa Palatia montis*) is a programmatic pointer to the influence of Gallus, which is confirmed by the highly neoteric style used throughout.[79] Gallus' contribution will probably never be identified, which leaves Propertius' own originality obscure. But at least the elegy's surprising duality of function can be discerned: in literary terms Propertius 4.9 is indeed a fully fledged hellenistic poem close to the various strands of the *Aetia* tradition; but as a mythico-religious elegy it is also near to the heart of contemporary political, social, and religious reality. Similarly, the apparent inconcinnity of elegiac genre of content (*kômos/paraclausithyron*) and epic subject-matter, which, if accepted at face value, could suggest that Propertius' main aim was humor, assumes a richer significance once the manifold literary traditions lying behind Propertius 4.9 have been disentangled. Certain elegies of Propertius Book 4 may have been written for ritual public performance: 4.6 seems a likely candidate.[80] Conversely, such performance of 4.9 seems most unlikely; and yet the context of its composition and publication, the fourth book of Propertius' elegies, is one in which literature and contemporary life approximate very closely throughout.[81]

[79] For discussion of "neoteric" style (with bibliography), cf. Pinotti 54ff.; Pillinger 183-7.
[80] Cairns (1984).
[81] My thanks for their comments are due to many fellow-participants at the Symposium, and in particular to Charles Segal and Thomas Hubbard. I am also grateful to Ian Rutherford for discussion of *Paean* 6 and Theoxenia, and to Malcolm Heath for criticism of an earlier draft of this paper. I alone am responsible for opinions and remaining errors.

ADDENDUM Lawler (which came to my notice at a late point in the preparation of this paper) brings to light suggestive links between Heracles, the term *kallinikos*, the *kômos*, and transvestism. Although not all her theories can be considered proven, some of these links may constitute further reinforcement of the views advanced above.

BIBLIOGRAPHY TO PROPERTIUS 4.9:
"HERCULES EXCLUSUS" AND THE DIMENSIONS OF GENRE

(NB: Commentaries on Propertius are referred to in the paper by author's names only.)

Alfonsi, L. (1971), "Sul mito di Ercole e Caco in Properzio" in *Fons Perennis. Saggi critici di Filologia Classica raccolti in onore del Prof. Vittorio d'Agostino* (Torino) 1-6.

Amandry, P. (1939), "Convention réligieuse conclue entre Delphes et Skiathos," *BCH* 63.183- 219 and *Pl* 44f.

Anderson, W.S. (1964), "*Hercules Exclusus*: Propertius IV, 9," *AJP* 85.1-12.

Boetticher, C. (1856), *Der Baumkultus der Hellenen* (Berlin).

Bowra, C.M. (1964), *Pindar* (Oxford).

Brouwer, H.H.J. (1989), *Bona Dea. The Sources and a Description of the Cult (Études préliminaires aux religions orientales dans l'Empire romain* 110) (Leiden).

Cairns, F. (1972), *Generic Composition in Greek and Roman Poetry* (Edinburgh).

_____, (1975), "*Splendide Mendax:* Horace *Odes* III.11," *Greece and Rome* 21.129-39.

_____, (1979), *Tibullus. A Hellenistic Poet at Rome* (Cambridge).

_____, (1984), "Propertius and the Battle of Actium (4.6)," in Woodman-West 129-68, 229- 36.

_____, (1989), *Virgil's Augustan Epic* (Cambridge).

Coli, E. (1978), "Propert. IV 9 e il culto della Bona Dea," *Giornale Italiano di Filologia* 9.298-305.

Copley, F.O. (1956), *Exclusus amator: a study in Latin love poetry (Philological Monographs published by the American Philological Association 17)*.

Deneken, F. (1881), *De Theoxeniis* Diss. (Berlin).

Dover, K.J. ed. (1971), *Theocritus: Select Poems* (Basingstoke).

Eitrem, S. (1932), "Zur Apotheose," *Symbolae Osloenses* 10.31-56.

Färber, H. (1936), *Die Lyrik in der Kunsttheorie der Antike* (Munich).

Fedeli, P. (1983), "'*Propertii monobiblos*': struttura e motivi," *ANRW* II.30.3.1858-1922.

Festugière, A.J. (1955), *Epicurus and his Gods* tr. C.H. Chilton (Oxford).

Flückiger-Guggenheim, D. (1984), *Göttliche Gäste. Die Einkehr von Göttern und Heroen in der griechischen Mythologie* (*Europäische Hochschulschriften* III.237 [Bern]).

Fowler, A. (1982), *Kinds of Literature. An Introduction to the Theory of Genres and Modes* (Cambridge, Mass.).

Galinsky, G.K. (1972), *The Herakles Theme. The Adaptations of the Hero in Literature from Homer to the Twentieth Century* (Oxford).

Gill, D. (1974), "*Trapezomata:* A neglected aspect of Greek sacrifice," *Harvard Theological Review* 67.117-37.

Griffin, J. (1985), *Latin Poets and Roman Life* (London).

Harrison, S.J. (1989), "Augustus, the Poets, and the *Spolia Opima*," *CQ* n.s. 39.408-14.

Harrauer, H. (1973), *A Bibliography to Propertius* (Hildesheim).

Heath, M. (1988), "Receiving the κῶμος: the Context and Performance of Epinician," *AJP* 109.180-95.

Hoffman, R.J. (1989) "Ritual License and the Cult of Dionysus," *Athenaeum* n.s. 77.91-115.

Holleman, A.W.J., (1977) "Propertius IV 9: An Augustan View of Roman Religion," *Revue Belge de Philologie et d'Histoire* 55.79-92.

Howie, J.G. (1989), "Greek Polytheism" in *Polytheistic Systems*, ed. G. Davies (Edinburgh) 51- 76.

Kirkwood, G. (1982), *Selections from Pindar. Edited with an Introduction and Commentary* (American Philological Association Textbooks Series 7).

Lawler, L.B. (1948). "*Orchêsis Kallinikos*," *TAPA* 79.254-67.

McParland, E. (1970), "Propertius 4.9," *TAPA* 101.349-55.

Maltby, R. (1991), *A Lexicon of Ancient Latin Etymologies* (Arca 25, Leeds).

Meuli, K. (1946), "Griechische Opferbräuche," in *Phyllobolia für Peter von der Mühll* edd. O. Gigon, K. Meuli, W. Theiler, F. Wehrli, B. Wyss (Basel) 185-288.

Milani, C. (1976) "Osservazioni su Lat. *Lectisternium*," *Istituto Lombardo*: *Rend. Cl. Lett.* 110.231-42.

Mischkowski, H. (1917), *Die heiligen Tische im Götterkultus der Griechen und Römer* (Diss. Königsberg).

Neutsch, B. (1961), "Der Heros auf der Kline. Zu einer Grossen Terrakotta-Matrize im Nationalmuseum von Tarent," *Mitteilungen des Deutschen Archäologischen Instituts, Römische Abteilung* 68.150-63 and Plates 62-73.

Newman, J.K. (1967) *Augustus and the new poetry* (*Coll. Latomus* 88, Brussels-Berchem).

Newman, J.K., (1985) "Pindar and Callimachus," *ICS* 10.169-89.

Nilsson, M.P. (1906) *Griechische Feste von religiöser Bedeutung. Mit Ausschluss der attischen* (Leipzig).

Nock, A.D. (1944) "The Cult of Heroes," *HTR* 37.141-75; repr. in *Essays on Religion and the Ancient World* II, ed. Z. Stewart (Oxford 1972) 576-602.

Ogilvie, R.M. (1965) *A Commentary on Livy Books 1-5* (Oxford).

Palm, J. (1965-1966), "Bemerkungen zur Ekphrase in der griechischen Literatur," (*Kungl. Humanistiska Vetenskaps-Samfundet i Uppsala, Arsbok*) Stockholm.

Piccaluga, G. (1964) "Bona Dea. Due contributi all'interpretazione del suo culto," *Studi e Materiali di Storia delle Religioni* 35.195-237.

Pillinger, H.E. (1969) "Some Callimachean Influences on Propertius, Book 4," *HSCP* 73.171-99, 182-9.

Pinotti, P. (1977) "Propert. IV 9: Alessandrinismo e arte allusiva," *Giornale Italiano di Filologia* n.s. 8.50-71.

Poliakoff, M. (1980) "Nectar, Springs, and the Sea: Critical Terminology in Pindar and Callimachus," *ZPE* 39.41-7.

Radt, S.L. (1958) *Pindars Zweiter und Sechster Paian. Text, Scholien und Kommentar* (Amsterdam).

Ravenna, G. (1974) "L'ekphrasis poetica di opere d'arte in latino. Temi e problemi," *Quaderni dell'Instituto di Filologia Latina, Università di Padova* 3.1-52.

_____, (1980), *Ekphrasis, Descriptio: teoria, pratica e generi letterari* (Padova).

_____, (1980a), *Giasone e "enargheia:" ekphrasis ed economia narrativa (Val. Fl. 2, 629 —fine)* (Padova).

Richardson, N.J. (1986), "Pindar and later literary criticism in antiquity," *Papers of the Liverpool Latin Seminar* 5.383-401.

Russell, D.A.—Wilson, N.G. edd. (1981), *Menander Rhetor* (Oxford).

Sbordone, F. (1941), "Il Ciclo Italico di Eracle. 3.—Eracle e Caco," *Athenaeum* n.s. 19.149-80.

Schönbeck, G. (1962), *Der Locus Amoenus Von Homer bis Horaz* (Diss. Heidelberg).

Shapiro, H.A. (1980), "Jason's Cloak," *TAPA* 110.263-86.

Slater, W.J. (1969), "Futures in Pindar," *CQ* n.s. 19-86-94.

Slater, W.J. (1978), "Artemon and Anacreon: no text without context," *Phoenix* 32.185-94.

Thönges-Stringaris, R. (1965), "Das Griechische Totenmahl," *Mitteilungen des Deutschen Archäologischen Instituts, Athenische Abteilung* 80.1-99 and Pl. 1-30.

Thomas, R.F. (1983), "Virgil's Ecphrastic Centerpieces," *HSCP* 87.175-84.

Thomas, R.F. (1983a), "Callimachus, the *Victoria Berenicis* and Roman poetry," *Classical Quarterly* n.s. 33.92-113.

Thomas, R.F. (1988), "Turning Back the Clock," *CP* 83.54-69.

Wächter, T. (1910), *Reinheitsvorschriften im griechischen Kult* (*Religionsgeschichtliche Versuche und Vorarbeiten* 9.1) Giessen.

Warden, J. (1982), "Epic into Elegy: Propertius 4,9,70f.," *Hermes* 110.228-42.

Weniger, L. (1923/24), "Theophanien, altgriechische Götteradvente," *Archiv für Religionswissenschaft* 22.16-57.

Winter, J.G. (1910), "The Myth of Hercules at Rome" in *Roman History and Mythology* (University of Michigan Studies, Humanistic Series IV) (New York) 171-273.

Woodman, T. and West, D., eds. (1984), *Poetry and Politics in the Age of Augustus* (Cambridge).

Wissowa, G. (1912), *Religion und Kultus der Römer*, 2nd ed. (Munich).

Yardley, J.C. (1978), "The Elegiac Paraclausithyron," *Symbolae Osloenses* 76.19-34.

THE LIMITS OF GENRE
Response to Francis Cairns

I have no doubt that most readers will join me in finding Professor Cairns' method of approaching Propertius 4.9 and the conclusions he draws highly exciting and challenging. Ranging far back into the fifth century for his principal literary illustration and far outside the limits of literature for insight into Propertius' aetiological significance, he has indeed stretched the dimensions of genre and stretched our imaginations in a most refreshing way. I have no intention, then, to respond to him as Hercules did to Cacus, storming his lair and rescuing my cows from him. But I do perhaps feel a little like Hercules outside the shrine of the Bona Dea, teased by the sound of the girls inside and thirsty for the waters that are promised by the place. I am genuinely intrigued by the Propertian poem that Cairns has developed for us and I hunger and thirst to share it. Let me stop at that particular line, before I try to decide whether he is Bona Dea herself or rather her alluring *puellae*, and get down to the proper business of response.

Professor Cairns is one of the great exponents of the value of genre as an empirical tool for working with Latin poetry, and we are all in debt to him for his book and many articles which apply his methodology. In this paper, however, the range and versatility of his use of genre and his patent intention of exploring the dimensions—or, we might say, of testing the limit—of genre suggest that his mastery of the empirical tool has transformed it into a genuine hermeneutics, a definitive way of interpretation. Rejecting the constraints of the simple genres such as elegy and epic, which indeed have very limited utility in the discussion of Propertius 4.9, and putting his emphasis instead on "genres of content," he has invoked a number of new and tantalizing aspects of potential significance for the poem and invited us to consider a new Propertius, whose literary sophistication and his position in that complex Augustan blend of Roman and Hellenistic cultural currents (including those of religion) enable him to embrace in this poem not only the traditions that come to focus in Callimachus but also those which existed in his native town of Assisi and throughout Roman Italy in religious life and cult. By this hermeneutic, then, it becomes significant to talk of 4.9 as a "mythico-religious and cultic elegy."

I trust that it is clear that I share Professor Cairns' impatience with naive dependence on traditional generic labels and wish to explore the dimensions of genre with him. But I wonder whether we need to have some empirical tests to determine how apt a so-called genre of content is to the poem or passage under discussion. Is there perhaps some minimum number of parallel elements which must be observed before we would feel entitled to identify a particular genre? I say this because I believe that his use of *kômos* lacks clear definition. It seems to be the means by which he wants to look at Propertius from the start; it then becomes a viewpoint on Pindar's paean; and thereby we move toward mythico-religious elegy. But what elements of what definition of *kômos* are functioning? It could be said, I think, that the paraclausithyron, the song sung at the closed door of a girl, was under certain conditions a *kômos*, but can we claim that under *any* conditions it was such? A serenade praising the beauty of the girl differs rather drastically from a song of self-praise and importunity: are both properly *kômoi*? Is the erotic component a necessary and expected aspect of *kômoi* or an accidental feature? Recent controversy among students of Pindar has focused on the question of whether or not the epinikians were often first performed as solos or, as has traditionally been believed, by a choral group; and part of the problem has been to understand what Pindar meant by talking of the performance as a *kômos* and the performer as *komazon*.[1] I trust that we can agree that the principal emphasis of *kômos* in the epinikians rests on energetic celebration. When the Pindaric komast asks a place or a deity to receive him/it in celebration, he might perhaps be similar to Alcibiades in the *Symposium*, who gains entrance to praise Socrates, and to a fond serenader who craves to be heard by his beloved, but does the request for reception of the komast connote a closed door or prepare us for the erotic purposes of the paraclausithyron? I am not sure, then, from the use of the generic term *kômos*, that Pindar and Propertius are aptly brought together.

Apart from the relationship between the various examples of the *kômos* and komasts in this paper, I find myself concerned with the analysis of Paean 6 and its "illustrative" connections with Propertius 4.9. Cairns has come up with some dazzling potential parallels between the two poems, especially between the opening situation of the Paean and the setting for the approach of Hercules

---

[1] M. Heath (cited in Cairns' bibliography), who extends the views of M. Lefkowitz in the same volume of *AJP*, pp. 1-11, has been forcefully answered by C. Carey, "The Performance of the Victory Ode," also in that volume, pp. 545-65, and by Anne Burnett, "Performing Pindar's Odes," *CP* 84 (1989) 283-93.

in 4.9 to the shrine of Bona Dea. Although we might pause over some of the details of the argued parallels, for example, the postulation of an erotic element in the very words "receive me" of the Paean[2] or the suggestion that the sexual dichotomy of male chorus asking to join a female chorus, which is already singing and dancing for Apollo, puts that male chorus in a position analogous to Hercules at the door of Bona Dea; or the way Cairns groups word units to interpret the sound (8) as that of water and to isolate the phrase *orphanon andrôn* (9) as similar to Propertius' *nullis sacra retecta viris* (26),[3] nevertheless what is perhaps more pertinent is to inquire into the very conception of the illustrative use of Paean 6. When we are using, not a relatively definable literary genre, but a cluster of motifs which we call a genre of content, how do we control free association and determine the pertinency and possibility of the supposed illustration?

We know the conditions in which paeans were performed in fifth-century Greece, and we have the central portion of Paean 6, in which the chorus did its principal business and celebrated the role of Apollo at Troy and his subsequent punishment of Neoptolemos. Granted that Pindar was a highly sophisticated poet, capable of considerable wit and irony about his material, does it seem likely that his personal poetics, the expectations of the audience and occasion for the paean, and the general cultural and religious background of the early fifth-century in Greece could aptly be combined to create a significant illustration for the very different audience and poetic occasion of Propertius' aetiological elegy and for the cultural and religious conditions which influence reception? The scenario for the business of the paean, celebrating Apollo, might be argued to be so conventionally prooemial and so determined by the serious focus on Apollo as to exclude the kind of special emphasis that Professor Cairns has assigned it; it becomes in his view perhaps a Hellenistic illustration before its time, anachronistically. (If we discard as unproven and unprovable the isolated line of Alcaeus which Cairns considers the earliest extract from an ancient erotic *kômos*, then there is no

---

[2]   It is a conventional opening of epinicians for the komast or the chorus to ask that they or their song be received. Cf. *O*. 5.1-3, *P*. 8.5 and 12.1-5, and *N* . 11.1-3.

[3]   The flexibility of word-order in Greek poetry and the requirements of logic support the usual interpretation of the passage as meaning that the komast and chorus of *Paean* 6 has heard by the waters of Castalia a sound lacking a chorus of males.

contemporary warrant for any erotic overtones in this paean.)[4] The combination of religious with erotic purpose in the Paean is questionable, and on the other hand the combination of erotic with religious purpose in Propertius 4.9 remains to be proved. For all the fascinating lore that Cairns elicited from it, then, how pertinent is Paean 6 as an illustration?

That brings me, then, to Propertius' poem itself and to the provocative suggestion by Cairns that it is a mythico-religious and cultic elegy as well as what we all recognize: an intelligent adaptation of the aetiological techniques of Callimachean elegy and of the forms and interests of erotic elegy which Propertius had practiced heretofore in Book 1-3. I want his suggestion to be true not only because it has some personal appeal to my own ideas of religious sophistication but also because it would enhance and enlarge my appreciation of Propertius, which is already fervent. It seems to me that the attractive proposals of Professor Cairns recommend themselves in this paper largely by analogy with other genres of content or with the general religious attitude of Greeks and Romans who, like the people of the Latin countries today, were able to be both playful and serious about their gods and cults. What we seem to need, to anchor this interpretation of Propertius, is more detailed presentation of the facts of this poem and of the deity and cult with which it deals.

Professor Cairns suggests that Propertius 4.9 falls into the genre of a hymn, along the lines defined by the rhetorician Menander under the rubric *mythikos hymnos*. It recounts the achievements of a god (Heracles) and ends with a hymnic envoi. If all hymns were of one religious tone, that generic classification could help us to fix the tone of Propertius and the way his audience received the poem. However, if the Romans of this period enjoyed using the hymnal pattern for un-serious purposes, either to "divinize" a mortal of questionable credentials or to concentrate on the discreditable and comic achievements of immortals, as we can see that they did in the poetry of Horace and Ovid,[5] then the hymnal genre proves nothing conclusive about the religious intentions of Propertius.

---

[4] Hephaestion, *Ench.* 5.2, who has preserved it, cites it solely as an example of the iambic tetrameter catalectic, without context or interpretation. Most editors are more cautious than Radke and refuse to postulate a specific komastic situation for the single line.

[5] Cf. Horace *C.* 1.30 and 32; 2.7 and 8; 3.11, 13, 21, and 26; Ovid, *Am.* 1.13, 3.6 and 10; and the mock-reverent presentation of Jupiter in *Met.* 1.163 ff., 589 ff., and 2.846 ff.

Another way of throwing light on audience expectations would be to check the practices of Propertius both in the remainder of Book 4 and in the earlier books. In the first part of the program poem of Book 4, as is well known, the poet declares confidently that he intends to make his topic the sacred rites and days of Rome (*sacra diesque canam* 4.1.69). However, he then creates a voice of opposition in Horus (who has some Callimachean features, perhaps, but also evokes the familiar features of the love elegy of Books 1-3), and the program ends up in ambivalence. Of the ten remaining poems, it would be hard to name one (apart from this Hercules elegy) which conveys religious understanding and appeals to the broad Latin view of cult. The presentation of Vertumnus in 2 gives us an amiable talking statue, a deity who does not really know the etymology of his own name, but is tickled to go over all the transvestite roles he can play. Elegy 10 talks of the cult of Jupiter Feretrius, but not in religious terms, focusing rather distantly on the martial (un-elegiac) victories of three Roman generals who then made the rare offering to Jupiter. Elegy 6 features Apollo of Actium, whose presentation Professor Johnson and many others have found highly problematical. Elegy 8 turns from the chaste rites at Lanuvium, at which Cynthia was an unchaste onlooker, to the wild erotic scene on the Esquiline, which eventually includes Cynthia: patently, the *sacra* yield to non-religious, erotic material. The rest of the poems do not involve sacred rites or cult at all. In light of that performance in the other elegies of Book 4, it would of course be possible, but not probable or expectable that Propertius would produce a mythico-religious or cultic elegy in 9 that would touch the full range of traditional Roman religious life. I do not need, I think, to review the earlier books for religious breadth: that was not in the purpose of the love elegist. I call attention only to 2.31, which is a description of the Temple of Apollo on the Palatine. An ecphrasis, not a religious or cultic poem, it insists on the amatory element by starting from an apparent complaint of the girl over the lover's lateness, who then claims interest in the new temple as his excuse (real or otherwise). Audience expectation for religious, cultic elegy in 4.9 would, I think, have been low.

Propertius recounted two myths on Hercules' Roman exploits in 4.9, as is well known. In 20 lines he covers the story of Cacus, which had already been related by both Livy and Vergil and would be told less than twenty years later by Ovid in *Fasti* 1.543 ff. Propertius' version is the briefest and least engaging of all four accounts; and it is plain that he uses it as an introduction to the much longer and more detailed story of Hercules and Bona Dea (50 lines) with which we are chiefly concerned today. Our only other surviving Roman source for this second myth is Varro (cited by Macrobius); and it is not clear whether he told the same story or even laid it in this Roman setting.[6] Propertius is the only writer known to us to link these two myths, which present Hercules' encounters with Evil and Good, both of which he masters in the same violent manner.

Earlier this year, I was in Rome, where I had spent the two weeks of my spring vacation partly in pursuing some research on Bona Dea and the topography of this poem. Bona Dea frustrates research today, of female as well as of male scholars. The famous rites, such as those which Clodius violated in 62 B.C., had nothing to do with the scene of 4.9: they always took place in a magistrate's house and involved only the most august matrons and Vestals. Bona Dea had some strange stories and rites that included snakes, and she had a shrine, which Augustus' wife Livia would later restore. Ovid briefly talks about the goddess in connection with May 1 (*Fasti* 5.147-58). He locates the shrine below what he calls The Rock, and Roman topographers, without ever finding secure traces of the spot, have generally agreed that it was on the slopes of the Lesser Aventine.[7] I am not sure what we can assume about the attitude to this goddess of the males, at least 50% of Propertius' audience; but it does seem evident that Propertius himself in the poem gives few indications of informed understanding or feeling about the goddess, far less than Ovid in the *Fasti*.

I do think it worthwhile to emphasize the topographical facts, because they may provide a clue as to tone. The action of the episode involving Cacus takes place near the Velabrum and the Forum Boarium underneath the precipitous slope of the Palatine Hill that towers up there. Propertius specifically locates the scene in line 3-6; and he agrees, as Jocelyn P. Small and

---

[6]   Macrobius, *Sat.* 1.27-29, seems to be citing Varro (whose authority he has clearly invoked for the tradition that Bona Dea is the daughter of Faunus). He goes on to say that no man enters her temple, then connects that fact with the ritual of Hercules' worship, at which no woman is permitted. This myth provides the reason: "quod Herculi cum boves Geryonis per agros Italiae duceret, sitienti respondit mulier aquam se non posse praestare, quod feminarum deae celebraretur dies, nec ex eo apparatu viris gustare fas esset." There, his account ends, without indication that Hercules broke into the shrine (which seems to be involved) and slaked his thirst. Note that Macrobius-Varro locates the encounter vaguely "in the fields of Italy," not specifically in Rome, and draws no connection with Cacus or the Ara Maxima.

[7]   The older topographers, such as Platner, Ashby, and Lugli, and the present generation, notably Coarelli, all agree in locating the Rock on the Lesser Aventine.

others observe, with the pre-Vergilian tradition which makes Cacus a shepherd living on the Palatine with other shepherds.[8] The commemorative founding of the Ara Maxima in the Forum Boarium fits this setting perfectly. For his own poetic reasons, Vergil in *Aeneid* 8 turned Cacus into a hellish monster and moved his cave to the Aventine (outside Evander's territory). But that cave was also in the tall sheer face of the hill which towers above the Tiber; it was not somewhere along the gentler slope that flanks the Circus Maximus.[9] Thus, the first episode of the two in Propertius' elegy takes place on and below the heights of the Palatine closest to the Tiber, and it concludes at the Ara Maxima only a stone's throw from the river water. With a fussiness that his usual gargantuan tastes belie, Hercules turns his back on the ready water (as if living in Propertius' more polluted era) and the sources available on the Palatine, and he is made to rush thirstily on a course which the Roman audience would recognize as straight down the Circus Maximus, over 500 meters, and on to the shrine of Bona Dea, a total distance of over a half mile.[10] No wonder he arrived with dust-caked beard (31). Although, then, the speech he manages to utter is reminiscent of the words of a komast, poor Hercules is in a condition very different from the well-oiled state of the traditional komast. His words, his actions and his appearance are far below those appropriate to a god. And the vague description of the shrine and devotees of Bona Dea does not enhance the religious or cultic tone, I think.

I have tried to find in the text of Propertius' elegy some details that would match and support the suggestions of Professor Cairns as to its status as "a mythico-religious and cultic elegy." I have not been successful. It seems to me that Propertius is not the man to pursue such generic enlargement, and this elegy is more obviously preoccupied with flaunting the tour de force of the poet who has combined stories of Bad Cacus and Good Goddess, of rites that forbid men and rites that ban women and linking them with this un-heroic,

---

8   J.P. Small, *Cacus and Marsyas in Etrusco-Roman Legend* (Princeton 1982), Chapter 1, places Cacus on the Palatine in the pre-Vergilian tradition, with which, as she notes, Propertius also agrees. E. Montanari, art. "Caco," *Enciclopedia Virgiliana* (Rome 1989) emphasizes that, of the Augustans, only Vergil and Ovid assign Cacus to the Aventine; the others (Propertius, Livy, and Dionysius) all put him on the Palatine by the Scala Caci.

9   Vergil's description of the attack on Cacus, as he hides in a cave on the Aventine, in *Aen.* 8.228 ff., imagines a precipitous rocky approach to a cavern near the river. Cf. especially 236 and 240.

10   The modern location for the Shrine of Bona Dea is regularly connected to the site of Santa Balbina, on the side of the Lesser Aventine overlooking the Baths of Caracalla. To reach that place from the end of the Circus Maximus, Hercules would have had to struggle another 200-300 yards.

comically human Hercules. Nevertheless, this has been an occasion for a very valuable exploration of techniques of interpretation. We should all be grateful to Professor Cairns for a provocative paper that forces us to see how wide the dimensions of Roman elegy might be and to test his suggestions against the brilliant achievement of Propertius 4.9.

EMPIRICAL AND THEORETICAL APPROACHES TO LITERARY GENRE

Critics who intend to deal with poetic genres would do well to abandon the false dilemma of empiricism versus theory. It might seem that they could accomplish this by practicing good empiricism and healthy theory; but it is obvious that two one-sided and extreme positions cannot be ennobled simply by adding a positive adjective to them. Instead, we should perhaps think of good criticism as Aristotle thought of *aretê*, as a summit rising between two symmetric vices, one due to excess and the other due to insufficiency. Now, just as one cannot produce courage by wedding a good cowardice to a good rashness—that is, by ennobling two vices and thereby algebraically canceling them out—so too good criticism does not spring from the correction of a methodological near- or far-sightedness by merely enlarging or restricting the visual field. When good criticism succeeds, it does so by discrediting both the kind of empiricism whose attention is directed obsessively to naturalistically understood details (that is, to naked data, to evidence presumed to speak for itself) and the kind of theory which is nebulous and abstract, which loses sight of how a text is put together and of its fine and specific texture. Hence, good empiricism is neither directed at single "lived realities" nor does it compare with one another fragments of *Realia* and of poetic texts, adding if necessary a wider horizon of interpretation as a simple corrective. Vice versa, and complementarily, healthy theory does not search for a recipe for poetic composition which simply needs to be "filled" with empirical contents. Thus the dispute between one-sided empiricism as contrasted with theory, and one-sided theory as contrasted with empiricism, is one, in Aristotelian terms, between two low-level notions, both far removed from the "summit" of *aretê*. To put this in other terms, flaws of method are made manifest by actual critical research—when it fails.

My own position is beset with many difficulties. For example, my stubborn refusal to believe in genres as handbooks of poetic composition ends up forcing me to deny myself a critical position I would have every interest in having as an ally, given that I too wish to indulge in the vice of believing in the usefulness of genre in the interpretation of texts. What makes matters worse is that, as must be clear by now, my ideas do *not* represent an attempt to mediate between these two hostile camps. I admit at once that my position is a response to my dissatisfaction at constantly trying to perfect an imperfect instrument which nevertheless allows me to go ahead in my work. Hence I am unhappy with my own results, but I am also dissatisfied with the way in which many classicists continue to study (and also, fail to study) literary genre:[1] this is a general impression, but the field I shall be considering today is itself a large one—that of classical Roman poetry.

Given that much of what I shall be saying is problematic and controversial, I would like to begin by establishing at least one point. In my view, at least one function gives meaning to the critical concept of genre and makes its study useful: that is, the function of associating elements of content and of form, putting them into relation and correspondence with one another. Only if the category of genre succeeds in establishing a non-arbitrary and non-impressionistic connection between these two levels, does it seem to me useful and also, if I may say so, reasonable. A category of genre based exclusively upon formal features is clearly unacceptable: what scholar, for example, would be willing to consider all poetry written in the Aeolic dialect as a single genre? Such a connection would be not only merely formal, but contingent and superficial. But it is just as dangerous (and it is more common in recent studies) to think of genre as a typology founded exclusively upon typical contents: *topoi,* recurrent themes and motifs, situations. A classification by contents runs the danger of never indicating the boundary between the general

---

[1]   The paper by L.E. Rossi, "I generi letterari e le loro leggi scritte e non scritte nelle letterature classiche," *BICS* 18 (1971) 69-94, which is important on many counts, has the great merit of having reopened the discussion on genres. The need to renew that debate arose from the fact that the Positivist sleep in Germany had made genres an "obvious" category—a static, mechanical interpretative modulus—while, in the following generation, in Italy, the Crocian school had unwisely excluded genres from critical consideration. In line with Rossi's paper, even if with a few significant differences, there has been the contribution by M. Fantuzzi, "La contaminazione dei generi letterari nella letteratura greca ellenistica: rifiuto del sistema o evoluzione di un sistema?," *Lingua e Stile* 15 (1980) 433-450. A valuable recent paper by T.G. Rosenmeyer, "Ancient Literary Genres: A Mirage?," *Yearbook of Comparative and General Literature* 34 (1985) 74-84, especially 81 f. (with useful bibliography) argues that the ancients tended to think less in terms of genres than in those of the imitation of specific poetic precedents. Rosenmeyer is undoubtedly right, but it must be pointed out that, if imitation is to be successful, it necessarily involves a degree of *generalisation,* in the sense that the imitative process requires the poet who is imitating to set up a relationship whereby an acknowledged textual model becomes a generally applicable matrix for the production of new texts. I trust Dr. Horsfall will forgive me a brief excursion into jargon if I say that the special relationship between a recognized model and its successful imitation makes possible a "transfer of competence." The capable imitator does not engage in an act of literary theft, but reaches the point where he is able to "write in the manner of" his predecessor (for example, in the way a great epic poet had written). To be able to do this, he chooses certain distinctive features of the exemplary text, identifies them as being typical of and essential to the poetic quality of the text as a whole, and then makes them part of a new (personal) matrix that he himself becomes able to apply.

and the particular: if for example we agree to call "a dying man's last words" a genre, there is no reason to stop there, and we could just as well accept such genres as "the poet meets Cupid at night" or "the poet is transformed into a swan." To argue in this way is to fail to set a clear boundary between the genre as *generative matrix* on the one hand (more on this below) and the individual classification of single texts on the other, for it is to lose sight of the connection between structures of content and structures of expression. Genre thereby becomes downgraded to a (fixed) recipe, to a mechanical handbook of production, and ceases to be an optional strategy of literary composition.

There have always been scholars who are skeptical about the interpretative usefulness of literary genres and have preferred to argue in terms of "real life" and literature, in terms of lived experience, of Realia, to be set against the distinctive individuality of single texts. For these empirically minded critics, there are only naked facts on the one hand and literature on the other: the middle is populated by such unserviceable abstractions as, precisely, "genre." Often these stubborn empiricists start out from a justified polemic, reacting against the kind of historicism which regards the pedigree of a notion as a sufficient explanation of its meaning and tells us about genres in terms of the birth, life, and death of organisms. If my foreigner's ear does not mislead me, your very word *genre* is somewhat vaguer, less assertive and triumphant than its German equivalent *Gattung*: evidently in this case, too, the fundamentally empirical Anglo-American tradition feels a certain reluctance to adopt such weighty, demanding abstractions.

But the empirical attitude, too, is open to serious objections, with regard both to its treatment of literature and to its presuppositions about real life. The naturalistic illusion, the *naturalistic fallacy*, tends to believe that there are such things as naked facts, by contrast with literary elaboration and with culture: but the facts that interest us always, so to speak, have clothes on. It is the bizarre habit of a certain kind of historicism (which seems to provide the framework for a certain kind of scholarship) to forget that history is a process and hence to immobilize it in the form of a series of isolated facts directly affecting the poet's consciousness (conceived as a wax tablet upon which events impress themselves). The old vice of naturalistic reductionism imagines that real historical events are naturalistically present, evident in themselves, that they can be separated from the system of interpretation, from the very way in which they are experienced; and it forgets, too, that in general neither history nor any consciousness of experience whatsoever can exist without having already passed through the historical forms of linguistic and perceptual codes and cultural codes.

Facts acquire meaning only in connection with one another. A genre is not made up by "stuffing" it with isolated fragments of content, but by a total system of reciprocal, structured relations: the single element must enter into a constellation with others if it is to be transvalued and redefined until it too is able to connote, by itself, the presence of a whole genre. Ovid, for example, is a poet who is very interested in the relative nature of genres and in the possibility of using certain elements derived from different codes. He is fascinated by coincidences and overlapping images. Consider a word like *arma*: within a certain constellation, this announces an epic theme, and the very word can even be considered an unambiguous symbol, a connotative signpost pointing to the genre of epic poetry. Thus the first love-story of the *Metamorphoses,* that of Daphne, is introduced by a prologue which stages an emblematic dispute between Apollo and Cupid:[2] to whom does a military weapon like the bow properly belong, i.e. within whose competence does it lie? of which literary genre is it the sign? The dispute arises from the fact that, as Ovid notes, Cupid too has *arma*, which are a distinctive feature of the elegiac code: Ovid can hinge his discourse upon this coincidence and let it pivot from epic to elegy.[3] Or consider Mercury's magical *virga*. As a divine attribute, this is an element of epic; on the other hand, we all know that the *virga* is used by shepherds too, including the shepherds of the bucolic genre. One scene of the *Metamorphoses* is typically epic: the father of the gods charges Mercury with a mission to be performed on earth. But the monstrous Argus he will have to deal with there is a guardian of herds. At once the scene is transformed from epic to bucolic, and Mercury starts to speak in a bucolic style. Yet he still has his *virga* with him—it has simply changed function (now it is the stick with which the shepherd directs the flock), and its polyvalence

---

[2]   It has been observed that Ovid returns here to the dilemma which he had "staged" in the proem of the *Amores:* there Cupid had dissuaded the poet intent upon singing *arma . . . violentaque bella* and imposed upon him the elegiac rhythm by simply stealing a metrical foot; the episode continued with a dispute about spheres of competence and ended with an arrow well aimed by Cupid (a love-affair). Cf. W.S.M. Nicoll, "Cupid, Apollo and Daphne (Ov., *Met.* 1.452ff.)," *CQ* 30 (1980) 174ff.; cf. also E.J. Kenney, "Introduction" to *Ovid. Metamorphoses,* trans. A.D. Melville (Oxford-New York 1986), pp. xvii-xviii.

[3]   At the very moment he drags Apollo out of the epic world to carry him into the world of elegy (just as in the proem of the *Amores* the poet himself was carried from epic into elegy), Cupid significantly takes on the language and gestures of the epic hero: hence the proclamation of a challenge (*Met.* 1.463-65), the "formula of transition to action" *dixit et . . .,* the description of the warrior-archer's gestures and weapons, finally (this is the custom in epic) the description of how the missile reaches its target: *laesit Apollineas traiecta per ossa medullas (ibid.* 473).

underlines even more the change of code and of world. The task of changing
the whole structure in this way is assigned to a difference in the constellation of
the signifying elements: before this "metamorphosis," Mercury is depicted as
the epic messenger with winged sandals, petasus and magic wand; in his new
guise, the only element which has remained, the *virga*—in metamorphosis one
cardinal element is present both before and after—becomes the signal of the
world of shepherds by entering into relation with the other characterizing
elements, such as she-goats and shepherds' pipes.[4] Behind the unchanging
objects and words emerges the power of the relations and systems of signs
which are literary genres.

It is a fact, for example, that the lyric poets drink a lot and the elegiac
ones much less. Wine helps the lyric poet to sing and to compose poetry, while
in general the elegiac poets seem to regard wine at most as a kind of antidote
for unhappy love, and they speak emphatically about drinking pure water.[5]
The elegist Propertius who comes home tipsy one evening is a swallow that
does not make a summer. Our ways of reacting to this simple fact can be very
diverse: to begin with, we might think of it as merely a reflection of
biographical, historically authentic preferences—a possibility we should not
exclude, as I suspect that Horace was a true connoisseur of wines. On the other
hand, it has been convincingly demonstrated that poetic alcoholism is a special
case and belongs to a controversy in poetic theory: as you know, Callimachus
had ascribed his own initiation as a poet to the water of the "holy spring,"[6]
while Alcaeus (at least to judge from the fragments) talks about hardly
anything except wine.[7] In short, drinking water and drinking wine had also
become symbols of two different poetics. Both activities entertain metaphoric
or metonymic relations with the literary genre they designate, but at the same
time (a very important point) they *enter into a systematic relationship* with

---

4   *Met.* 1.674ff.: *illic tegumenque removit / et posuit pennas, tantummodo virga retenta est:
/ hac agit ut pastor per devia rura capellas, / dum venit, adductas et structis cantat avenis.*
5   Cf. e.g. Prop. 3.1.3 *puro de fonte;* 3.1.6 *quamve bibistis aquam?;* 3.3.5 *admoram
fontibus ora;* 3.3.51f. *lymphisque a fonte petitis / ora Philitea nostra rigavit aqua.* Useful
comparative material and numerous bibliographic indications can be found collected in the
commentary of P. Fedeli on the passages cited.
6   This is the source of later epigrammatists' polemical image of the Callimachean poet as
hydropotes: cf most recently P.E. Knox, "Wine, Water, and Callimachean Polemics," *HSCP*
89 (1985) 107-19.
7   In a well-known, amusing passage in *The Deipnosophists* (10. 430a-d) Athenaeus, who
has, in fact, preserved many of these fragments, makes one of his characters say that Alcaeus
appears to be such a *philopotes* that he "drinks wine in all seasons and circumstances: . . . in
winter, . . . in summer, . . . in spring, . . . in misfortune, . . . in happy times" (cf. also *ibid.*
429a , 436f).

their own opposite, and produce meaning in this way as well. In other words, speaking emphatically about the drinking of water is meaningful precisely because the effects of wine have been recommended and extolled. Speaking more generally, a phenomenon can become meaningful only on condition that it enters into a system, so setting up a relationship with something that is not already a cultural or literary sign.

Now it might be objected that what I am proposing really amounts merely to a new version of the familiar dichotomy between experience and literature, between empiricists and conventionalists, perhaps with an implicit preference for art over life; but in fact my point is quite different. For there is no reason to believe that the "system" (let us call it this) which I have outlined functions only in literature. "Real life" too is structured by cultural images and models, by symbolic choices, by communicative and perceptual codes: in real life too—in that of the Romans, for example—drinking wine is certainly an everyday activity motivated by familiar gastronomic qualities, but at the same time it can also act as a directed signal, understandable within a complex system of references such as water, blood, luxury, Dionysus, the symposium, the consumption of Greek products, virility, death, etc.; each of these elements then enters into a constellation with its opposites and contraries, corollaries, connotations, etc. Hence poetry does not work on "primary" realities, naked, isolated objects for collection, but instead deals with a cultural (or, if you prefer, culturalized) reality, one which is semiotic, already marked by conventions and tensions. That is why the biographical approach does not do justice to reality.

So much for reality, for "real life." But matters are no better with regard to literature. As Jasper Griffin has well observed,[8] the fact that there were many young Werthers in Europe around 1800 and Don Juans around 1820 has to do with the success of these works, and with their influence upon reality, rather than with their realism. Literature acts on cultural models which act on "real life" and transform it. Is Roman elegy the description of a world or the blueprint for a world? Our understanding of it benefits from the adoption of the second view.[9]

---

[8] *Latin Poets and Roman Life* (London 1985) 3.

[9] This point can be developed further, extending J. Griffin's observations and, like him, speaking in terms of examples. Don Quixote decides to set out for adventure because he has read handbooks of chivalry; in his readings he has admired the deeds of the famous knight-errant Amadis of Gaul and now he wants to imitate the model represented in chivalric literature. This model is the "mediator" of the form of life which Don Quixote wants to act out. Between the reality to be experienced and the subject of this experience intervenes the mediation of the

What is the place of genres in this view? I have already suggested that genres are matrices of works, to be conceived not as recipes but as strategies: they act in texts not *ante rem* or *post rem* but *in re*. They are like strategies, procedures whose own functioning can only be completed by the response of an addressee whom the very form of the text renders precise and recognizable. If poetry is conceived more as the blueprint for a world than as mimesis, then, as we shall see more clearly below, it is hard to do without genres.

Here too we must deal with the effects of a "realistic" approach which tries to create a short-circuit between individual texts and naked biographical realities. One influential Horatian scholar, discussing an *Epode* dedicated to the sexual desire of a woman who is no longer young and beautiful, not only sets about reconstructing the typology of this character in the social reality of late Republican Rome but even goes so far as to postulate an autobiographical importance for her: "Horace shows that he has endured the lust of one or two of these ladies" (one or two? well, well!) "(one or two depending on whether or not the lady in Epode 12 is identified with the one in Epode 8)."[10] The same critic declares that he is inclined to believe that we are dealing here with the poet's real experience: was Horace supposed to give the impression that it was false? But is it really the critic's job to feel on his palate the "bitter taste of life," perhaps by so arranging his own senses as to recapture the reek of a libidinous old lady (or even of two: the number, alas, as you have seen, is destined to remain uncertain even for those who wish to bring the unflattering catalogue up to date), or is it not rather his task to explain the text better as a literary work? What is gained by wondering about the biographical reality of these encounters? Perhaps it would be better to ask why in the *Epodes* Horace continually meets caricatures of eager lovers and of old grandmothers but in the *Odes,* as far as we can tell, almost only delicate blondes, ripe young maidens available for existential speculation: a fortunate twist of fate? If readers do not understand that they have changed "worlds" (as a first step towards understanding the individual poems), it will be dangerous for them to

---

literary model as a "form of experience," a model of the perception and elaboration of reality itself. Amadis (it will be objected) is a fictional character; of course, but the author of the fiction, the story, is not Don Quixote: the mediator is imaginary, the mediation is not. And, to take another example, it will once again be literature that "produces," so to speak, Madame Bovary's form of experience and determines her desire: the heroine's imagination is completely full of literary examples encountered in the course of reading popular romances and the passionate love stories of the scandal sheets, which constitute the "mediators" between real life and ideal life, between reality and the model according to which reality is perceived.

10   A. La Penna, *Orazio e la morale mondana europea,* introd. to *Orazio: Tutte le opere,* Firenze 1968, p. XXIf.

wonder about the spiritual and sexual development of Horace as a historical individual.

What usually bothers those who do not like to work with genres is their schematic and reductive character, their apparent over-simplification: if our purpose is to explain realities as complex as poetic texts, why should we wish to pass through such simplified "lattices?" But genre, as I am trying to describe it here, is not so much a problem for us as for *them*, the authors. Even if we admit the substantial difference between ancient culture and our own, we must still agree that literature functions according to a model of communication which is fairly universal and recurrent. The scheme offered by genre is a means of projection—projection as a way of making oneself understood: it is the poet's instrument of expression before it becomes our instrument of investigation. The programmatic nature inherent in the codification of a genre calls for *literary competence* in anyone who sets about writing a new text, and thus it determines not only the place of certain written works within the genre, but also that of those works which can still be written: a place of expectation, a road which is waiting to be traveled. Let us recall, then, that genre is not only our descriptive grid, inferred from our empirical research; it is also an expectation inscribed within the experience of the authors themselves.

Examined closely, the whole development of literary production from Catullus to Ovid can be considered as a process of the construction of genres, that is, of a literary system articulated in single areas, each of which determines its identity by comparison with the others. By signaling the boundaries of its own specific language, each form also delimits the language of the contiguous forms by differentiation. We are accustomed to think of this literature, behind which stands the experience of Alexandria, as being characterized by a congenital *poikilia* which ought to make the category of the literary genre highly problematic as an instrument of interpretation. And yet, even though the Latin poets derive their poetics from Alexandrian models, they themselves work in substantially the opposite direction.[11] In all the poetic departments of Alexandrian derivation or inspiration, the Latin poets, starting out from a reality which is often heterogeneous in form, work instead to select, to seek out dominant features around which they can construct organic forms of literary discourse—that is, to construct genres. Virgil worked with an

---

[11] There are important observations on this score in M. Labate, "Da Catullo a Ovidio: forme della letteratura, immagini del mondo," forthcoming in *Storia di Roma* (Turin: Einaudi).

edition of Theocritus which included *Idylls* of various kinds (bucolics, mimes, encomia): but there is no doubt that his own *Eclogues* construct a coherent pastoral world by restricting the possibilities of the Syracusan Muse (understood as hexametric poetry of lower-middle level): every exception in Virgil will present itself as just that.[12] When compared with the multiform variety of Hellenistic elegiac poetry, Roman elegy is certainly characterized by a unified project which selects and retains only those traits which, once they are put into systematic relation with one another, make elegy the specific representation of a tormented and unbalanced love relationship (suffering and *servitium*).[13]

Once the world has been trimmed according to a *partial* intention, the rhetoric codified in the genre produces an ideology and a language, that is, it reformulates the world by extracting from it only certain contents (which thus take the place of the whole of reality) and by constructing a mode of expression appropriate to such a partiality (this means constructing a language which is a selection from the linguistic possibilities but suffers no deficiencies, a language which is reduced but at the same time full and complete, coherent). The rhetoric of the genre is, in short, a perspective which is limited but which can reduce everything to itself, and make everything in its own image. Thus a great literary theoretician, Julius Caesar Scaliger, observed in the sixteenth century: "Pastoralia cuiuscumque generis negotium semper retrahunt ad agrorum naturam" [14] ("Pastoral poetry reduces any business, any matter to a bucolic nature, any element of this world is 'told' in the language of country-life"); this means that bucolic poetry is constructed as a closed and self-sufficient discourse, in which every element becomes a symbolic figure connoting the whole pastoral world: things enter into the text only if they agree to be spoken of in the language of the world of shepherds, only if they know how to adapt to that system of the poetic imagination. Genre, modelling the world in accordance with its own language, invites us to believe that nothing exists outside the image which it knows how to give of the world. And, even if it is true that this reduction of the world to a partial view is the way every literary genre, as the process whereby discourse is formed, inevitably

---

12   The most obvious case is certainly that of the Fourth Eclogue, which is introduced by the explicit programmatic declaration *paulo maiora canamus* so as to signal a slight distance from the homogenous and codified level of the bucolic genre. Even so, the very theme ("greater") of the new "aurea aetas" which is announced here is modulated by Virgil in pastoral terms and according to the bucolic imagination.

13   Cf. Labate, *op. cit.*

14   J.C. Scaliger, *Poetices libri septem*, III, 150, A. Buck, Stuttgart 1964 (=1561).

manifests itself, it is still true that the genre of Latin love elegy practices this restriction even more consciously, inasmuch as it makes this the keystone of its poetics. For the elegiac poet bases his identity upon diversity, declares that he is enclosed within one part of the world (within a "model of the world") which seems to him *self-sufficient.*

The sensitivity of Roman poets towards genres *a parte subjecti* is confirmed by the curious phenomenon of "empty slots." The development of Roman poetry towards a canon of genres provokes a tension so strong that it raises expectations around "unoccupied" spaces, *blanks* created and delimited at the borders of already fulfilled genres. Thus, for example, Ovid notices in some of Propertius' elegiac experiments the potential for an unoccupied genre (Ovid actually calls it *opus,* "specific form of poetic creation"): and his *Heroides* are written to fill up just this generic space, which is still free, *ignotum aliis* according to Ovid's well-known definition (*Ars Amat.* 3.346). Once the Augustans' work has in fact satisfied the most ambitious expectations, substantially completing the work of construction of an articulated literary system (the long-awaited Roman Alcaeus, Hesiod, and Homer are no longer lacking), it becomes easier to see slots which remain empty and perhaps will never be filled: Horace's letter to Augustus is dominated by the sense of a lack, a hole left open in the system of genres by the absence of a modern theater: cultural and social conditions which cannot be easily modified make the undertaking impossible by now, even for a generation of talented poets.[15] The very awareness of these lacunas indirectly confirms that by this time the system of genres has become a fully constituted reality which contemporaries have begun to recognize—and of which even the schools too will be taking notice before long.

Correspondingly, we must suppose that ancient readers attached considerable significance to the question, "To what genre does this new text belong?;" for otherwise the complexity of many ancient texts—for example

---

[15]   Attempts at tragedy had not been lacking in the modern period: Varius' *Thyestes* was a success and had gained for its author an extraordinary reward which was perhaps also an encouragement to continue along this path; long before Ovid's *Medea* pleased Quintilian (10.1.98), it had delighted its author, who boasts that he is quite up to so difficult a task (*Am.* 2.18.13f.); and yet individual successes are not enough to satisfy expectations for a new Latin theater (the Greek tragedians and the archaic Latin tragedians had produced a corpus of works which could be staged in regular theatrical "seasons"): Varius' *Thyestes* is not enough, *Romana Tragoedia* in person can still ask Ovid "nunc habeam per te . . . nomen" (*Am.* 3.1.29f.). And not even Ovid's *Medea* will suffice: Quintilian will judge that Ovid had demonstrated what could be achieved by a talented but undisciplined poet, one capable only of touching upon a genre, not of giving it life and vitality.

Persius' choliambs—verges on senselessness. Naturally, when the question, "To what genre do you belong?" is directed to the text, it provokes not only obvious answers, but also novelties, displacements, disequilibria and new equilibria: that is why it is such an interesting question. As I have already pointed out, the genres I find most interesting in this perspective are the most traditional ones: epic, bucolic, elegy, satire, etc. I believe in fact that it is these genres—their relations, boundaries, conflicts, redistributions of territory, etc.—that are at stake in the really important games played out between author and reader. To define genres differently makes the game lose interest, at least for me. I do not believe that an ancient reader trembled with emotion when assailed by the doubt, "but is what I am reading a *propempticon* or an *epibaterion?*"

As you certainly know better than I, hermeneutic criticism in its deconstructionist version is enjoying increasing success in many places, if for no other reason than because it answers to a widespread need. Many people seem in fact to believe that our relation with the classic texts is running the risk of becoming tired, static, unadventurous. The idea that these texts have shot all their bolts of meaning and have been definitively understood is truly frightening: we would then be left with sluggish readers on the one hand, and texts that are no longer interesting on the other. Deconstructionist hermeneutics responds to this crisis with a new movement that gives an undeniable impression of vitality: it draws its motto from a recognition that "there is no peace in the texts." As a struggle against conformism this is certainly positive (and also—but let us not say this too loudly—because it promises to provide a living for a larger number of interpreters, a promise all the more attractive for classicists, who are obliged to work on a finite body of material—a source of energy which cannot be renewed!). As a pre-deconstructionist critic, I wish these developments good luck; but I refuse to limit myself to a static and rigid vision of my own hermeneutic practice. I do not believe that literary criticism, as I understand and practice it, needs this medicine.

Take the question of genres. It is certainly possible to use genres in a static, classificatory, descriptive and almost tautological way. I need not give examples: we know that in this way we run the risk of a rather funereal peace (and in that case it is easy to prefer perpetual motion, the unlimited production of meaning, the construction and deconstruction of the text, etc.). But in my view the genres are not at all (at least, not *merely*) a factor of order, stability, and identity: precisely the opposite is the case.

For example: to many people the didactic epic may seem a quintessentially peaceful genre, one based upon clear and elementary rules, practically a container indifferent to the specificity of the discourse it puts forward. A similarly static conception of the didactic genre is often applied to Lucretius too, who is said to have wedded (with some adaptation) a new ideology to a traditional "generic" structure. Interpreted in this way, the didactic character of the *De rerum natura* is fragmented into many tiny, entirely superficial generic signals—like the formulas of transition and of persuasion—or is reduced to recalling the function of the addressee Memmius. In my own view, the new form which the didactic genre takes on in Lucretius finds its necessary complement in the creation of an addressee who knows how to adapt himself to the sublime level of an overwhelming experience: the doctrine on atoms is not only described in its own terms but is also seen in the reaction of vertigo which it can generate.[16] If the addressee of the *De rerum natura* is to know the sublimity towards which the poet wants to elevate him, he must become sublime himself. The sublime transforms the didactic genre by providing the model to which the poet adapts his discourse and to which the reader must adapt his behavior so that this too will be lofty and resolute. At this point the didactic form and the teacher-student relation are no longer unproblematic, as they were, say, in Aratus or Nicander. The sublime form of the text and of the addressee are the result of the transformation which the didactic genre had to undergo when it chose to become the means of communicating a moral journey—they are the obvious signs of an agonistic interpretation of the didactic experience. The relation between teacher-bard and addressee-disciple is not a tranquil agreement, but a tense wager which may fail. The teacher-student relation, which had been a stable framework in the traditional didactic genre, becomes in the *De rerum natura* a center of tension and a problematic theme in itself. The transformation of the genre into a proselytizing, missionary discourse is afflicted by incessant anxiety and doubt. And to understand how new this is, let us recall, by contrast, the bland, relaxed didactic structure of poems on snake venom, on the constellations, or on gastronomy. As we shall see below, genre can become a problematic—even an unruly—ingredient of the work itself. And perhaps it might even be suggested that this deployment of genre as the problematic or "theatrical" contents of a work is a characteristic of Roman poetry, of its tendency to put

[16] Cf. G.B. Conte, "Insegnamenti per un lettore sublime. Forma del testo e forma del destinatario nel 'De rerum natura' di Lucrezio," Introduction to *Lucrezio: La natura delle cose* (Milan: Rizzoli, 1990) 27-42.

the choice of language and of genre in "dramatic" terms, almost to "stage" the problem of the choice of literary form.

To the prescriptive immobility which menaces the notion of genre, scholarship has tried to respond with an image which seems more dynamic: the formula of the "Kreuzung der Gattungen." Scholars like Deubner and Kroll analyzed Alexandrian and Roman poetry as the production of hybrid and cross-bred texts. Now the idea of "Kreuzung" is not false in itself, even if it often relies upon examples which are rather mechanical and superficial. The fact that Callimachus writes a hymn in elegiac distichs is certainly remarkable, but it does not constitute by itself the great novelty of his poetics. The real fault of "Kreuzung," anyway, is its recipe character, which ends up making it look at literary questions only in terms of the production of texts: we can explain by "Kreuzung" how a text is "put together" with various genres. The idea behind this is that of the *workshop*, while for me (as I have said) genre functions instead as a *strategy*.

Let me take as an example Virgil's Tenth *Eclogue*, if only because some years ago I ventured an interpretation of it.[17] Kroll insisted upon the fact that the bucolic genre is a miscellany of various genres: on this view the Tenth *Eclogue* in particular is a hybrid of bucolic and elegy. But that is certainly not the most important fact for readers and interpreters of this composition: otherwise Klingner would be mistaken in considering it one of the texts which most resist interpretation.[18] I think instead that Kroll's line of reading should be completely reversed. This *Eclogue* is not the result of a combination of influences: bucolic does not renounce its own literary individuality by becoming contaminated in some way with elegy; indeed, the meaning of the Tenth *Eclogue* is founded precisely upon flaunting the difference between the two genres, on the one hand the bucolic world of Virgil, on the other the elegiac world of Gallus, a momentary "guest" in the shepherds' world. Upon the limited terrain of a shared space, elegy and bucolic take on life and confront one another, compete with and define one another in turn. The fact that the specific individuality of each of the two opposed genres can be measured is entirely due to a shared space which allows the comparison: it is only because the same *carmina* can be intoned in both the elegiac register and

17   *Virgilio: il genere e i suoi confini* (Milan: Garzanti, 1984) 13-42 (=*The Rhetoric of Imitation. Genre and Poetic Memory in Virgil and Other Latin Poets*, trans. from Italian, ed. and with a foreword by Charles Segal [Ithaca-London: Cornell University Press, 1986] 100-29).
18   F. Klingner, *Virgil. Bucolica, Georgica, Aeneis* (Zürich-Stuttgart 1967) 166: "The Tenth Eclogue is the most peculiar, so peculiar that to a large extent its interpreters have exercised their ingenuity on it in vain."

the bucolic one (by Gallus' mouth in the second part of the *Eclogue*) that we can become aware of the "formative" function which each register possesses. The Tenth *Eclogue* presents itself, then, as the exploration of the boundaries of one poetic genre (the bucolic) at the moment in which its specific and distinctive features are defined, dialectically, by the comparison arising from its juxtaposition with another genre. Thus we see how the various genres of a literary culture can be defined precisely in their reciprocal and systematic relations, each with regard to every other one. In the final analysis, the space of the Tenth *Eclogue* becomes the *confrontation between two genres* which mediate two worlds, and two models of life, as well.

For the proponents of "Kreuzung der Gattungen" in interpreting the works of Latin literature, perhaps no other text seems to lend itself so well as Ovid's *Heroides:* are they not an exemplary case of a continual mixture of tragedy, epic, bucolic, elegy? are they not obviously an intersection of different genres? And yet here too it would be easy to demonstrate the falsity of such a perspective. For Ovid reinterprets all this material of heterogeneous provenance organically and dynamically according to a new literary code, the language of elegy:[19] and in particular he precipitates out a model of life which is the elegiac one. In this case, elegy becomes a form of the world that reproduces with greater precision the life of women, a life of suffering, of true *servitium,* of humiliation. The *Heroides* represent that literary genre which is almost ingrained in the socio-cultural condition of women, they are the declension of the elegiac paradigm in the feminine gender.[20] Ovid's consciousness of genres permits elegy to rediscover its original vocation as poetic lament, becoming women's expressive form—the form of their voice.[21]

With regard to genres, the Augustan poets seem to experience a level of anxiety without precedents and without analogies: their attitude is one of problematic self-interrogation, and they thereby testify to the existence and importance of the question. Even more significant, and more characteristic of my own approach, is the fact that the reader becomes involved in this process. Such problems are so familiar for us that we tend to consider the whole

---

[19] Cf. in this connection A. Barchiesi, "Narratività e convenzione nelle *Heroides,*" *MD* 19 (1987) 63-90, esp. pp. 67ff. Cf. also the same author's "Problemi di interpretazione in Ovidio: continuità delle storie, continuazione dei testi," *MD* 16 (1986) 77-107.

[20] Indeed, this specific "declension" of the elegiac paradigm comes to constitute, as it were, a sub-genre of elegy (the elegiac epistle), an expressive form adapted to representing the voice of a marginal or marginalized character, upon whom the very distance at which she finds herself confined imposes a subjective filter through which events are interpreted.

[21] Cf. G. Rosati, "Introduction" to *Heroides* (BUR).

phenomenon natural. Propertius, all in all a pure elegist, is also one of the first to transform his own poetic career into an *object of representation* (even a superficial comparison between the books of Propertius and that of Catullus shows a significant difference in this regard). What readers are shown is not only Propertius the lover, but also Propertius the poet facing genres, facing the elegiac genre, which is built and dismantled: it should suffice to recall the sequence of metaliterary reflections which lead from the poetic comparison with Ponticus in the first book to the proem and envoi of the second one, and to the programmatic elegies which open the third book.

Then, in the fourth book the poet offers, so to speak, a *dramatized* representation of his own generic consciousness: we are present at a dialogue in which the two interlocutors impersonate two possibilities of the elegiac form which are felt *by now* to be decisively different, indeed almost opposed to one another. In fact, the fourth book of Propertius contains both Roman aetiologies in the manner of Callimachus and love elegies (though these latter have new elements with regard to the elegies of the earlier books). As is well known, the interpretation of its proem is extremely difficult and controversial;[22] but if we agree with the majority of Propertian scholars nowadays that the figure of Horos is not simply a caricature, then we must also admit that Propertius has decided to make us participants in a *hesitation* between two modes of practicing elegy, indeed, I would say, between two distinct elegiac genres.[23] It has also been suggested that 4.1 is a *recusatio* quite similar to other Propertian *recusationes*, for example 3.3 and 3.9: but you will agree with me that the ambiguity of the character who intervenes here to dissuade the poet from a "grander" project (Horos is not authoritative like Apollo or Calliope) makes this composition a true *haesitatio* rather than a toned down *recusatio*. Propertius' new elegiac experiment does not make the status of this genre more uncertain, but sets the *new* attempt against "traditional" love elegy, by now codified in its genre. It is significant that, for those who, like Horos, pose as conservatives and antiexperimentalists in literary issues, elegy means love elegy *tout court: at tu finge elegos* (4.1.135), as though by now *elegi* meant only love poetry and hence *servitium* .[24] Hence Propertius'

22   A good recent discussion is offered by C.W. Macleod, "Propertius 4.1," in *Papers of the Liverpool Latin Seminar 1976*, pp. 141-53 (= *Collected Papers* [Oxford 1983] 202-14).
23   This has been well seen by W. Suerbaum, "Der Schluss der Einleitungselegie zum 4. Properzbuch (Zum Motiv der Lebenswahl bei Properz)," *RhM* 107 (1964) 360-61.
24   To a large extent, this still holds good even for those who are inclined to endorse the clever hypothesis of C.W. Macleod (*loc. cit.* , p. 147 and n. 41), who suggests that ll. 135-146 may be a kind of quotation from Apollo's past orders. In any case, according to Horos,

hesitation, so far from signifying indifference to the generic codification, indirectly reinforces the very concept of genre, and indicates its boundaries more decisively.

In short, the most characteristic, most constant element of Augustan poetry is the poet's insistence on letting us know that he could also be doing something else. The genre "stages" itself, becomes spectacle: the *recusationes* are better explained as a parade of literary genres and of related genres of life. At *Remedia Amoris* 381, Ovid prepares the reader according to simple expectations: *Callimachi numeris non est dicendus Achilles: Cydippe non est oris, Homere, tui*, that is, he reminds the reader of a natural coherence of matter and form; but the rest of his career will go on to demonstrate the limits of this canon. It will remain true that heroes like Achilles are not suited to the elegiac distich, but the *Heroides* show that this too can be done: Achilles is a character in the *Heroides*, as is Cydippe. On the other hand, everybody knows that love-affairs like Cydippe's were made for the elegiac distich, and yet in the *Metamorphoses*, a hexametric epic, love is the most important theme (even more than metamorphosis itself). I do not mean to imply that the work of Ovid consists solely in destroying the traditional codifications: to limit ourselves to the *Metamorphoses*, we must admit that this work shows respect for a hierarchy and for an order which are relative but not nonexistent.[25] What, however, seems most obvious in Ovid—who is perhaps an exceptional author in this regard—is his incessant consciousness of the system of genres. 1) He justifies the *Amores* as a form in search of a theme: Cupid has stolen a foot from a hexameter, and the result is the production of the elegiac distich (as though to say, in jest, *numeros tene, res sequentur*); 2) The *Tristia* explain the conversion of the same metrical form to a different theme: this time the pentameter is the lame foot of an exile in distress; 3) Sappho writes a "Herois" in distichs to her beloved Phaon: "You will wonder"—she says to him—"why I am not writing lyric: it is the subject matter—a sad one: my unhappy love— which demands the weeping song of elegy."[26] As you see, either the form

---

Apollo's commands *still* retain their full validity. If this is so, composing aetiological elegy is not an acceptable way of complying with that injunction to compose elegiac poetry.
25   These problems formed the subject of Richard Heinze's controversial monograph (*Ovids elegische Erzählung*, Leipzig 1919 = *Vom Geist des Römertums*, Stuttgart 1960, 3rd edition, pp. 308-403); now S. Hinds, *The Metamorphosis of Persephone. Ovid and the Self-Conscious Muse* (Cambridge 1987) has returned to them with a new theoretical awareness.
26   It might be objected against my use of this passage in *Her.* 15 that the poem's Ovidian authorship is still *sub judice*, even if the tendency to consider it authentic has been prevalent for some time (most recently on the opposite side, but often with forced arguments, R.J. Tarrant, "The Authenticity of the Letter of Sappho to Phaon," *HSCP* 85 [1981] 133-53). Examined

chooses the theme or vice versa. 4) The *Fasti* are practically obsessed with their own generic status: the poet asks himself to what extent *elegi* can sustain themes of heroic, hexametric song (*heroi res erat ista pedis: Fasti* 2.126); inversely, he is delighted that the distich has grown so far after having sung the humble poetry of love: 2.8 *ecquis ad haec* (to the *Fasti*) *illinc* (from the *Amores*) *crederet esse viam?*[27] What had been the hesitation of Propertius 4.1 thereby becomes the open exhibition of the problem: indeed, genre and the difference among the genres become spectacle. Every new text, as it unfolds, justifies its own relation with the system of literary genres, which it simultaneously takes as norm and evades.

The example of Ovid may suggest to us that the poet can only choose between respecting the canons—so endorsing the tradition codified in terms of genres—and upsetting them. It may make us wonder whether anything else exists besides genres and texts which respect them, violate them, or discuss them. But we have also seen more complex examples: the Tenth *Eclogue* has reminded us that genres not only represent themselves but are also forms of meaning, articulated models of possible worlds. In short: genres are particularized in texts, life is generalized in models. Between genres and models there is a profound osmosis.

To return, in conclusion, to the problem I posed at the beginning, I cannot agree that it is absolutely necessary to oppose the fiction of poetry to the reality of the empirical world: true, literature is different from reality, but it is not the exact contrary of reality.[28] What we should avoid is thinking of reality naturalistically, as though it were a simple datum. In fact, reality is nothing but a system of perceptions determined by cultural codes and is therefore itself a construction, even if one at a different level from literature. The empirical world, in order to be perceived, must of necessity be translated into something which it is not—into a model of reality, endowed with a meaning and therefore with a form. Genre functions as a mediator, permitting certain models of reality to be selected and to enter into the language of literature: it gives them the possibility of being "represented."

---

closely, indeed, the verses considered here (5-8) can provide a further argument for the Ovidian authorship of the epistle: for such consciousness of the problem of genres hardly belongs to an imitator-forger's capacities and intentions.

27   Hinds, *op. cit.* 115.

28   I had occasion to offer some reflections on this subject in the course of my discussion of the interpretation of Roman elegy proposed by P. Veyne (*L'élégie érotique romaine. L'amour, la poésie et l'occident*, Paris 1983), in "L'amore senza elegia: i 'Remedia amoris' e la logica di un genere," Introd. to *Ovidio: Rimedi contro l'amore*, ed. by C. Lazzarini (Venice 1986) 49-50, n. 19 (= *Poetics Today* 10.3 [1989] 458f. with n. 19).

The empiricist too could agree that, in comparison with the extraordinarily rich variety of reality, literature operates by *selection:* where he probably would end up disagreeing is in his notion that the selection acts directly upon naked facts rather than upon conventions and models which preexist literature. The selection cannot be conceived without certain procedures, which, as strategies of communication, guide the reader to understand the selective processes which underlie the text. The strategy of communication is to make things speak, to charge them with meanings and symbolic values: but, in culture, things already have their own voice, they already mean something independently of the fact that they enter into one system of selection rather than another. That is why it is incorrect to believe, for example, that the elegiac poet's refusal of *militia* (or of a career) must necessarily refer to empirical and personal choices on the part of characters who, unlike their contemporaries, recoiled from committing themselves to a promising military campaign;[29] or else to believe, in precisely the opposite direction, that such a refusal, insignificant in itself, becomes significant only as a formal characteristic of rhetorical literary expression. Both the "realistic" interpretation and the "formalistic" one miss the point. Instead, we should say that the elegiac poets whom we cite as an example work on models and concepts of reality which have already become active and operative (in this case: what military service *represents* in the Roman cultural system). These strategies of selection, in short, function as just so many programs, they correspond to just so many genres: indeed, they are the genres themselves. A genre does not add new information, but it shows things from a new point of view: the specificity of each genre resides in the combination, indeed in the recombination of elements of reality. In this way the reader is set on the path towards constructing an imaginary situation or world, in which only some of the many conventions found in the extraliterary world enter into systematic relation with one another. That is why it is easy to discover in literature many of those conventions which regulate culture, society, empirical reality: this is the starting point for the naturalistic fallacy of much empiricist criticism.

Conversely, the force of empiricism, which tries to give an account of genres as *historically* fulfilled possibilities, becomes obvious by contrast with the purely formalistic perspective which—if only in principle—would like to imagine indefinitely many possible genres. Theory and empiricism coincide in

---

29   It should suffice to recall here Propertius' elegy to Tullus (1.6) or Tibullus 1.3 *Ibitis . . . sine me . . .*

the need to explain critically the various forms of literary language of a given culture and to describe the system of genres with their relative internal variations and their reciprocal delimitations. Behind those forms of language which assure recognizable lines of communication between author and reader, the cultural project of the author and at the same time the expectations of his addressees must be sought out: the reader finds in the genre an interpretative model of reality, a simulacrum of meaning, which, drawing him strategically into a network of presuppositions, "provokes" him and makes him capable of reacting to the impulses which the author has transmitted to him. Evanescent though it is, it is the genre which suggests a sense of the totality of the text and provides a meaning to the various components by ordering them typologically: in this way the "déjà vu" precipitated out in cultural experience and in the literary tradition can activate an effective "rhetoric of difference," by means of which—practically, that is, by comparing and contrasting—the reader can recognize what is new, and at the same time perceive the specificity of the individual text which is offered to him.[30]

But nothing would be more useless than to conceive of genres as simple, immobile abstractions, or as lifeless specimens to be collected in sterile bell jars: genre lives only in individual works. Just as we see not Man, but many individual human beings, whom we are capable of distinguishing from fleas or from horses, so too we see not the epic genre or the elegiac genre, but individual works which belong to particular genres, as we can recognize even in the case of hybrids. And not only because they share a family resemblance, as it were, but because genre lives in the individual totality of each work. We may say that the genre constitutes the bone-structure of a text, inasmuch as it sustains it and holds it together; but we must be careful not to think of it as a fleshless skeleton, for otherwise we will lose the very substance of the living text. In the *Dialogues of the Dead,* Lucian recounts the Cynic Menippus' meeting in the Underworld with the skeleton of Thersites, the ugliest of all the

---

[30]   On the other hand, it is true that the changeable and interpenetrative structure of genres often renders too rigidly schematic a definition of them useless for the work of interpretation. Even if the genre can be thought of in the pure state as a working hypothesis, its real action (in texts) is subject to many possible deformations: it can undergo procedures of combination and aggregation, of inclusion and of selection, of reduction and amplification, of transposition and reversal, it can undergo functional mutations and adaptations; it can also happen that contents and expressions already strictly codified become dissociated so that they can be associated with other expressions and with other contents. But it remains true that within the system of the Classical literatures any discursive combination, however complex and disparate it may be, still always respects one discursive project (one genre) which predominates over all the others that go to make up the text and subordinates them to its own intention.

Greek warriors who went to Troy, who points out to the philosopher the skeleton of Nireus, the fairest of all who went to Troy. But in fact, there is no visible difference between the two skeletons. For those of us who are looking for texts, and want to read them and distinguish between them, it is the flesh that makes the difference, that lets us distinguish every time between Nireus and Thersites.

(Translated by Glenn W. Most)

OF GENRES AND POEMS
Response to Gian Biagio Conte

Professor Conte's characteristically subtle and perceptive paper brings
out the falsity of the opposition between "empirical" approaches, insisting on
the relationship of poetry to the facts of real social life, and those which
disregard living experience in favour of schematic and theoretical lines of
thought. The level of discussion is rising in a way which we should all find
welcome, as unsophisticated and over-simple arguments and approaches begin
to learn from each other's shortcomings and to do more justice to the
complexity of such poems as the elegies of Propertius and the *Eclogues* of
Virgil.[1]

Continued meditation on the difficult problems posed by the relation of
poetic genres to individual poems has led me to think that in my own work in
this area I have tended to disregard the question of the genres. Certain over-
emphatic and one-sided treatments impelled me to redress the balance.
Anxious to emphasize the mutual interplay between literature and life, I
conducted the analysis much more in terms of works than of genres. I take this
opportunity to look more seriously at that aspect.

We must welcome Professor Conte's insistence that to possess real value
for these studies the idea of genre must include elements both of form
(expression) and of content. Only in that way can sterile disputes be

---

[1]   Not quite everywhere, however.   Thus R.F. Thomas writes: "It is a curious
phenomenon that this type of criticism" (*i.e.* that of my *Latin Poets and Roman Life* [London
1986] and other, alarmingly unnamed, "influential quarters") "is confined to Latin lyric and
elegy. Critics of Greek poetry take it for granted that their subject is literary, and their approach
to it addresses literary concerns, the relationship of lyric diction to the Homeric poems, the
treatment of myth, the use of metaphor, and so on. The reason for the discrepancy is, I think,
that we know so much more about Roman society and history of the first century B.C. . . ."
(*CP* 83 [1988] 61f.). By a delicious logic, a procedure hard to avoid in an area where a certain
kind of evidence is absent—and yet much of the most important work on Greek poetry has
succeeded in going beyond it—becomes the sole permitted model for work in an area where that
evidence exists. Thomas assumes as eternally orthodox a present fashion for isolating literature
from the society in which it was produced and enjoyed; "the critic's business" is sharply
distinguished from "that of the historian" (*ibid.*). Books, then, are begotten by books, and a
description of pretty girls swimming is influenced neither by painting nor—still less—by life,
but "for my money [Catullus] provided an erotic embellishment of *Argonautica* iv.940" (*ibid.*
58). One misses only an explicit reference to the setting in which, doubtless, the ancient poet,
like the modern scholar, did his work: the university library.

transcended. Such an approach will yield dividends. For instance, I was struck by the perception that the *virga* of Mercury, retained in the First Book of the *Metamorphoses* as the god turns from divine messenger to oxherd, glances at the genre of bucolic: "At once the scene is transformed from epic to bucolic, and Mercury starts to speak in a bucolic style." The retention of the *virga* and its changed function "underlines the change of code and of world." This is very attractive. We might add it to another touch, from the Second Book, when Mercury falls in love with the Athenian princess Herse and comes down to make love to her. He takes care to look his best:

> tanta est fiducia formae;
> quae quamquam iusta est, cura tamen adiuvat illam,
> (*Met* 2.731f.)

combing his hair, adjusting the fit of his tunic, and seeing to it:

> ut teres in dextra, quae somnos ducit et arcet,
> virga sit.   (*ibid.* 735f.)

(that in his right the staff, with which he brings
and keeps away sleep, might be well polished).

Here the commentators observe that Ovid makes his amorous god observe the instructions to be careful about their appearance, which the poet gives to mortal lovers in his *Ars Amatoria*.[2] The ordinary lover in Augustan Rome did not call on his girl with a stick in his hand, like a gentleman of 1900, and so the *Ars* gives no specific instruction for the smartness of one's cane. Mercury, however, is the god who always carries a staff—is recognized by carrying it, like a saint in religious iconography—and so it is available to the poet for witty and ingenious applications. In the Io story it becomes a herdsman's oxdriving stick; in the Herse story it shares in the general smartness appropriate to all the accoutrements of the men about town when bent on pleasure. For the latter is set in a town and in a palace, while the former is set in the open air, on the hill-side, among the herds.

So far, so good. But we have not exhausted the question. How important is the specific question of poetic genre? In the episode of Herse the

---

2   *Ars* 1. 511f.; cf. *Remedia Amoris* 679f.

poet clearly meant to glance at his own notorious poem the *Ars* and—as so often—to make a connection between its hedonistic world of urban sophistication and the archaic setting of the myths. Franz Bömer, in his commentary on the passage, remarks grimly that this is "frivoles Spiel des Dichters mit dem Bereich des Göttlichen (oder, nach neuester Auffassung, Humor.)"[3] What is added if we insist that the genre of the *Ars*, rather than the atmosphere, is important?

I approach the question by returning to Book One and Mercury driving the cattle with his divine staff. Other parallels suggest themselves. Thus: in Theocritus 24th Poem, the *Herakliskos*, the poet tells us that Heracles, a baby of ten months old, was attacked by two horrendous serpents sent by Hera. The poem opens with a charmingly Biedermeier scene: Alcmena bathed her twin sons, gave them their fill of milk, and

> "laid them to rest in the bronze shield, that fair piece of armour of which Amphitryon had spoiled Pterelaus when he fell. And stroking the boys' heads she [uttered a short lullaby]. And with these words she rocked (δίνησε) the great shield, and sleep came over them." (Theocritus 24.3-10; trans. Gow).

Now, the defeat of Pterelaus was the one great heroic exploit of Amphitryon (it is splendidly described in the *Amphitryo* of Plautus); this shield, therefore, must have been his greatest trophy. We remember the heroic pride and passion which center on the winning of armour from the vanquished in the *Iliad*, and we see, with a special educated pleasure, the very different scene of two babies being rocked to sleep in a captured and heroic shield. As for the rocking: in the *Seven against Thebes* the gigantic Hippomedon intimidates the besieged by brandishing in their sight a mighty shield emblazoned with the figure of the fire-breathing monster Typhoeus:

> ἅλω δὲ πολλήν, ἀσπίδος κύκλον λέγω,
> ἔφριξα δινήσαντος (Aeschylus, *Septem* 489f.)

> (When he whirled a mighty orb around, I mean the circle of his shield, he made me shudder).

3　　F. Bömer, *P. Ovidius Naso: Metamorphosen. Kommentar 1* (Heidelberg 1969) 410 on 2.731. Not for the first time, one wonders what makes a scholar decide that he is by nature the right man to comment on a particular poet.

Same verb, διvέω, but a totally different ethos: from heroic threatening to maternal tenderness.

The procedure here seems to me to have a strong family resemblance to that of Ovid in describing Mercury keeping the kine with his divine staff of office. But when we ask for the role of genre, it is hard to know what to reply. The Theocritean poem has just begun: the audience can hardly have formed a definite conception of the genre to which they are to assign it. *Idyll* 24 does not begin, like 22, with words which unambiguously suggest a particular generic nature. So they can hardly be relying on the contrast with a different genre in order to understand and appreciate this passage. The piquancy which it contains is much less a matter of specific poetic genres than of general stylistic levels, and of the normal setting in which a piece of paraphernalia like a hero's shield makes its appearance: the shield which failed to protect a man's life now shelters the infant children of his slayer, and the triumphant boast of the warrior gives place to the tender lullaby of the nursing mother.[4]

Another aspect of the Ovidian passage presents itself, too. Mercury drives the cattle with a *virga* normally reserved for other and grander uses. A memorable passage of the *Aeneid* makes a similar point. In his abuse of the Trojans as effeminate Orientals, the Italian prince Numanus Remulus stresses the toughness of the Italians:

> Omne aevum ferro teritur, versaque iuvencum
> terga fatigamus hasta. (Virgil, *Aeneid* 9.609f.)

> (All our life is lived out with weapons, and we goad our
> oxen's backs with a reversed spear).

The warrior's spear, too, can serve as cattle-driver: as Donatus comments *ad loc.*, "una atque eadem species et ruri servit et bello." But the specifically bucolic aspect is surely not present in this passage, which is concerned to deny the existence of any opposition at all between agricultural and military prowess:

---

[4] On εὐχωλή and cognates see E. Benveniste, *Le vocabulaire des institutions indoeuropéennes* (Paris 1969) ii.237ff.; A.W.H. Adkins in *CQ* 19 (1969) 20-33.

at patiens operum parvoque adsueta iuventus
aut rastris terram domat aut quatit oppida bello.
(*ibid.*, 607f.)

(But bearing toil and being inured to want our young men
tame the earth with hoes or shake cities in war).

The passage recalls, as the commentators seem not to bother to say, that strand
in the Homeric epics which emphasizes the identity of the herdsman and the
hero. Even the less obvious activity of ploughing is placed in a similar light by
Odysseus, when the suitor Eurymachus insults him by saying that he would not
dream of accepting a job, reaping or ploughing: "I am unsurpassed," Odysseus
tells him, "at ploughing with a team of oxen, and if war were to come, you
would see me in the front rank." The ploughman is the hero in mufti: the
hero is the ploughman in arms.[5]

On the one side of the Ovidian passage, then, we see a kind of
composition which takes pleasure in depicting objects from the heroic world
re-used in ways and in settings which convey a profound change of ethos: such
passages may work by glancing at a specific poetic genre and contrasting it
with that of the main text, but that may be, as with the shield re-used as a
cradle, at most a very small part of their effect. On the other side, there are
passages, no less effective in their own style, which are concerned rather to
annihilate any distinction than to flaunt it: thus Numanus emphasizes not the
polar opposition of bucolic and epic, but on the contrary their compatibility
and even their identity. But in terms of ancient literary theory both are *epos*.

Something rather similar can be said, I think, also about the interesting
suggestion that the dispute between Cupid and Apollo, as to which of them
should wear and use the bow and arrows, introduces the generic question of
epic *versus* love elegy. The idea is appealing, and certainly Ovid was, as Conte
rightly emphasizes, keenly self-conscious on the question of the relation of
elegy and epic. But a related motif is also known to us, which was at home in
the Alexandrian epigram: that of Aphrodite ὁπλισμένη, wearing armor.
Leonidas wrote two epigrams on the theme[6] and six others—a total of eight—

5   Homer, *Odyssey* 18.371. Cf. J. Duchemin, "A propos de l'*Hercules tueur de lion*"
Miscellanea di studi alessandrini in memoria di A. Rostagni (Torino 1963) 311-21; J. Griffin,
"Heroic and Unheroic Ideas in Homer," *Chios,* edd. J. Boardman and C.E. Vaphopoulou-
Richardson (Oxford 1986) 3-14.
6   *Hellenistic Epigrams* edd. A.S.F. Gow and D.L. Page (Cambridge 1965) 2107 and
2585.

are preserved in the *Anthology*. The question "Why Venus in Sparta wears armor" was a theme in the schools of the declaimers.[7] Apollo's objection to the unwarlike Cupid using the bow is of a similar kind. Even closer to the dispute in the *Metamorphoses* are other epigrams: one by Meleager explaining that it is nothing strange (οὐ ξένον) if Eros shoots blazing arrows, as his father is Ares; another by Philip (69 Gow-Page) describing Eros wearing the lion-skin and arrows of Heracles.[8] The question of the appropriateness of unwarlike deities parading in weapons goes back to the fifth Book of the *Iliad*.[9] It is one which of its nature recalls the epigram at least as much as the developed love-elegy. When we do find an elegy on such a theme, as with Propertius 2.12 (*quicumque ille fuit, puerum qui pinxit Amorem*), a poem which does indeed develop the question why Cupid is armed with bow and arrows, the epigrammatic content and movement can easily be detected.[10] These considerations must be added, I think, to the statement that "Cupid, too, has *arma*, which are a distinctive feature of the elegiac code." And we remember that in the epic of Apollonius, in its most celebrated part, Eros fires an arrow at Medea which makes her fall in love with Jason.[11] In view of the use made by Virgil of that book of Apollonius, Ovid must have been familiar with it. Even in the epic, then, the archer Eros had figured conspicuously, as well as in the epigram. It seems to follow that, while it may indeed be true that the Ovidian passage is intended to evoke the elegy, that is not its sole resonance: and even, to put the point in another way, that what is to be evoked in the mind of the reader is less specifically the generic point (elegy *versus* epic) than a vaguer and more complex constellation of ideas: love poetry and its traditional armory; the archer Eros of Apollonius who lies behind the Virgilian Cupid and the passion of Dido; the epigram, and the love elegy which enlarges and develops it. I agree that the word *arma* has an epic colouring and recalls the epic, and one element of the effect aimed at here is an emphasis on the fact that Ovid's poem is not an epic of a certain sort—above all, of a Virgilian sort. The specific work, the great poem of the previous generation, the lion in the path for Ovid and the rest, is perhaps more urgently present than the genre of epic. It was the first thing which the word *arma* would evoke.

---

7   Quintilian 2.4.26.
8   *The Garland of Philip*, edd. Gow and Page (Cambridge 1968) 4038; 3090.
9   Homer, *Iliad* 5.330ff.
10   E.g. A. La Penna, *L'integrazione difficile: un profilo di Properzio* (Torino 1977) 60.
11   Apollonius Rhodius 3.280-7.

What emerges from this is that my difficulty is not with the kind of analysis which Conte offers—that seems to me very enlightening, a judicious balance of detail and theory—but with his estimate of the importance of the genres and of generic analysis. I think there are a number of cases in which the genre is of less significance for the understanding of a poem than some particular other poem or work of literature. I say "work of literature" because the significant model can itself be a poem. For instance, the first *Ode* of the Second Book of Horace is addressed to Pollio and discusses his *Roman History*. Five of its ten stanzas evoke the atmosphere and the events of that stirring and tragic time:

> iam nunc minaci murmure cornuum
> perstringis auris, iam litui strepunt,
>   iam fulgor armorum fugaces
>   terret equos equitumque voltus . . .
>   (Horace, *C.* 2.1.17-20).

Nisbet and Hubbard comment that Horace's *Ode* reflects the tone and substance of the *Historiae* . . . and particularly of the proem, which he surely had read. After a highly colored and pathetic development of the themes of the war, Roman suffering and Roman guilt, the poet recalls himself, at the end of his poem, to the proper task of his own lyric poetry—smaller and less serious themes and effects. An allusion to the Greek lyric poet Simonides helps to clinch the transition and forms an elegant and literate close. I dwell for a moment on this familiar example because it shows, I think, that genres can even be brought into explicit contrast without it being a principal role of the poem to define or delimit them. In writing of disaster and guilt Horace would not, it seems, be leaving the province of lyric poetry altogether: the dirges of Simonides were classics of the lyric. In as far as Horace defines his own practice, for the rest of Book Two at least, it is *within* the possible lyric space. Potentially, lyric could accommodate such material in such a tone; it is the lyric poet Horace who declines to write it.

I turn to another and perhaps more central example. The Tenth *Eclogue* has received from Conte some penetrating analysis, for which we are all grateful.[12] And yet I find myself wondering whether the conception of genre

---

[12]   G.B. Conte, *Il genere e i suoi confini* (Torino 1980) 11-45 = *The Rhetoric of Imitation* (Ithaca 1986) 100-29.

which he has developed—one which includes, as he rightly insists, both formal elements and elements of content—is the single key to the poem in quite the way which he suggests. Conte's analysis concludes that "the meaning of the Tenth *Eclogue* is founded precisely upon flaunting the difference between the two genres" of bucolic and elegy; the two genres define each other and themselves by their comparison. "The Tenth *Eclogue* proposes itself as the exploration of the limits of one poetic genre (the bucolic) at the moment in which its specific and distinctive features are defined, by dialectical comparison, by its bordering upon those of another genre."

Do all the elements of the poem really fall into place with such an analysis? I think it hard to be convinced. The poem opens with the statement that what follows, the last of the *Eclogues*, is meant as a tribute to Gallus and his love: it will tell the story of his amorous sufferings, in the hope that both Gallus and his fickle beloved Lycoris may read it. *Sollicitos Galli dicamus amores*—a phrase which seems to include both telling of his passion and also (if, as seems likely, Gallus called his elegies *Amores*), retelling his own versification of that passion. The reader at once wonders why Lycoris, if she did indeed read the poem, should be expected to be vitally interested in the question of the definition of poetic genres. What would interest her, we might think, would be not a problem in literary theory, but an account of the sufferings and devotion of her lover, with praise of her own irresistible power.

That, however, is a smaller point than the question of the attitude envisaged in Gallus himself. "In the final analysis," writes Conte, "the space of the Tenth *Eclogue* becomes the *confrontation between two genres* which mediate two worlds, and two life projects, as well." The ancients constantly speak of their poetry in terms less of literature, in our sense, than of music; and I think that musical analogies are often, for us, the most illuminating. Here, then, we have an example of a device so common in music as to need no explanation, but in poetry much rarer and more problematic: *tema con variazioni*, variations on a theme.

Gallus, poet and friend of Virgil, has already received high praise and made a personal appearance in the Sixth *Eclogue*. There he appears in the context, it seems, of the characteristic subject matter of the neoteric poets of Catullus' generation: Hylas, Pasiphae, the sisters of Phaethon. At least one such poem, the *Io* of Calvus, is actually quoted.[13] Then we see Gallus "wandering by the River Permessus," led by one of the Muses into the presence

[13] Virgil, *Buc.* 6. 47 and 52.

of Apollo, and presented with the pipes which once belonged to Hesiod, on
which he is to sing of the Grynean Grove (*Buc.* 6.45-73). Apparently what is
envisaged is a short learned hexameter poem, on a subject touched on by
Euphorion and Parthenius. In the Tenth *Eclogue* he appears again, this time
not in Boeotia but in Arcadia. In an evocation of the first *Idyll* of Theocritus,
Virgil makes the gods Apollo, Silvanus, and Pan all vainly remonstrate with
the poet in his unhappy state, pining away in the Arcadian solitude and
mourning for the beloved Lycoris, who has left him to follow a soldier
through ice and snow.

It appears from the coincidence of *Buc.* 10.46ff. with Propertius 1.8.5ff.
combined with Servius' comment on line 46, that the motif "Your soft feet are
at risk from the ice," comes from a celebrated poem of Gallus himself.[14]
Gallus, it seems, lamented the loss of a fickle beloved, abstained from blaming
her, and hoped the bitter cold would spare her dainty feet. Virgil has
transposed this plangent note from the elegy, with its characteristic metre and
also ethos (urban, sophisticated), to an Arcadia of fantasy, where a love-lorn
singer is naturally a herdsman, his comforters are not *amici* like those of
Catullus or Propertius but rustic gods, and publication is by means of carving
in the bark of a tree. The elegiac poet's characteristic utterance is transposed
into another key. But are we right to infer that what we witness is "the
confrontation of two life projects?"

Surely Gallus felt the poem to be, in the first place, a tremendous
compliment. Virgil is saying that Gallus as a poet is the appropriate figure to
stand at the end of his book of *Eclogues*; and he flatters both Gallus and
himself by showing how a masterpiece of his friend's production can be
elegantly and melodiously varied in his own bucolic style. There is no question
of a serious choice of life for Gallus, who of course in reality was no
moonstruck lover but a capable officer on campaign, and who as a poet is not
being challenged to turn to bucolic; and the juxtaposition of bucolic with
elegiac mode is less a confrontation than a musical refinement. The point, that
is, lies much less in any abstract significance of the fact of genre than in the
pleasure of seeing a delightful poem which is also, by a stroke of cleverness, a
recognizable variant on two other delightful poems: the Latin elegies of
Gallus, and the Greek hexameters of Theocritus. A poem in Latin but in

---

14   Cf. J. Hubaux, "Parthénius, Gallus, Virgile, Properce," in "Miscellanea Properziana,"
Atti dell' Accademia Properziana del Subasio-Assisi 5.5 (1957) 31-9.

hexameters, with Gallus recognizable but transformed in a Theocritean setting, combines and varies all the elements in a new and surprising whole.

These remarks have tended to play down the importance of purely generic considerations, at least in some cases. That is not to say that they are never important; such obvious instances as the constant glances at tragedy in Old Comedy show how vital they can be. But I suspect that we have tended, in recent years, to exaggerate the extent to which Augustan poets were constantly thinking of the question of epic in the abstract rather than of the *Aeneid*, or of a genre of literature rather than a scene or a poem. Professor Conte has broadened and refined our idea of genre; we now, I think, need to broaden and refine our conception of the way in which that conception is relevant to particular texts.

Response to Jasper Griffin's Response

To Jasper Griffin's polite question, "what is the use of the notion of genre compared to the concrete notion of the poetic work?"—for example, "what is the use of speaking about the elegiac genre, given that certain elements are shared by epigram and elegy?"—I think I would answer that I use the distinction in order to *avoid confusion*, to grasp literary specificities, and to make clear the different functions which particular elements have in different contexts.   Let me take an example.   The armed Cupid is a theme of Alexandrian epigrammatic literature (the epigram asks wittily about the significance of those weapons); but the tension between the space of eros and that of weapons, which in the epigram is occasional and witty, becomes in Ovid a specific contrast between elegy and epic. It would be easy to show that this is the case in Ovid by systematic analyses of Ovidian texts (and by literary historical investigations of elegy, contrasted for example with the love lyric of Horace, who often likes implicitly to compete with elegy); but here it will be enough, I believe, to recall the programmatic scene of the prefatory elegy of the *Amores,* in which we see precisely a "confrontation" between epic and elegy.   The systematic implications involved in the dilemma which is "staged" by the poet in this poem are all well known: Cupid dissuades the poet intent upon singing *arma . . . violentaque bella* and imposes upon him the elegiac rhythm by simply stealing a metrical foot; the episode continues with a dispute about spheres of competence and ends with an arrow well aimed by Cupid (a love affair).

My purpose is not to point out in the ancient authors passages which could be subjected to sophisticated analyses possibly relevant to the question of genre.   My purpose is to find a way to *interpret* these passages: and in this question Jasper Griffin's perspective and my own differ perhaps somewhat from one another, alas.   It seems to me that this is made clear by at least one other example.   He recalls the well-known passage in the *Aeneid* in which Numanus makes a claim for the unity of the peasant element and the warrior element in Italic culture as contrasted with foreign cultures.   An index of this unity is the reversibility of the warrior's *hasta,* his spear, ready to become a cattle-driver.   Griffin maintains that in this passage, as far as the reversed warrior's *hasta* is concerned, "the specifically bucolic aspect is surely not present," and that Numanus "emphasizes not the polar opposition of bucolic and epic, but on the contrary their compatibility, even their identity."   I must confess that this argument leaves me rather confused. I do not understand what bucolic has to do with this, and in fact I do not see how it could possibly have anything to do with it: for the reversed *hasta* is indeed used to urge on cattle, but these are cattle that are drawing the plow, not ones that are going to pasture. The man who is holding the *hasta* is not a *pastor* but a *georgos*. It is entirely true that no opposition between the georgic world and the epic world is presented here: but this is precisely because Virgil's *Georgics* had been constructed upon the ancient ideological premise which saw the Roman as a farmer-soldier. This does not mean, however, that there is not a georgic specificity as well as an epic specificity. Rather, it means that in the text we witness an ideological operation which proposes their partial identity. It assumes an existential model which is at least partially shared in common (something that I doubt Nicander and the Alexandrian georgic didactic poets would have contemplated). In short, I would wish the motif of the "reversed spear" not to be treated only in terms of content nor simply in formal terms, but in terms of how form and content necessarily interact and reshape each other. By the way, let us not forget that the motif of plowing with the spear has a precise genealogy which derives specifically from heroic epic: this is just what Jason does in Apollonius Rhodius 3.1321-30, "he grasped his resistless spear wherewith, like some ploughman with a Pelasgian goad, he pricked the bulls beneath, striking their flanks . . . They moved on at the bidding of the spear."

It should be clear from this discussion that I am not advocating an exclusively generic approach to poetry. Literary genres are one component of poetic discourse, as are syntax, meter, or narrative and rhetorical procedures. It is simply a matter of seeing whether referring to genre makes the texts we study more interesting, richer in meaning and in problems. The advantage is that of discovering behind the apparent fixity of the texts a more mobile perspective: one which is programmatic, dynamic, close to the very act of poetic composition and to its richness in problems.

One last point. Friedrich Klingner, my teacher many years ago in Munich, left me rather cold when he practiced criticism in musical terms, and I must confess that the notion of "theme and variation" seems to me too vague to put matters in order, given that it is applicable to any artistic procedure whatsoever. Besides, as far as I know, genres exist in the musical tradition as well, and composers expect the audience to react to their specific choices.

Above all, what I really don't want to happen is for my position to be unintentionally distorted into a reductive formalism (fifteen years ago I might have been considered perhaps something of a formalist, at the time I wrote my book about allusion and intertextuality). It seems to me that Jasper Griffin tends to restrict my interpretation of the Tenth *Eclogue* to a problem of literary theory. Well, I am afraid it is not so. As far as I am concerned, the confrontation between two genres also *mediates* two worlds, two ideologies, two ways of life, and two kinds of mental horizon.

BOUNDARIES, WORLDS, AND ANALOGICAL THINKING, OR
HOW LUCRETIUS LEARNED TO LOVE ATOMISM AND STILL
WRITE POETRY

If I could choose an epigraph for this paper it would be the scenes in Stanley Kubrick's film, *Dr. Strangelove,* in which the mad general fiercely protects the perimeters of his base on the one hand and is obsessed with the idea of conserving bodily fluids on the other. It is a jump, I know, to Epicurus; but he too is deeply interested in boundaries and, judging from his negative view of sex ("It never did anyone good, and it is lucky if it did not do harm," frag. 62 Usener) he too is not happy about the loss of bodily fluids. Indeed the Garden is itself a safely bounded world; and Lucretius' metaphor, in the famous proem of Book 2, of the sage's vision from a celestial citadel, fortified by the philosophy of his master, may have its roots in Epicurean thinking about boundaries.

Boundaries and their violation play an important role in Lucretius' thought, as they did to some degree in that of Epicurus. Lucretius imbues with new poetic feeling what was a perhaps latent tendency in his Master's view of the world. This venture will also take us into the thorny problem of applying modern psychological theories to an ancient poet. This is the hermeneutic side of this paper and I shall come back to it at the end. I shall be arguing, in part, that the mental operations of displacement and analogy, which play a large role in Freudian (and other psychological) approaches to the self help us understanding the ways in which Lucretius has made Epicurus' thought his own and has interpreted in his own personal, poetic way Epicurus' moral mission of rescuing mankind from the fear of death and making his fellow-men more serene and happier with their lives.

The fear of mutilation or dismemberment constitutes what psychologists label "primary boundary anxiety," anxiety about the invasion, transformation, or deformation of one's corporeal being.[1] Such concerns about the integrity

---

[1] The standard works are Seymour Fisher, *Body Consciousness* (Englewood Cliffs, N.J. 1973) and *Body Experience in Fantasy and Behavior* (New York 1970). For applications to classical texts see R. F. Newbold, "Boundaries and Bodies in Late Antiquity," *Arethusa* 12 (1979) 93-114 and "Discipline, Bondage, and the Serpent in Nonnus' *Dionysiaca*," *Classical World* 78 (1984-85) 89-98; also my essay, "Boundary Violation and the Landscape of the Self in Senecan Tragedy," *Antike und Abendland* 29 (1983) 172-87, reprinted in my *Interpreting Greek Tragedy* (Ithaca 1986) 315-36.

of one's body exist, to a greater or lesser degree, in all of us and are closely
related to our feelings of security and our basic instincts for survival. The fear
of death is a heightened form of such boundary anxieties, for it is often
accompanied by the terror of total self-annihilation, the dissolution of one's
personal identity into an infinite, all-swallowing ocean of non-being, to use
Lucretius' own metaphor and one also used by Plutarch to argue against
Epicurus' confidence in dispelling the fear of death *(It Is Not Possible to Live
Happily According to Epicurus* 30.1106E).

   Ovid's *Metamorphoses* may suggest a helpful analogy. Ovid shows us,
again and again, the violation of the body's form by changes of shape or
substance. The verisimilitude expected in this genre of narrative poetry
produces something of the same *frisson* of terror as the accounts of death
produce in Lucretius.[2] Such passages draw their power from anxiety similar
to the fear of death: the helplessness, disorientation, self-alienation in seeing
one's familiar corporeal form change into something that is "not yourself," that
is, watching and experiencing the end of what "you" are.

   The least rational, and therefore most powerful, components of the fear
of death appear in implicit rather than explicit forms, that is, in the recurrent
images of primary boundary violation, such as mutilation and putrefaction.
These surface as an explicit subject of the poem just at the point where
Lucretius confronts those terrors of death that are suppressed in Book 3: his
account of the depression and anxiety of those who are caught in the process of
painful dying in the plague. Here physical dissolution is not merely a value-
free atomic process but a dreadful experience. The victims, day by day, watch
the deteriorating changes going on in their own bodies.

   Among most of the peoples of the world, as anthropologists like Mary
Douglas and Susan Postal point out, the boundaries of the body receive the
greatest symbolic elaboration, in clothing, masks, markings, rituals, and other
expressive forms.[3] Every society and every individual use such "defensive
barriers," both literal and figurative; and the nature of these defenses is an
important clue to the conceptual framework with which the individual or the
society operates in the world.[4] "The body," Mary Douglas observes, "is a
model which can stand for any bounded system. Its boundaries can represent

---

2   See my "Ovid: Metamorphosis, Hero, Poet," *Helios* 12 (1985) 57f.
3   See Mary Douglas *Purity and Danger* (1966; reprint, London 1979) 114-28; Susan
Postal, "Body Image and Identity: A Comparison of Kwakiutl and Hopi," *American
Anthropologist* 67 (1965) 455-60, passim.
4   See Seymour Fisher and Sidney Cleveland, *Body Image and Personality* (Princeton
1968) 206.

any boundaries which are threatened or precarious."[5] Given the interchangeability between microcosm and macrocosm in Epicurean physics, however, the converse of this statement also holds true. In the Lucretian universe the stress at the boundaries of the world magnifies to cosmic proportions the stress upon our individual bodies.[6] In both cases, the outer perimeter is the vulnerable area.

Epicurus had insisted on infinite worlds and their dissolution (*To Pythocles*, D.L. 10.88). In Lucretius the death of the world is a drama of its outer boundaries, enacted between the "walls of the world" (*moenia mundi*) and the atoms constantly battering them from outside.[7] The process reflects some of our most basic fears about the violation of bodily boundaries. Early in the poem he tells how age and time threaten to reach "inside" living matter and "devour it entirely" (*penitus peremit consumens materiem omnem*, 1.225f.). The doom of things threatens to destroy them "beneath its very teeth" (*leti sub dentibus ipsis*, 1.852), not unlike Catullus' "evil shades of Orcus" that "devour all that's lovely" (*malae tenebrae / Orci, quae omnia bella devoratis*, 3.13f.).

At the end of Book 1, refuting the view that the ethereal fire will move to the edges of the universe, Lucretius gives a vivid image of "the world's walls flying apart, dissolved through the great void" and the "sky's thunderous regions collapsing from above" while the "earth is drawn away from beneath our feet" so that "in a point of time there is nothing left except desolate void and dark first-beginnings" (1.1102-1110). The conclusion of the next book corrects this false cosmology, but the results are not very different: "The walls of the great world all around, overrun in the attack, will give forth their collapse and crumbling ruin" (*sic igitur magni quoque circum moenia mundi / expugnata dabunt labem putrisque ruinas*) (2.1144f.).[8]

---

5   Douglas 115.
6   The analogy between microcosm and macrocosm was probably used by Democritus and is well established in Greek scientific thinking, e. g. in the Hippocratic corpus and in Plato. See G.E.R. Lloyd, *Polarity and Analogy* (Cambridge 1971) 252-67; David Furley, *The Greek Cosmologists*, vol. 1 (Cambridge 1987) 157f. For a thorough study of the importance of the argument from analogy in Lucretius see now Alessandro Schiesaro, *Simulacrum et imago: Gli argomenti analogici nel De rerum Natura* (Pisa 1990).
7   For the image of the "walls of the world" in Lucretius' "dramatic conception" of the universe see Friedrich Klingner, "Philosophie und Dichtkunst am Ende des zweiten Buches des Lucrez," in *Studien zur griechischen und römischen Literatur* (Zurich 1964) 146f. (originally published in *Hermes* 80, 1952, 3-31).
8   On these two passages see Gerhard Müller, "Die Finalia der sechs Bücher des Lucrez," *Fondation Hardt, Entretiens, Lucrèce* (Vandoeuvres-Geneva 1978) 199f.

The consistent analogy in this passage with the vital processes of a living being (cf. "food," "eating," "nurture," "veins," 2.1125, 1127, 1136, 1147) makes it clear how intimately our own bodies share in these experiences of the "body" of the macrocosm. Indeed, the same terms that describe the world's disintegration here recur for the end of an individual life in Book 3. There the soul's departure leaves the body "changed by so great a collapse that it falls crumbling" (*tanta mutatum putre ruina / conciderit ut corpus*, 3.584f.); here the world's walls crash "into crumbling ruins" (*putris ruinas*, 2.1145).

Staying alive, according to Epicurean physics, is quite literally a matter of defending your physical boundaries. It is at the outermost surface of the body, *in summo corpore*, where the issue of life and death is decided. In describing the soul in Book 3, Lucretius explains that its movements and disturbances are generally limited to this outer zone (*plerumque fit in summo quasi corpore finis / motibus*), and in this way we can hold on to life (3.252-57). Our death is most clearly visible in or on the "outermost perimeter of the limbs," *extima membrorum circumcaesura* (3.219), as Lucretius observes when he notes that this external surface can be intact even when the vital soul is gone and no life remains (3.216-20).

Every creature, as a compound of atoms, needs to keep on taking in matter (nourishment) in order to sustain its borders and thus resist the constant hammering of atoms from outside (2.1133-40). So it is with our world. When a world or a human being no longer has a sufficient supply of atoms to maintain its "walls" it disintegrates or dies. Lucretius describes this process a number of times, most fully at the end of Book 1, on the creation and eventual destruction of our world (1.1021ff.). Given infinite numbers of atoms and an infinite space (void), our world came together through the chance blows and unions of atoms and will continue to exist as long as new atoms replenish those that are lost. In this way the rivers and seas are renewed and "the earth, warmed by the sun's heat, continues to renew its offspring; and the race of living beings, thus sent up, flourishes, and the fires of the heavens, gliding [through the sky], live" (1.1028-34).

A few lines later Lucretius draws a comparison between this process in the universe and an individual human being (1.1038-1043):

nam veluti privata cibo natura animantum
diffluit amittens corpus, sic omnia debent
dissolui simul ac defecit suppeditare
materies aliqua ratione aversa viai.

nec plagae possunt extrinsecus undique summam
conservare omnem, quaecumque est conciliata.

For just as the nature of living things, deprived of food, flows
apart, losing its bodily substance, so all things have to be dissolved
as soon as material fails to supply it, for some reason turned aside
in its course.

Just as the macrocosm of the world's "body" and the microcosm of the
invisible "bodies" (*corpora*) of the atoms teach us about the inevitable
destruction of our own bodies, so our bodies teach us about the death of the
world. Hence the diseases of the world described in Book 6 cause the deaths of
men and also provide analogies to the frailty of human flesh. In the argument
for the mortality of the world in Book 5, Lucretius describes its subjection to
"diseases" (*morbis*) in exactly the same terms as the human body.[9] In both
cases "some harsher cause" will bring not just sickness but total destruction (cf.
5.346f., *ibi si tristior incubuisset causa,* "if some grimmer cause had pressed
upon things;" 3.485f., *paulo si durior insinuarit causa,* "if a somewhat harsher
cause slipped within"). A few lines later, in expounding the physical basis for
this inevitable destruction of our world and everything in it, Lucretius repeats
verbatim the verses about the mixture of atoms and void that he had used for
the mortality of the soul in Book 3 (the passages are 5.351-63 = 3.806-18; for
our argument it does not matter which passage was written first: see Bailey, ad
loc.).

The death of worlds is just as "natural" as the death of individual
persons, and just as inevitable. Yet by keeping before us the physical processes
of decay and dissolution in the world's body, Lucretius indirectly reminds us
of the decay and dissolution going on, at every moment, in our own bodies,
particularly after we have passed our prime and begun the downward slide
toward death (cf. 2.1120-32).

World-death at the end of Books 1 and 2 leads into the inexorable death
of the individual in Book 3 and the futility of hoping for the survival of our
souls after the physical disintegration of our bodies. Books 5 and 6 show us
our world's frailty and certain end. The imbedding of personal death in the

---

[9] On the importance of "disease" as a link between human mortality and the mortality of
the world see D. Clay, *Lucretius and Epicurus* (Ithaca 1978) 260. The relationship, however,
as this paper tries to show, is more than just a method "of reducing his reader's awe before
what is extraordinary in nature," as Clay here suggests.

death of the world at the conclusions of Books 1 and 2 is balanced, finally, by
the imbedding of personal death in the death of an entire society at the end of
the poem. By letting us envision and accept this process writ large in the
natural world, Lucretius aims at overcoming something of our refusal of
death, and he can thereby begin to free us from fearing it. The first step is to
overcome our denial of the world's mortality, which Lucretius recognizes as
"something new and wondrous" and hence "difficult to persuade in words" (*res
nova miraque menti*, 5.97; *quam difficile id mihi sit pervincere dictis, 5.99*).
The proof of the world's mortality is largely the task of Books 5 and 6, but
Lucretius prepares the way by his preliminary accounts of cosmic destruction
in Books 1 and 2. Even we moderns, faced with global warming, the erosion
of the ozone layer, and (more modestly) the disintegration of the pyramids
(Horace's example of indestructible monumentality, *Odes* 3.30), are reluctant
to admit the fragility of our world. How much more solid did the world seem
to the ancients, lacking modern technology's power of destroying or radically
transforming the face of nature.[10] In both Greek and Roman poetry, in fact, it
is a commonplace that the natural world endures though we humans die: *soles
occidere et redire possunt* or *damna tamen celeres reparant caelestia lunae*.[11]
Lucretius, then, has to emphasize repeatedly how flawed, faulty, and
vulnerable it is.

In giving his detailed account of the end of the world, Lucretius may
well be working out his own images. The extant writings of Epicurus show
little of the detail and attention that the subject has in Lucretius. Epicurus' lost
Great Epitome or *On Nature* may have supplied such details, but the one
surviving text that does discuss the end of the world gives us a sense of how
much personal coloring Lucretius has added *(To Pythocles*, D.L. 10.88):

> A world (*kosmos*) is the enclosing circuit of the sky, including stars
> and earth and the phenomena; and when this is dissolved everything
> in it will receive its dissolution, since it is a fragment of the infinite
> and it has its end in a limit (*peras*) that is either rare or dense, either

10   There are, of course, exceptions: e.g. the Stoic *ekpyrosis,* the Platonic myths of cyclical
cataclysm and renewal in the *Politicus,* or the idea of a great deluge that destroyed mankind in
the remote past. as in Ovid, *Met.,* Book 1. But such views still have to overcome the same
resistance as the Epicurean destruction of the world.
11   "Suns can set and rise again," Catullus 5.7; "Nevertheless the swift moons can repair
the losses in the heavens," Horace, *Odes* 4.7.13; cf. pseudo-Moschus, *Epitaph for Bion* 99-
107; in general Marco Fantuzzi, "Caducità dell' uomo e eternità della natura: variazioni di un
motivo letterario," *Quaderni Urbinati di Cultura Classica,* n. s. 26 (1987) 101-110.

revolving or in a state of rest, and it is round or triangular, or has some such outline (*perigraphé*).

We may contrast the much more vivid images of the boundaries of the world at the end of Lucretius' second book and the other passages discussed above.[12]

The same earth that is the mother of all things is also their common grave (5.259). The converse of this process is the Epicurean principle of *isonomia*: life and creation are always counterbalancing death and decay, and vice versa. Early in the poem Lucretius briefly explains how organisms live only "until a force comes against them that beats them apart by its blows or else penetrates into them through their empty spaces and dissolves them" (*donec vis obiit quae res diverberet ictu / aut intus penetret per inania dissolvatque*, 1.222f.). The atomic substance into which they disintegrate, however, is not destroyed, for if time and decay should consume what it destroys, Venus, the life force, would have no way to "lead back the race of living creatures, each after its kind, into the light of life" (*unde animale genus generatim in lumina vitae / redducit Venus*, 1.227f.). Warming to the theme of nature's regenerative energy, Lucretius gives more emphasis to creation than destruction at this point of the poem; and he goes on soon after in his celebrated verses on the new lambs that gambol over the grass on unsteady legs, drunk with the pure milk (1.259-61). The disintegrative processes, so far, have no such vivid language—a balance that he will reverse in the closing sections of the work.

Cosmic destruction comes home to us mortals simply and tangibly in the account of the earth's waning fertility at the end of Book 2. In contrast to Epicurus' extraordinary vision of the world's periphery at the beginning of the poem (1.72-74), the onlooker here is only a humble farmer.[13] Lucretius thus puts the spectator of world-decay very much inside the dying world, and also inside the poem. We, as readers, become spectators of an unphilosophical spectator who "does not grasp" (*nec tenet*, 2.1173) the truth of the death going on constantly around him.

---

[12] See W. M. Green, "The Dying World of Lucretius," *AJP* 63 (1942) passim, especially 52ff.; also Klingner, "Philosophie und Dichtkunst" 136-44, who takes up Bignone's suggestion that Epicurus' theory of the mortality of the world is part of his polemic against Aristotle.

[13] On the effect of this lowly personage here see Klingner, "Philosophie und Dichtkunst" 147f.

This scene qualifies the misplaced, superstitious worship of earth as Great Mother in the middle of the book (cf. 2.645-660).[14] But it also balances the proem of the book, with its very different kind of spectator, one who is momentarily outside the struggles between life and death, growth and decay, because he has attained the privileged viewing-place of the gods, occupying the "lofty, tranquil regions fortified by the learning of the wise" (*munita tenere / edita doctrina sapientum templa serena*, 2.7-8). Such a metaphorical "fortification" is far more secure than the physical boundaries of a living being, "fortified by vital forces" that will eventually fail (cf. *vitalibus ab rebus munita tenetur*, of the mortal soul, 3.820). These metaphorical walls of philosophy are even stronger than our own world as a whole, whose walls, as we have seen, will be "stormed" by the battering of atoms from outside (*expugnata*, 2.1145).[15]

In the proem of the next book Lucretius will make himself into just such a philosophical spectator of the world-processes as he experiences both "divine pleasure" and mortal "awe." He looks out over the mysteries of the infinite universe revealed by Epicurus (3.25-30):

> at contra nusquam apparent Acherusia templa
> nec tellus obstat quin omnia dispiciantur,
> sub pedibus quaecumque infra per inane geruntur.
> his ibi me rebus quaedam divina voluptas
> percipit atque horror, quod sic natura tua vi
> tam manifesta patens ex omni parte retecta est.

But nowhere appear the regions of Acheron, nor does the earth stand in the way to obstruct the view over all those things that go on throughout the void beneath my feet. At these things a certain divine pleasure seizes me and a shuddering awe, because nature has been revealed and opened up to clear view in every direction by your force.

---

14   On this relationship see Müller 205 and the "Discussion," 226f.
15   On the possible Epicurean sources of the image of the philosopher as a fortified city see Clay, *Lucretius and Epicurus* 65 and 186-88; cf. Epicurus, frag. 339 Usener and *Kyriai Doxai* 7, 13, 14. The image, however, seems far stronger in Lucretius. Clay's arguments for its importance in Epicurus' own writings are not strong.

The farmer at the end of the previous book, however, possesses no such transcendent vision. He stands in full immanence, totally involved with the earth and its fruits. Aged himself, he both identifies and is identified with his aging fields. Unable to see the system in which he participates, he can only "weary the heavens" with misplaced complaints, ignorant "that all things are gradually wasting in decay" (*nec tenet omnia paulatim tabescere,* 2.1173).[16]

The vision that Epicurus' *ratio* has brought to us is so far from this blind enclosure in process that it in fact opens upon a kind of anti-world. This is the lucid divine space whose untouched, inviolate condition only sets off more clearly the constantly attacked, ever-decaying world in which we (and everything else) exist. The parting of these "walls of the world" (*moenia mundi discedunt,* 3.15f.) reveals the blessed peace of the gods that frees us from fear (3.18-24):

> apparet divum numen sedesque quietae
> quas neque concutiunt venti nec nubila nimbis
> aspergunt neque nix acri concreta pruina
> cana cadens violat semperque innubilus aether
> integit, et large diffuso lumine ridet.
> omnia suppeditat porro natura neque ulla
> res animi pacem delibat tempore in ullo.

> There appears the divine majesty of the gods and their peaceful abode, which no winds shake or clouds besprinkle with mists, nor does any white-falling snow, congealed with sharp frost, violate it, but the cloudless ether covers it over always, and it smiles with broadly radiating light. Nature supplies all things, nor does anything at any time mar the peace of their spirits.

In our world, however, the parting of the "walls of the world" is the ultimate stage of mortality (1.1094f., 2.1144f.).

In the gods' world nature "supplies everything," whereas for mortals there will come the inevitable time when not enough substance will be

---

16   Note the progression of the motif of old age and decay in this passage, from the rather neutral attribute of the farmer as "old," *grandis* (1164), to the "old and wrinkled vine" (*vetulae vitis sator atque vietae,* 1168, with Heinsius' emendation), and to the closing image of "all things going to the tomb [?], worn out with the aged span of time" (*omnia . . . ire / ad capulum [?] spatio aetatis defessa vetusto,* 1173f.). For some interesting thematic links between the end of Book 2 and the proem of Book 3 see Müller 200-4.

"supplied" to fend off disintegration *(suppeditare*, 2.1138; cf. 1.231). This sky is unshaken by wind or cloud, in contrast to the skies of the mortal world, "struck," pierced, or traversed by lightning, rain, heat, and the other atmospheric disturbances. These prove its imperfections and signal its eventual collapse (cf. 6.281ff., 513ff., 591ff., etc.). In his account of thunder early in Book 6, for example, Lucretius describes how "everything seems so shaken by thunder" *(tonitru concussa)* that even "the vast walls of the capacious world seem to be rent and to gape apart" *(divulsa repente / maxima dissiluisse capacis moenia mundi*, 6.121-23). The "cloudless aether" of the gods' realm is never "violated" by snow or ice, whereas in our world we must take care not to believe that heavenly bodies are "inviolable in their strength" *(inviolabilia haec ne credas forte vigere* (5.305; *inviolabilis* occurs only here in Lucretius).

Although descriptions of growth, decay, and disintegration pervade nearly every part of the poem, there is a strong progression from the somatic terms describing the death of our world at the end of Book 2 to the mortality of the soul in Book 3. The brief glimpse of the inviolate abode of the gods in the proem of Book 3 sets off the ineluctable mortality of our bodies and our world in the rest of the book. The old farmer at the end of Book 2, then, helps form the transition between the impersonal, cosmic disintegration of worlds and the deaths of individuals in our world.

Having used the world's death in the first and second books to prepare us for the personal deaths of the third, Lucretius can then draw on that personal knowledge of death to convince us in Books 5 and 6 of the counter-intuitive truth that our entire world will perish. Each of us constitutes a miniature atomic world. The imperfect "vessel" of our bodies is the exact counterpart, in microcosm, of the *moenia mundi*, the vast walls of the world. Just as these latter will eventually fly apart and scatter to the void all the atoms that lie within (cf. 1.1103-13, 2.1143f.), so the vessel of our body will eventually be unable to protect the vital soul which it contains and at its collapse will scatter the soul-atoms within to the winds (3.440-444; cf. also 554-57 and 936).

Given the fact that boundaries are the zone where life is threatened, it is not surprising that images of walls, fortresses, armor, and the like describe the vulnerable areas of both worlds and of people. Such imagery is clearest in the accounts of cosmic destruction that we have already mentioned (cf. 1.1102ff., 2.1144ff., 5.1213f., 6.121ff.). And, as we have observed, Epicurus' privileged knowledge and status as sage derive from his heroic journey to the boundaries of the world (1.73f.) and his vision out beyond them. The philosopher experiences these boundary-places without the fear of death, and Lucretius benefits from his Master's vision (3.16-17): *diffugiunt animi terrores, moenia mundi /discedunt, totum video per inane geri res* ("The mind's terrors scatter in flight; the walls of the world part, and I behold nature's operations being carried on through the entire void"). In this vista the opening of the world's walls brings not panic but the "scattering of the mind's fears." The careful chiastic balance between *diffugiunt animi terrores* and *moenia mundi discedunt* enhances this philosophical response to this more tranquil dissolving of the world's boundaries. Immediately after comes the vision of the gods' invulnerability (*apparet divum numen*, 3.18ff.). This vision of an indestructible divine abode is hard to reconcile with Epicurean physics[17] and is, I think, to be regarded as at least in part metaphorical and rhetorical. It forms a pendant to the dissolution or penetration of boundaries that is the inevitable fate of every organism in the universe, our bodies included.

Just as the collapse of a being's outer perimeter means its death, so the creation of boundaries is a first step toward making life. Life in the human body results from the interior knitting together, at birth, of soul and body, in the sheltered space formed by "the limbs of the mother and the womb" (3.344-47): "From life's beginning the reciprocal contacts of body and of soul, laid up in the mother's limbs and womb" (*maternis etiam membris alvoque reposta*), "so learn their vital movements that separation cannot take place without illness and suffering." The spatial condition of our life, in other words, is this sheltered removal (*reposta*) of the newly formed being inside the mother's body.

The creation of our entire mortal world begins with the closing off of boundaries as aether, spreading out in all directions, "in greedy embrace hedges in all the rest of things" (*avido complexu cetera saepsit*, 5.466-70). Lucretius draws a beautiful analogy with the morning mists rising from the newly formed earth "weaving" a kind of web of cloud beneath the sky (*subtexunt nubila caelum*, 5.466). This subtle fabric forms the world's necessary enclosure; but we are also reminded of the creative embrace of Venus in the proem of Book 1 and her attempt to "surround" Mars with her sacred body (*circumfusa super*, 1.38f.), also in the service of life and creation.

The knowledge of boundaries and limits also provides emotional security against the threat of disorder and arbitrariness in the life of the universe. This sense of fixed limits, as Lucretius expresses it in his repeated metaphor of the

---

[17]   See A.A. Long and D. Sedley, *The Hellenistic Philosophers*, vol. 1 (Cambridge 1987) 147f.

"deeply clinging boundary stone," gives the Epicurean the confidence in reason that sets him apart from his ignorant fellow-mortals (cf. 1.77, 107-11, 595f.).

The "enclosures of life," *claustra vitai*, protect our vital essence and are "dissolved" or "totter" in collapse when we are old or suffer disease (1.414f., 6.1153; cf. 3.396ff.). Yet so far are we from immortality that penetrability is the very condition of our existence. Our vital processes, like perspiration or the growth of hair, depend on this porous condition of our physical being. We owe our sense-perceptions to the same penetrability. Hearing, for instance, depends on voices that "fly between the barriers and enclosures of the house" (*inter saepta meant voces et clausa domorum / transvolitant*, 1.354f.).[18] The corollary of these life-sustaining penetrations of our corporeal boundaries is their eventual disintegration. The rupture of these defenses at any point creates the "gate of death" through which the delicate soul atoms stream forth (*ianua leti*, 1.1112, 5.373).[19] The body forms the shield-like "covering" (*tegmen*) that protects the soul from dissolving into the winds, and thus the soul dies when that "covering" is "dissolved" or "removed" (*resoluto corporis omni / tegmine*, 3.576f.; *tegmine dempto*, 604; cf. 649).

The *claustra vitai* are to the microcosm of the individual human body what the *moenia mundi* are to the world as a whole. Lucretius makes the connection explicit in his lengthy analogy between water dripping through rock in the cave, perspiration, nourishment, and the growth of hair to which I referred above (6.921-44). He goes on here to explain how cold pierces metals, how voices pass through the "stony barriers of houses" (*dissaepta domorum saxea*, 6.951), and how clouds or storms traverse the zones "where the breastplate of the sky closes in (the heavens) all around (*denique qua circum caeli lorica coercet*, 6.954). This metaphor is the exact analogy, in the macrocosm, to the *tegmen* ("shield," "covering") that protects the individual human soul from dissolution into the air (3.576f., 604). Lucretius uses *tegmen* only some fifty lines later of the literal "shield" of the warrior (3.649). Epicurus' own language, which Lucretius seems to have in mind, is the neutral *to stegazon*, "that which covers" (*To Herodotus*, D.L. 10.65).

Unfortunately, there is a lacuna (perhaps of only a single verse) after the "breastplate of the sky" in 6.954; but the generalizing conclusion on the "rare"

---

18   Cf. Epicurus, *Letter to Herodotus*, D.L. 10.49.
19   Similarly, one who is close to death stands "at the threshold of doom," *in limine leti*, at a kind of boundary point (2.960, 6.1157, 1208). To be born, correspondingly, is "to enter the threshold of life" (*vitae cum limen inimus*, 3.681) or, in a broader spatial field, to come "into the shores of light" (*in luminis oras*).

(i.e. penetrable) texture with which all bodies are woven together makes it clear that the same conditions govern the human constitution and the remotest reaches of the heavens (*quandoquidem nil est nisi raro corpore nexum*, "since there is nothing that is not woven of rare body," 958).

The great plague at Athens, some two hundred lines later, arrives as a foreign invader, "arising deep within the borders of Egypt," crossing those boundaries on a long journey, and then coming at last to "rest heavily upon the whole people of Pandion" in Athens (6.1141-43):

> nam penitus veniens Aegypti finibus ortus,
> aera permensus multum camposque natantis,
> incubuit tandem populo Pandionis omni.

The plague is thus a specific instance of that invading "force of disease" described earlier in the book: "The force of disease slips into (us) from outside" (*morbida visque simul, cum extrinsecus insinuatur*, 6.955). The effect of this "force of disease" is to move "through the throat," "fill the breast" and then "flow into the saddened heart of the sick," where "the enclosures of life totter" (6.1151-53):

> inde ubi per fauces pectus complerat et ipsum
> morbida vis in cor maestum confluxerat aegris,
> omnia tum vero vitai claustra lababant.

As plague is the hostile invasion of a political territory, individual illness is the invasion of a body's interior territory. Harmful substances can "strike diseases" into us (*morbos incutere*, 6.772). "Many hostile atoms," Lucretius continues, pass through the ears, many slip through our very nostrils, harmful and rough in their contact" (*multa meant inimica per auris, multa per ipsas / insinuant naris infesta atque aspera tactu*, 5.777f.).

The poem's most striking example of individual boundary violation is the account of early man being eaten alive by wild beasts in Book 5, "seeing his living flesh disappearing into a living tomb" (5.990-93):

> unus enim tum quisque magis deprensus eorum
> pabula viva feris praebebat, dentibus haustus,
> et nemora ac montis gemitu silvasque replebat
> viva videns vivo sepeliri viscera busto.

For then each one of them, caught, was providing living food to
wild beasts, gulped down by the teeth, and he would fill the groves
and mountains and forests with his groaning, seeing his living flesh
being buried in a living tomb.

The gratuitous detail of the mangled person's "seeing" (*videns*) his
"living entrails" disappear into his killer's maw adds psychological horror to
the scene.[20] Burial "alive," as it were, here takes the most extreme form of
primary boundary anxiety, the absorption of one's life-substance, violently and
painfully, into the engulfing life of a cruel and powerful creature. The
interlocking repetitions of the same sound for "life," "seeing," and "flesh"
(*viva . . .viva . . .vivo//vi-dens . . .vi-scera*) tie together the different parts of
this anxiety: concern for basic life-process and survival; the horror of being
conscious of the event; and the exposure of one's interior organs to destruction
and engulfment in the vitals of another being.

This horrific event, accompanied by the victim's screams of agony is
bracketed, as it were, by being set in the remote time of prehistory.
Interestingly, however, it occurs in our time as a psychological event, as a
nightmare, described in Book 4. This is the dream of those who "as if they are
being eaten by the biting of a panther or savage lion, fill everything with great
shouting" (*et quasi pantherae morsu saevive leonis /mandantur magnis
clamoribus omnia complent, 4.1016f.*) The recall of the previous book may be
Lucretius' way of recognizing that anxieties about the physical integrity of our
body, the enclosing "vessel" of our soul, are a fundamental part of our
psychological make-up, surfacing in dreams and in a different way in our
reconstruction of our remote past.

This passage also brings us into the poet's contemporary world in
another way, for the scene invites comparison with the foolish man's concern
about the laceration of his body after death in 3.885-87:

nec *videt* in *vera* nullum fore morte alium se
qui possit *vivus* sibi se lugere peremptum

---

[20]   On the verbal power and pathos of 5.990ff. see Bonelli 237f. The passage intensifies
the similar effect of *per viscera viva per artus*, of pain, in 2.964. It would be interesting to view
this passage as a macabre, destructive inversion, characteristically Lucretian, of Epicurus'
concern with the belly as the seat of pleasures (on which see J. Pigeaud, *Maladie de l'âme*
(Paris 1981) 226, following Logre, calls "la situation menacée de ce corps épicurien tel qu' il est
conçu originellement, corps poreux . . .")

stansque iacentem se lacerari uri*ve* dolere.

The pre-civilized man in Book 5 is *"*alive" to "see" (*vivus, videre*, 5.993) his body's terrible suffering. The foolish man of 3.885, though belonging to the civilized and indeed urban present, "does not see" the non-existence of that self that, "alive," can mourn that "he" is being torn apart (*nec videt . . . vivus . . . se lacerari*, 3.885-87).

The psychological invasion of our boundaries can be no less deleterious than the physical violation, particularly as we receive fantasies or dreams as *simulacra*, that is, the outer shells of things that penetrate the surface of our body. Fear of the gods can "slip into our breasts" (*insinuarit pectora*, 5.73f.). Passionate love is a wound (4.1015ff.), and its poisonous sweetness "drips into our heart" (*in cor stillavit*, 4.1059f.). Such love also takes the form of a deluded and empty attempt to cross physical boundaries as the lovers "fasten their bodies (together) greedily and join their mouth's saliva" (4.1108f.), but it is "all in vain because they can tear nothing away nor penetrate and depart with entire body into (the other's) body" (4.1110f., *nec penetrare et abire in corpus corpore toto*). Since lovers can take in no solid substance to sate their impossible desires, they can exchange only empty images and so remain in a state of tormented, ever-renewed frustration. Thus they are caught in a morbid situation of non-nurture and decay, a kind of living death, as they "waste away with a hidden wound" inside their bodies (*tabescunt vulnere caeco*, 4.1120).

The analogies between worlds and persons has a middle term in the boundaries of cities. Fortified cities and their destruction, as we have seen, bulk large in Lucretius' depictions of death.[21] Human civilization reaches its apogee with the building of "strong towers" and the dividing up of the earth (5.1440f.):

> iam validis saepti degebant turribus aevum
> et divisa colebatur discretaque tellus.

> And now they passed their lives hedged in with strong towers,
> and the earth, divided and partitioned, was being tilled.

---

[21] To the examples mentioned earlier we may add 6.239-42, the power of lightning bolts to "lay open towers" (*turris discludere*), destroy homes, tear wooden timbers away, and move the "monuments of men."

The rapid enumeration of civilization's triumphs soon follows, including walls (1448), sailing, agriculture, laws, and so on. But this material fortification of boundaries as the acme of human evolution is ironically undercut by the fragility of all the walls and enclosures of life, whether of the world or of the individual. The only truly "pure security," Epicurus wrote, comes from the spiritual "tranquillity" (*hesychia*) of his philosophy and from "withdrawal from the many" (*Kyriai Doxai* 14).

Although the extant fragments of Epicurus show little of Lucretius' acute sensitivity to somatic boundaries, his admonitions against sexual intercourse (frag. 62 Usener, D.L. 10.118) suggest that such boundary anxiety is not entirely Lucretius' invention.[22] In a celebrated saying, for example, Epicurus wrote: "Against everything else it is possible to provide security; but as far as death is concerned all of us mortals inhabit an unwalled city" (*polin ateichiston,* fragment 339 Usener = *Sententiae Vaticanae* 31). Nevertheless, Epicurus' terms for the "boundaries" of the world are rather neutral and abstract words like "limit" or "enclosure" (*peras, periochê, periechein, emperilambanein*).[23] When Philodemus quotes Epicurus' remark about death and the unwalled city (frag. 339 Usener, above), his context is the general ephemerality and uncertainty of life (*De Morte* 37.18ff.). This is an important theme in Epicurus, to be sure,[24] and the image does bring together walls and the motif of death; but it does not receive the elaboration that Lucretius' poem gives it.

The plague at Athens is the logical culmination of the vulnerability of boundaries. It is, as we have seen, an invasion of Athenian territory. In following its manifestations, Lucretius traces in excruciating, step-by-step detail, how the deadly "force of disease" enters and destroys a living human organism. And in its larger role in the book, the plague is the ultimate example of that porous, permeable state that is the condition of both life and death for all physical organisms, whether these are all the worlds in the *summa summarum* of the universe or all the human bodies in a great city.

Conclusion

In using psychological and anthropological models like those of Seymour Fisher or Mary Douglas, I am raising the large hermeneutic question—perhaps

---

22   On sexual intercourse and fears of "boundary pollution" see Douglas 125f.
23   See Epicurus, *Letter to Herodotus* (D.L. 10.73f.) and *Letter to Pythocles* (D.L. 10.88-90); also fragment 303 Usener.
24   See *Kyriai Doxai* 7, 13, 14. In the last of these (14) Epicurus derives the "purest security" not from material goods but "from peace of mind and withdrawal from the many."

the central hermeneutic question of our field today—of whether concepts and procedures that are completely extraneous to the culture and historical moment of an ancient text can validly be brought to bear on it. There are, of course, various ways out of this problem. The simplest is perhaps to recognize that we are all creatures of our own time and can never wholly escape its influence, however much imaginative sympathy and historical understanding we bring to the classical texts we are studying. The more positive side of this solution is that certain categories of human experience are universal; and we might even profit from bringing the experience of the ancients into contact with our own. We all have bodies and we all fear death, and we respond therefore to a poet who deals with the inconveniences and disadvantages of having a body and of being mortal.

But there is also a more complex answer, and this lies in the need to combine both historicizing and universalizing approaches. Thus for the aspects of Lucretius' poetry and thought that I have analyzed here, the modern concepts of boundary violation and displacement need to be applied against the historical background of their Epicurean equivalents. It may be possible—and it is perhaps inevitable—that the contemporary reader who comes to the poem with no previous knowledge of Epicureanism will translate Lucretius' terms into his own. But the task of the classicist is, or could be, to aid or supplement that translation on the one hand while on the other correcting and refining it with the necessary historical information.

Lucretius' concern with body boundaries, for example, is perhaps a nascent form of that obsession with the mutilated, suffering body that one sees in the literature of the late Augustan and early Imperial periods, from Ovid's *Metamorphoses* to Lucan and the tragedies of Seneca.[25] The same factors may also be operating, albeit in milder form, for Lucretius as for the later poets, that is, anxiety about the definition of clear identity at a period of crisis and changing values, a sense of helplessness and loss of control over the outside world, and a feeling that the body politic is in a state of corruption or decay. The body becomes the site on which is projected wider, more general, less tangible feelings of fragility, disorientation, moral degradation. When Ovid, for instance, juxtaposes the uncovered muscles and visible veins and entrails of

---

[25]   See my remarks in "Boundary Violation" in *Interpreting Greek Tragedy* 315-36, especially 316f., 333ff.; also Glenn Most, "The Rhetoric of Dismemberment in Neronian Poetry," in Daniel L. Selden and Ralph J. Hexter, eds., *Alexander's Cook: Rethinking Writing from Antiquity*, forthcoming. I am grateful to Professor Most for allowing me to see his paper in advance of publication.

Marsyas' flayed body with the nymphs, dryads, and shepherds of the forest, he is showing us a world very different from the innocent, pastoral beauty of Virgil's *Eclogues*. Ugliness, cruelty, and horror invade the *locus amoenus*.

In this spirit, we may also take another, historical look at the mental operations of displacement and analogy that I have used in this paper. Within Epicurus' atomistic system, we stand not just in a relation of analogy to the cosmos but in fact in a relation of continuity, since we share the same substance and non-substance (atoms and void) as everything that exists. The death of the world, then, is not just a displacement or projection of anxieties about our bodies upon the natural world; it is, also, a magnificently terrible blow-up on the vast screen of the universe of the gradual, inevitable dissolution continually going on, visibly and invisibly, within our physical frame. Logically, Lucretius has little need for such a displacement, since in his materialist system microcosm and macrocosm are not just analogues of one another but parts of the same continuum.

Even here, the ancient and the modern reading may not, ultimately, be so far apart. Within the terms of Lucretius' avowed intentions, namely to improve human life by banishing the fear of death, the psychological effect of the argument is of fundamental importance. And psychologically the analogies between the death of the world and the death of the person do help prepare the reader to confront the reality of his own individual death in Book 3. For this reason, perhaps, Lucretius anticipates the arguments of Book 5 by ending each of his first two books with vivid accounts of cataclysm.[26]

If we probe still more deeply, Lucretius may in fact not be so very far from the modern notion of displacement. The displacement of anxiety from one area (physical suffering and the violation or annihilation of bodily integrity) to another (the afterlife) is in fact consistent with Epicurean psychology, as David Konstan has pointed out in a monograph on the subject, for the Epicureans recognized the fear of the Underworld as a displaced form of fear in this life.[27] Lucretius himself formulates the principle near the end of Book 3 (3.978ff.) when he gives an allegorical interpretation of mythical

---

[26]   Klingner, "Philosophie und Dichtkunst" 139-44 has excellent observations on the shifting of this topic in Lucretius' argument, but I do not agree with his analysis of the reasons (the poet's fascination with destruction, pessimism, and the lack of complete integration of the poetry and the philosophy).
[27]   David Konstan, *Some Aspects of Epicurean Psychology*, Philosophia Antiqua 25 (Leiden 1973) 25-27.

sinners like Tantalus and Sisyphus: *sed Tityos nobis hic est, in amore iacentem* . . . ("This is Tityos for us, the one who lies sprawled in love," 3.992).[28]

This form of displacement, however, operates at a relatively conscious level and follows a traditional technique of the allegorical interpretation of myth.[29] Another mode of displacement, admittedly remoter and more speculative, may be at work if Lucretius's details of putrefaction, mutilation, and other destructive attacks on the body reflect a concern with a generalized moral decay, of the sort that Sallust, for example, castigates in his *Catiline*. Lucretius too frequently touches on this kind of corruption, particularly at the beginning of the book that has the most extended treatment of bodily injury (3.59-78). Lucretius here traces all of our vices and crimes to the fear of death. For these social and personal ills he also uses vivid images of filth or infection. Embittered, envious men complain that they are "rolled about in the mud" (*ipsi se in tenebris volvi caenoque queruntur*, 3.77). Power in the corrupt state has reverted "to the utmost dregs" (*ad summam faecem*, 5.1141). Epicurus himself saw how his contemporaries, in their insatiable desire for material things "as it were befouled everything with bitter taste" (6.22, *taetro quasi conspurcare sapore*), anticipating the literal infections of the plague at the end of the book (cf. 6.1154, 1200, 1205, 1271). This attention to the corruption, disintegration, or disfigurement of the whole body, then, may reflect feelings of malaise and disorientation at a time of turmoil and massive social and political change. There is perhaps no more immediate expression of disorientation than to lose the clear relation to one's own corporeal being or the sharp outline of one's own form in the world. The modern reader will think at once of Kafka's *Metamorphosis*.

Lucretius' aim is, of course, to rid human life of its crippling anxieties, the fears that constitute the "wounds against life," *vulnera vitae*, as he calls them at the beginning of Book 3. To depict these anxieties with the vividness that he displays in Book 3 and at the end of Book 6 might seem to be counterproductive; but I think rather that it is part of the poet's attempt to bring forth to the light of reason what he calls the "dark goad," the *caecum stimulum*, that lies hidden within the human heart. The historically determined

---

28   This statement also forms a pendant to *nil igitur mors est ad nos* ("Death is nothing to us," 3.830).

29   For such allegorizations see P.H.Schrijvers, "Sur quelques aspects de la critique des mythes chez Lucrèce" in *Syzetesis: Studi sull' epicureismo greco e romano offerti a Marcello Gigante* (Naples 1983) vol. 1, pp. 353-71, passim; also Elizabeth Asmis, "Lucretius' Venus and Stoic Zeus," *Hermes* 110 (1982) 469f.; E. J. Kenney, *Lucretius De Rerum Natura Book III* (Cambridge 1971) ad 978-1023 (pp. 222f.).

Charles Segal

Lucretius and the Lucretius who still belongs to the twentieth century, then, come together at the same point of juncture as that between Lucretius the poet and Lucretius the Epicurean philosopher. His displacement of anxieties about death into images of violating the boundaries of the body is not explicitly and systematically articulated, but it forms part of the therapeutic effect of the poem's argument. Looking at it in terms of the modern notion of displacement and boundary violation, I suggest, makes clearer to us this therapeutic effect.[30]

30   I have drawn heavily on material in my book, *Lucretius on Death and Anxiety: Poetry and Philosophy in De Rerum Natura* (Princeton 1990), especially chapter 5, but have elaborated on several points and recast some features of the argument. I am grateful to Princeton University Press for permission to reuse some of this material here. I prepared this essay during a Fellowship at the Center for Advanced Study in the Behavioral Sciences, Stanford, California. I am grateful for financial support at the Center, which was provided by the National Endowment for the Humanities (#RA-20037-88) and the Andrew W. Mellon Foundation.

MOENIA MUNDI: THE AKRITIC POET
Response to Charles Segal

At the conclusion of his paper, Charles Segal raises what he calls "the large, central hermeneutic question of our field today: whether concepts and procedures completely extraneous to the culture and historical moment of a text can validly be brought to bear upon it." The simplest way out, he notes, is to recognize that we have no choice but to apply them.

I am less sure than he is that this explanation is either a way out or simple. First we must recognize what those extraneous concepts are. I am not referring now to such models as that of deconstruction which signify their presence by their referents, but to those assumptions which are so much part of our cultural conditioning and scholarly training that we are unaware we are applying them.

In the proceedings of a conference like our own in Ottawa some ten years ago, Professor Palmer noted that "the premodern era in hermeneutics is 'the Golden Age of allegorical interpretation' . . . the modern era is something like 'the Golden Age of literalism.'" From the Renaissance on, he argued, the interpretation of the text focused on "the surface verbal meaning."[1]

Palmer's observation, Maija Väisänen has recently suggested in her brilliant study of Catullus, sets him among a minority of modern critics. "The idea," she contends, "that the listener is prone to pass over the most immediate meanings in favor of those which are more hidden is rarely considered by modern scholars." This assumption of the intentionality of the explicit, she notes, can be explained, at least in part, by our failure to keep in mind that most ancient poetic texts were designed for oral presentation, where the illusory clarity of surface verbal meanings—perhaps we should call them the *moenia verborum*—disappears. The apparent self-sufficient distinctness of an individual word is visual, not aural, obvious to the reader rather than to the listener: "Only the written word has a constant surface in space."[2] But then, of

1 "Allegorical, Philological, and Philosophical Hermeneutics: Three Modes in a Complex Heritage," in *Contemporary Literary Hermeneutics and Interpretation of Classical Texts*, S. Kresic ed. (Ottawa 1981) 23-4.
2 Maija Väisänen, *La Musa delle molte voci: studio sulle dimensioni storiche dell' arte di Catullo*, Helsinki (Societas Historica Finlandiae, Studia Historica 30) 1988, 23. Perhaps, we might add, this is why Plato insisted that language imitates phenomena "in letters and in

course, as Väisänen shows with an apt citation of Walter Ong: "A complex and polysemous utterance is no clearer when it is written down, nor is its meaning any simpler. We are surer that we can recover it word for word. That is all. But, word for word, it may convey only a very obscure sense."[3] Literalism, in short, does not take us very far in poetry.

The very insistence of Greeks on describing truth as "that which does not elude us" (*alêtheia*), safety as "that which does not trip us" (*asphaleia*), and *emphasis* as "the process of digging out the latent meaning of a word or phrase" should remind us that their fundamental world view was less positivistic, less sure of the apparently stable surface of anything than our own.[4] We should, therefore, beware of such casual assumptions as those which Charles Segal occasionally makes in his paper: "How much more solid did the world seem to the ancients, lacking modern technology's power of radically transforming the face of nature," or that "we all have bodies and we all fear death."

Even if we leave aside the Christian sense of the imminent end of the world in the first century A.D., we should recall that Lucretius and the Epicureans were by no means unique in Greco-Roman antiquity in envisaging the world as unstable and doomed to perish, or in viewing "personal boundary violation," most notably death, in terms of the destruction of all the world's boundaries. The Stoics had their own doctrine of final conflagration which would have rendered ironic Jupiter's promise to Venus in *Aeneid* 1.279, that Rome will have an empire without end: *imperium sine fine dedi*. And Seneca's chorus in *Trojan Women* takes almost Lucretian consolation in the universality of cataclysmic destruction (1009-55).

The concept of boundary violation and human fear of such violation to which Segal refers in his discussion of Lucretius is modern only in its phrasing. Far from being an extraneous, new construct, it is an idea of immemorial antiquity. In Anaximander's terms, the "Boundless," *to apeiron*,

---

syllables" rather than in words. See my "Ars est Caelare Artem (Art in Puns and Anagrams Engraved)," in *On Puns*, ed. Jonathan Culler (Oxford 1988) 17-43 (especially 27-8); cf. my *Metaformations. Soundplay and Wordplay in Ovid and Other Classical Poets* (Ithaca 1985) 44-7.

3   Walter Ong, *The Presence of the Word* (New Haven 1967) 147.

4   For *alêtheia* see Marcel Détienne, "La notion mythique d'*alêtheia, REG* 73 (1960) 27-35, F. Ahl, "Amber, Avalon, and Apollo's Singing Swan," *AJP* 103 (1982) 373-411, and W.G. Thalmann, *Conventions of Form and Thought in Early Greek Poetry* (Baltimore 1984)147-9; for *emphasis* see Quintilian, *Inst. Or.* 9.2.64 and my "The Art of Safe Criticism in Greece and Rome," *AJP* 105 (1984) 174-208.

is the "principle and element of existing things."[5] And the mythic act of creation is in *Genesis*, Hesiod, and Ovid's *Metamorphoses*, an act of separation: of breaking up the primal oneness of chaos, of creating boundaries, of achieving not *Struktur und Einheit*, structure and oneness, but structure and plurality.[6] The force which has the ability to draw these boundaries is variously described by the Greeks as god, mind (*nous*)or the ability to make distinctions (*logos*), and by the Christian evangelist, John, as "the word." These distinctions of boundaries are our means of defining ourselves and our universe, and are expressed in our languages, our grammatical rules, and the laws in terms of which we are all, in our different societies, educated, trained, and punished.

In Greek literature it is commonplace to read of infringement of boundaries being punished by *nemesis*, in a kind of restoration of pre-existing order, of *nomos*, whether *nomos* be used to refer to order prescribed by custom or law, or by the patterns of music and art. The Erinyes, the Furies, are, from Homer (*Iliad* 19.418) onwards, ready to punish both man and natural forces, even gods themselves, if they trespass beyond their assigned limits or boundaries.

Moenia Mundi

We can, without difficulty, see much of ancient thought, history, and myth in terms of the establishment and transgression of boundaries. Remus is punished for violating the protective boundaries of Rome's first walls either by Celer or by Romulus, his own brother (Plutarch, *Romulus*; Ovid, *Fasti* 4. 836-48). Often, of course, the punishment of border violation itself involves another violation of borders, and writers tend to favor those traditions where the symmetry is most complete. Thus the violation of Rome's walls by Remus is most often, as in Horace, *Epodes* 7, punished by his brother's act of fratricide—which itself oversteps the boundaries of *pietas*, the proper respect for family and civic ties.

Lucretius, in *De Rerum Natura*, understandably regards border violation not only on an individual but on a cosmic level as inevitable. Uniquely among Roman poets, he uses a puzzling expression, *moenia mundi*, "walls of the world," to describe the defining form and boundaries of matter, whose

---

5   Simplicius, *Phys.* 24.13 (DK 12A9); see Charles Kahn, *Anaximander and the Origins of Greek Cosmology* (New York 1960) 166 and 178-93.
6   See my discussion in *Metaformations* (note 2, above) and the sources cited there.

violation and disintegration lead to the destruction of men, cities, and even of the celestial bodies in the heavens. Since he insists throughout *De Rerum Natura* (as, for example, in 1.958-62) that the universe itself is not bounded in any direction, and that the atoms of which all things are composed are themselves imperishable, *mundus* appears to indicate the infinite number of complex organic, inorganic, and man-made structures found within the universe, structures which people often falsely assume to be the solid and permanent material basis of reality—rather, I suppose, as the scholar often assumes the written word to be the basis of meaning. Thus even the stars, symbolic to many in antiquity of divine eternity and immutability, are themselves as ultimately mortal as humans and their institutions.

His position on this matter, though fully in accord with the thinking of the Epicurean philosophers, was highly controversial in the eyes of others, and attacked by opponents of Epicureanism as impious, as we see in Cicero's *De Natura Deorum* 2.44. For the Epicureans were themselves attacking traditional sacred boundaries and definitions, smashing down the borders of conventional thought even while talking of the peace to be discovered when the walls of the world collapse.

The violation or breakdown of what Lucretius calls the *moenia mundi*, then, readily becomes a metaphor of human existence, especially for the Romans who called not only the world, but the augural center of their city the *mundus*. In Rome, the *mundus* was a trench into which, according to Plutarch (*Romulus* 11), Romans cast the first-fruits (*aparchai*) of all the natural (*physei*) necessities of life and of all things considered fine by law or tradition (*nomôi*). It was, Plutarch contends, circular in shape, and, from this central point, the boundaries of the city were themselves described in a circle.[7] *Mundus*, in this more specialized sense, both governs and is contained by the city boundaries, thus becoming a peculiarly apt, Roman metaphor for the limits of all matter. Indeed, the gates of the *mundus* were open only on three days during the Roman year which, as James Frazer, citing Festus, notes, were "deemed unfit for business because on them the gates of the infernal regions were supposed to be unbarred, leaving the spirits of that gloomy realm free to roam the

---

[7]   Whether Plutarch was right in his description of the shape and site of the trench, or wrong (as James Frazer and others have suggested in *Publii Ovidii Nasonis Fastorum Libri Sex* 3, London 1929, 386-7) is largely irrelevant. If he was reporting a tradition which Romans took to be correct, the analogy may well have been on Lucretius' mind.

world."[8] Frazer adds that the entrance to the *mundus* was kept closed "because the lower part of the structure . . . was sacred to the deified spirits of the dead," and argued that the creation of a *mundus* within the city was not only a sacrifice intended to secure the stability of the city walls, but to appease the spirits of the earth, whose own boundaries had been violated by the excavation of the trench.[9] The creation of one border involves the violation of another. But in Roman terms, the rupture of the *moenia mundi* would also suggest the rupture of the borders between life and death.

What one sees when one envisages the breakdown of the *moenia mundi* depends on what one expects to see. Segal characterizes the vision to which Epicurus' *ratio* brings us in Lucretius' poetic vision as an "anti-world:" "A lucid, divine space, whose untouched, inviolate condition only sets off more clearly the constantly attacked world in which we and everything else exist." He goes on to discuss Lucretius (3.15-24) where the parting of the *moenia mundi*, the walls of the world, allows us to see "the blessed peace of the gods that frees us from fear." It is an Elysium of the mind, not a haunted world of specters, Tartarus, and eternal darkness. It is also, as Phillip Mitsis points out, Epicurus' definition of piety which "consists in knowing the nature of the gods and their indifference to our world and thereby benefitting ourselves by approximating their state of *ataraxia*."[10]

In this sense Vergil's *pius Aeneas*, as he represents his vision of the parting of the veil of his vision in *Aeneid* 2.604-18, is the very antithesis of Epicurean piety, just as Epicurean piety is the antithesis of Cicero's.[11] For when Aeneas describes Venus (Lucretius' nature, his *Aeneadum genetrix*) tearing away the cloud that obscures his eyes, he opens up a scene of divine attack upon his city, Troy: Neptune is prying down the walls with his trident, Juno, armed for battle is calling the Greek troops from their ships. And Jupiter himself is giving them strength. It is a vision of what Aeneas says

---

[8]   Festus (pp. 144-7 [Lindsay]); Macrobius, *Saturnalia* 1.16. 16-18, and Frazer, *op. cit.*, 160, 388.

[9]   *Op. cit.*, 385.

[10] Phillip Mitsis, *Epicurus' Ethical Theory: The Pleasures of Invulnerability* (Ithaca 1988) 70, n. 30, drawing on Epicurus, *To Menoeceus* 123, 133.

[11] Scholars often wrongly assume Aeneas' *pietas* to be something unequivocal and absolute. It would probably help us understand the situation better if we recalled that the most famous of Vergil's contemporaries who assumed the epithet *pius* was Sextus Pompey, for whom even the ardent Republican Lucan had no use, dismissing him variously as a "Sicilian pirate" and a "degenerate spirit, unworthy of his great father." See my *Lucan: An Introduction.* Cornell Studies in Classical Philology 39 (Ithaca 1976) 130-49.

Venus called "the inclemency of the gods" that frees all human agents, including the narrator Aeneas himself, from any responsibility for the destruction of Troy's walls: the ultimate stage of Troy's mortality (601-3). What we see when what Lucretius calls the *moenia mundi*, the boundaries of common perception and understanding, are ruptured depends on who narrates the vision, and for what purpose.

Fear of life and love of death

While Lucretius proposes to liberate men from fear of death, Vergil gives us a hero who stands in that underworld whose very existence Lucretius denies, watching a Platonic troop of souls waiting eagerly to be reincarnated, but baffled by their fearful desire for the light: *quae lucis miseris tam dira cupido?* (*Aeneid* 6.721). His pity is for those about to live. Similarly, Seneca's chorus *Trojan Women* 371-7 seems unhappy that death might *not* be total. Lucan shows in the *Pharsalia* that many are motivated by *amor mortis* rather than *timor mortis*, as, for example Caesar's soldier Scaeva who comments in 6.245-6:

Pompei vobis minor est causaeque senatus
quam mihi mortis amor.

The causes of Pompey and the senate mean less
to you than love of death does to me.[12]

We should, then, be a little cautious of Segal's second generalization, mentioned earlier. Although we all have bodies, we do not all fear death— even ignominious death. Odysseus and Aeneas cry out at the thought of drowning at sea (*Odyssey* 5.306-312; *Aeneid* 1.94-101), but Lucan's Caesar, faced with the same doom, begs only that no trace of his body will ever be found (*Pharsalia* 5.655-71). Then there will be no proof that he is dead. Death will not have defined the limits of his power. He will have transcended the borders of history and leaped into myth. Because he wishes to be feared more than he wishes to live he earns the right to be feared because he is not afraid: *meruitque timeri/non metuens* (5.317-18).

---

[12]   See Werner Rutz's important study, *"Amor mortis* bei Lucan," *Hermes* 88 (1960) 462-75; also my *Lucan: An Introduction* 118-121.

Ironically enough, it is Lucan's act of portraying Caesar as the amoral borderer that contributed in large measure to Caesar's passing on from historical conqueror to mythic hero. And to become mythic is to defy the boundaries of mortality to join the ranks of what the Neoplatonist Sallustius calls "those things that never were and always are" (*Concerning the Gods and the Universe* 4.14-16)—a paradoxical anti-world of a different sort.

Walls and fortresses can imprison as well as defend their inhabitants. We should, then, modify Segal's remarks in his conclusion that "we all have bodies and we all fear death," to include the less socially acceptable reverse position: that of those who in antiquity as today regarded the body as a prison, *sôma sêma*, from which they prayed for release, or those who, like the Stoics, regarded life and death as "indifferent" to the wise man.

The poet as "borderer"

Within any given society, not least what Thomas Habinek calls the "guild" of Classical scholars, there will be those who see themselves primarily as almost sacerdotal guardians of traditional *nomoi*, of received borders, and those who cannot live within the borders to which they are assigned by nature, custom, and law, or whose own social and moral borders have been destroyed: Plutarch's Romulus, Vergil's Aeneas, or Ovid's Byblis and Myrrha in *Metamorphoses* 9.454-665 and 10.298-502. Greek tragedians often illustrate the mindset which induces their heroes to violate political and ethnic borders by showing them as violating the more familiar traditional social and family barriers by rape, incest, or murder.

We should remind ourselves that ancient poetry, especially epic, is, like the human experience, centered on the violation of borders. Epic heroes from Gilgamesh onwards are permitted to pass through the *mundus*, to violate that universal border of mortals, death, and return to life. Surely, in fact, that is the nature of the ancient hero. Being of divine descent he straddles the world of gods and men. He is like Digenis Akritas of Byzantine epic, a borderer, part Arab part Romaios, savior of a woman he rescues from marauding Arabian troops, restorer of her to her faithless lover, but also her rapist in a lonely oasis, simultaneously civilizer and outlaw. Such civilizer-outlaws, Hercules for example, have always had a certain appeal to those who are afraid of transgressing the borders within which they have been born and are, essentially, trapped just as their behavior is anathema to political philosophers, such as Plato, who want a more carefully balanced social order.

Occasionally an epic character will even become such a borderer hero despite himself. Silius Italicus' Hannibal, when recalled to Carthage from Italy where he has lived more of his life than he has lived in his native land, finds he has become so attached to the country he has been destroying that he wonders, as he leaves, whether Carthage is worth such a great sacrifice: *an tanti Carthago foret (Punica* 17.223-4).[13] In Statius' *Thebaid*, the seer Amphiaraus who crashes, through no desire of his own, chariot and all, straight into Pluto's realm while still alive, becomes a kind of mirror image of Pluto himself who had once intruded among the living in his chariot. He greets the god of the dead in modified Lucretian terms as "the great ender or definer, *finitor* of things, but also for me who once knew the causes and the elements, the great creator (*sator*)" (8.91-3). Although his spectacular demise—he is, essentially, buried alive—is Apollo's attempt to prevent him from lying unburied among the living because of Creon's decree which Apollo knows will forbid burial of the Argive dead after the war, Pluto assumes a) that the gods are attacking him, and b) that Amphiaraus is after Proserpina and decrees that, in retaliation for the violation of his stygian borders, he will leave the bodies of the dead among the living. Apollo's foreknowledge of Creon's decree thus becomes its cause. And priests back on earth will wonder what terrible evil Amphiaraus has done to deserve burial alive—a punishment reserved in the Rome of his day for religious criminals, as Statius knew well.[14]

Ancient poets too are "borderers"—and not just such revolutionaries as Lucretius with his onslaught against traditional religious views. One of the clearest explicit statements to this effect occurs in Statius' *Thebaid* 1.16-17 where the poet, after declaring that the muses are directing him to tell the tale of Thebes, decides: "Let the *limes*, the boundary of my song be the confused (*confusa*) house of Oedipus." He speaks in full knowledge of the arbitrariness of his definitions, recognizing that his motif of the house of Oedipus is not only part of a larger nexus of external causes reaching down into his own times, but that even the arbitrary external limits cannot define the internal confusion of conventional bounds and limits within the house of Oedipus.

Statius' view, of course, is arguably more Stoic than Epicurean. His *Thebaid* warns of the futility of intellectual borders, and his protagonists

---

13   See F. Ahl, M. Davis, A. Pomeroy, "Silius Italicus," *ANRW* 2.32.4 (1986) 2492-2561 (especially 2511-19).
14   See F. Ahl, "Statius' *Thebaid: A Reconsideration,"* *ANRW* 2.32.5 (1986) 2803-2912 (especially 2858-69).

behave as they do because they, like us, perhaps, have allowed their view of themselves and their roles to become bounded and fixed at some point or level. Even though circumstances and people change, Statius' men and gods continue to behave as if nothing has altered, can alter, or should alter. More seriously, they tend to see themselves, their lives, their ideas, as the ultimate reality.

Borders and their guardians

While the poet, like his ideals or heroes, is often a "borderer," we scholars usually wish to see definitions and borders affirmed rather than blurred. We lose patience with those writers we cannot pop into what Friedrich Dürrenmatt once called the "Kompottgläser der Literaturkritik." And this scholarly predisposition often has difficulty with the most obviously "borderer" poets such as Statius himself. Classicists are, by self-definition, dedicated to examining ancient poetry in terms of an ideal: the way something ought to look. We approve certain kinds of diction and expression as "natural," "golden," "classical," and incline to a rather priestly view of literature. Indeed, I so much agree with Michael von Albrecht's decision to throw out the designation "mannerist" when discussing Latin poetry after Vergil that I also wish we could toss out "classical." It fosters a mindset that makes us think of deviation from our agreed norms as archaic or decadent. We discuss familiar themes drawn from canonical texts—from our Isaiahs rather than our Malachis, our Vergils rather than our Claudians. We prefer newer or more elegant ways of reaffirming what our congregations already believe to radically fresh examination of our basic principles. Like the mad general of Kubrick's film to which Segal refers, we are fiercely protective of these boundaries and definitions of our discipline. As Lucretius senses how terrified man is of the dissolution of the boundaries of his being, we fear the dissolution of the boundaries of our discipline, our intellectual *moenia mundi*.

Latinists are understandably more priestlike than Hellenists. The Western world never had to rediscover Latin as it had to rediscover Greek. In our intellectual lineage there is well over around a millenium and a half of Christian thought, of clerics from whom we received Latin adapted for their theological purposes to express ideas consonant with a monistic view of god and nature—a view which had little in common with the pluralistic view of god and nature to be found in most Greek and Latin poets. While we have purged our *Oxford Latin Dictionary* of medieval usages, almost all of us remain monists, if not *monachoi*. We and our computers live and thrive in a binary world of god and no god, of one and zero, and all of us have difficulty coping with pluralistic thinking and polytheism. We therefore insist on discovering an artistic process in which order emerges from apparent chaos, rather than on one in which chaos lurks beneath apparent order.

Whereas the Hellenist has learned to take almost as much pride as Athena does in Odysseus' "borderer" duplicity, the more priestly Latinist still tries to rationalize Aeneas' "borderer" behavior away with all the zeal of a New Testament commentator trying to explain why Christ withered the fig-tree. Aeneas is given the moral epithet, *pius*. He obeys the gods, therefore he must be justified. Yet surely Vergil's contemporary, the brutal and unpopular Sextus Pompey, did something to devalue the purity of that epithet by applying it to himself.

In our tendency to see poets as defined by and defining borders rather than as akritic borderers we are at odds with major ancient critics of poetry. Plato, for example, took a rather different view. He regarded poets as subversive of the ideal state and therefore banned them—and particularly Homer—from it since their polyvalence and pluralism threatened civic morals and therefore had to be censored or banned.[15] Homer was, as Vergil's contemporary Dionysius of Halicarnassus points out (*On Literary Composition* 16), "the most many-voiced (*polyphônotatos*)" of the poets.

Socrates talks of "thoroughly cleansing (*diakathairontes*) again (*palin*) the city (*polin*)," by banning not only poets, but the use of complex musical forms and the instruments used to express them (*Republic* 3 [398C-399E]). The phrase is curiously resonant of Creon's words in Sophocles *Oedipus Tyrannus* 100-01, where Creon, recently returned from Delphi announces the gist of the Oracle's response as to the plague (*nosos*) can be removed from the city.[16] Socrates does not want "many-stringedness" (*polychordias*) or

---

15   *Republic* 2 (377D) - 3 (403C); 10 (606C-608B).
16   Creon: By banishing or paying out again (*palin*) killing for killing, since this bloodshed makes stormy going for our city state (*polin*). When Oedipus asks what "got underfoot (*empodôn*) to prevent an enquiry" at an earlier date (*OT* 128), Creon replies: "The complex riddle-singing (*poikilôidos*) Sphinx compelled us to look at what was at our feet (*pros posi*)" (*OT* 130. See also Jules Brody, *"Fate" in Oedipus Tyrannus: A Textual Approach*. Arethusa Monographs 11 [Buffalo 1985] 36-42). The Sphinx's riddle which Oedipus solves has, of course, a poetic form, since the Sphinx is, in Sophocles' terms, a singer of songs, a "rhapsode bitch" (*rhapsôidos kyon*) in *Oedipus Tyrannus* 391. Her complex, riddling song involves "foot" and "feet," *pous* and *podes* (either animal or metrical, as we see in Aristophanes *Frogs* 1323).If the idea of knowing the correct riddle of metrical feet or animal feet and purging the city of disease seems too farfetched, we should perhaps remind ourselves of *Republic* 3 (399E-400A), where Socrates observes: "Come on then," I said, "let's cleanse the rest too. Following

panharmonious (*panarmoniou*) music in his ideal state (399C). We won't rear workers, he declares, who manufacture instruments that produce *polychordia* or *panarmonia*. We want music characterized by *haplotes*, "oneness, simplicity."[17] He would therefore ban complex rhythms and scales along with complex poetry from his ideal city because they produce licentious behavior (*akolasian*) just as dietary excess causes disease (*noson*) (*Republic* 3 [404E]) . So too the complex-riddle-singing Sphinx was removed from Sophoclean Thebes to cure it of its disease by the scholarly act of resolving its ambiguities.[18]

If physical sickness and the image of the great Athenian plague are a metaphor, or, if you will, an act of mental displacement, for social disorder in Lucretius as Segal suggests, they are even more evidently so in Plato's *Republic*, written when the plague was still within living recollection. It is also worth adding that for Plato tyranny was perhaps the ultimate disease of both the individual mind and of the state.[19]

The scholar seeking to defend poetry against Plato often takes Platonic criticism too much to heart and tries to show that the poet is not really so subversive of definitions and ideals as Plato suggests. The most common assumption of modern critics of ancient poetry is quite the opposite of Plato's: that the poet is defined by, rather than a definer of, the borders within which he works. Thus if Pindar writes epinicians he must be intending to praise the victor's wealthy sponsors. And if the epic Jupiter gives an order, it must be right for a lesser god or mortal to obey it, however irrational or brutal it may appear to be. If the poet describes Jupiter ordering the human race obliterated because a single human killed a Dalmatian hostage, the poet must be trying to show how right and necessary such action was. And if he compares that

---

on from the scales (*harmoniais*) would come the matter of rhythms. We should not aim for those that are too complex (*poikilous*) or for the manifold variety of steps in phrasing (*baseis*) but look to see which rhythms suit an orderly and manly life. When we have seen these rhythms, we must compel the foot (*poda*) to follow the rationale (*logos*) of such a life—and the melody too. The rationale (*logos*) should not follow the foot."

[17]   And *panarmonia* in *Republic* 4 (404D) is compared to "much varied food" from Sicily, *poikilian opsou*. Food and nourishment of this kind is, Socrates notes, like music made in *panarmonia*, and not to be encouraged.

[18]   Perhaps Plato's point is that the state has enough difference already woven into its very plural texture than no additional pluralism of poetry or music seems advisable. For in *Republic* 8 (557), he compares the state "decorated with all its different lifestyles" (*pasin ēthesin pepoikilmenē*) to a *poikilon himation,* a "decorated tunic," decorated (*pepoikilmenon*) with all the flowers there are. How different a vision his is from the ideal *panarmonion tetrachordon* of the Homer-loving pagan pluralist Julian, in his *Banquet of the Caesars* 315C!

[19]   See *Metaformations* 81-3.

universal destruction to his ruler's unleashing of civil war to avenge his adoptive father, he must be trying to justify that action too. After all, that ruler brought unity and structure to the Roman world, and probably made the public post run on time. If this poet subsequently finds himself condemned to life-long exile by that same ruler, it must be because he gave poetic lessons in seducing women, some of the nicest of whom could be found watching great Caesar's triumphal processions.

Surely the time has come, if not to become "borderers" ourselves, at least to do what every student of rhetoric ought to do: test the opposite hypothesis, concede Plato to his point, and assume, for the sake of argument, that poetry may well be subversive of structure and unity, despite its illusion of formalism. Grant that the ancient poet, who takes outer, metrical form, perhaps even genre, as a given and thereby rhetorically submits himself to its strictures, does so in order to stretch those forms, pluralize them, even subvert them.

Poetry is arguably more often the product of a battle between form and energy, than of the imposition of form on inert matter. It deals with those very shadows of physical objects which Plato sets in the lowest segment of his divided line. Ancient poets often wrote in a self-consciously vatic way, and present a riddling song to their readers for them to solve. Like Sophocles' riddle-singing (*poikilôidos*) Sphinx (*Oedipus Tyrannus* 130), the poet's song carries more than one meaning in a single vocal utterance—a kind of orchestral symphony in reverse, where the sounds chosen and produced have the quality of pivotal chords. Poetry thus becomes a reverse form of musical notation, compressing concordant, even dissonant, themes into one line of writing rather than expressing them in the multiple lines of an orchestral score. Poets—especially the most polyphonic—are, then, in a sense, making words like polyphonic music, creating music from words and thus, in a real, not just a metaphorical way, "singing."

As such Homer and other ancient poets who emulated him almost automatically become subversive when their pluralism and polyphony confront any ideologically based or authoritarian state that has a single ruler—or a single god—not just Plato's.

Perhaps on three days a year, we could open the gates to the *mundus*, if not destroy its intellectual walls, learning from the Ancients and from our own legal practice the desirability of establishing at least an approximation of justice by making the strongest possible case against the prevailing borders of the explicit and what we have come to assume is the self-evident.

Discussion

Segal: When I spoke of the fact that we have no choice but to be part of our own world, I immediately qualified that. I would not want to take the proliferation of modern critical methodologies as a license to do anything you want with any text. Above all, it is the text itself which should direct us to the method rather than the other way around. That is the way I have always worked, and I have found, for good or ill, some aspects of contemporary theory which have helped me working through my own critical ideas in as close a relation to the ancient text as possible, and then to expand and to think about what relations there might be. It is not by any means a one-way process. One must always go back to the ancient work and be a devil's advocate and see if this is not simply totally irrelevant.

On the other hand, all of us, no matter how self-critical we are, do bring something of the assumptions of the contemporary world to the ancient text, we simply cannot help it. We are not first century B.C. men and women. We have the interesting and perhaps somewhat dangerous task of having our minds in both of these worlds and going back and forth between them. Even when we are doing strictly historical or strictly philological work, we have to examine with the utmost scrutiny our approaches to see if we are not in fact bringing in some unstated assumptions. Even empiricism, even denial of theory, is itself a theory. Professor Zetzel made the point yesterday that even our contemporary methods, in their most philological and historical aspects, are themselves the result of a long process of historical evolution from the ancients themselves, from Hellenistic scholarship, on through the Renaissance, and so on.

The other point is that contemporary approaches can illuminate an ancient text, they can bring it into relationship with modern thought and ideas, and I think classicists have a responsibility to be part of the modern world. Unless our discipline has something to say to our students and to our successors, we are not doing our job. If we are only explicating texts for a closed circle, for a guild to use Tom Habinek's term, and not concerned about the possible meaning of these great authors whom we all love, then I think we are dooming our field to become something like Babylonian or Hittite studies. We are lucky that we are working with material that remains rich, fruitful, valuable, and irreplaceable. It is our responsibility, by whatever means we can, to make sure that it remains alive, that it has a voice in contemporary culture, and does not become simply a narrow, specialized discipline.

Zetzel: It seemed to me that what you are doing in your argument was essentially what I would have called a combination of the history of ideas—that is the comparison of Epicurus and Lucretius—and good old-fashioned New Criticism, that is, following these themes and the repetition of phrases and words. Now is your use of modern psychological theory meant to be an analogy? Is it meant to be some insight into the psychological make-up of Lucretius himself? Or is it simply saying that the fact that we are all mortal, and are afraid of losing hands or life or whatever, is what makes Lucretius' approach important or interesting, simply that the ideas there are universals? If that is the case, I do not see value of modern psychological theory.

Segal: To be absolutely fair, I probably could have arrived at the same or similar conclusions without the benefit of theory. I could simply have dropped that part. The single most important thing—and I speak here among friends, in complete honesty—is that reading some of these people is what sensitized me to the importance of this theme. It provided a method and a coherent theory that helped me to go from the specific verbal echoes, following a New Critical approach, if you will, to the various levels of the various psychological implications of the poem, to see how important this theme was in dealing with the fear of death. So, it served as a kind of cement, but perhaps that is too static an image, and it may be better to leave metaphors out.

Zetzel: The psychological levels in whom?

Segal: One of the big problems with applying any kind of psychological criticism is to try to decide what is the object of the analysis. Are you trying to analyze the author; or are you trying to analyze the relationship between the reader and the text, in something analogous to what Freud called the transference; or are you trying to analyze a particular character? Here I would say it is most of all the mental phenomena, and this is where the universality is important. Some of the modern theory directed me to appreciating the importance of this particular attitude, this particular mind set, which is attuned to this problem. From there it led back into the poem and led me to re-read Epicurus and so on. That is not the only way to use theory, there are many ways of doing it.

One could also take this further. Then it enables one to see something of the ways in which Lucretius is not just an isolated phenomenon. I think what Fred Ahl was suggesting about the role of boundaries and limits in other authors of other periods is very suggestive. It is very useful to have a model which allows one to generalize from a single author and a single text both to other authors in the same period—I mentioned Ovid and Senecan tragedy, Fred mentioned Statius—or to make the further and riskier leap from antiquity to the present or to other periods.

Johnson: I was very taken with your discussion of displacement, and *Verschiebung*. That does seem to me to go way beyond *angoisse* in locating something that I think is probably very important. It's always been a problem to go from Lucretius to Epicurus, and notice the difference in emphasis. If you're right in going beyond displacement and saying it was an effort at therapeutics to say that we must face these evils in the microcosm and the macrocosm to get beyond this and be able to look at the entire universe, that would be fine. What the enlightenment liked, and what you find in Taoists and Walt Whitman is, "Hooray, there are millions and millions of worlds out there. Nature goes on always, if this one disappears there's plenty more." It's a very positive notion, which you do not get from Lucretius. You are left with what is essentially a very dispiriting poem to read, even while it's exciting in certain ways. I think you may be right that the poem ended with the plague, which is a dreadful way to end. But it seems to me the *Verschiebung* does pinpoint this and show the difference between the source and what Lucretius made of it.

Segal: You raise a number of interesting questions. What I present today is only part of a much larger and more complex argument. I think that Lucretius did in fact, whether consciously or not, respond to many of the ancient criticisms of Epicurus as an unsatisfactory philosopher of the fear of death. One finds this in Cicero in the *Tusculan Disputations* and the *De Finibus*, and very strongly on the Greek side in Plutarch's *Ad Colotes*. Perhaps he is reacting by exploring more deeply something that Epicurus had treated rather superficially. That is, as the ancient philosophers noted, Epicurus is very good at removing the fear of what happens to you after death, but he does not deal very directly with what it is itself to die. Here Lucretius is correcting him. On the other hand, I feel less sure about the so-called pessimism of Lucretius.

Ahl: About the curative power of Lucretius: the *De Rerum Natura* could be seen as a written-down psychoanalytic document to help you deal with your fears, in the sense that Aristotle, in the *Rhetoric*, talks of rhetoric in what we would describe as psychological terms. Perhaps it would be helpful to see the work in that light.

Griffin: In this very striking discussion about boundaries and the violation of boundaries, there is another poetical tradition one thinks of, connected with the Dionysiac *adflatus* and similar notions. Now that was not really of interest to Lucretius, but was of great interest to Horace, who regarded himself as an Epicurean. Dionysus is the god who abolishes the distinction between outside and inside, and different species and so on. The fact that two poets, coming from such similar intellectual backgrounds, can use such different strands coming out of the same tradition, shows how much it's up to the poet to choose.

Segal: In the *Bacchae* one of the focal points in Dionysus' attack on Pentheus is precisely the dissolution of walls. There is a kind of meeting in the Dionysiac religion, which was so emphatic about the flowing between boundaries, like the lovers that Lucretius describes, and that meeting takes the place precisely of attacking boundaries.

Wiseman: Coming back to the idea of the plague ending the work, being, as it were, the boundary of the text: if Fred Ahl is right that one should think of the text as a therapeutic act, and your brilliant idea of the plague as pre-Epicurean death is right, fine. But it's not explicit, is it? So I am a bit anxious about the idea that the boundary of the whole text, the ending of the whole work, is really what we have. I have always assumed in a rather careless classicist way that it's another of these unfinished masterpieces, and therefore he would have done it differently if he had lived longer. But it does need explaining.

Segal: I would not want to defend the notion that the poem is completely finished in every respect. But there are indications in the summary he gives in Book 1 and the repetitions of that at various places in the proems of the book, that he has a total design. I'm not sure whether the entire poem ended exactly as we have it, men fighting over the *corpora* in those last lines. It is a neat ending if it did, because men are fighting over the wring kind of *corpora*, *ne* *corpora desererentur*, "so that the bodies of the dead should not be abandoned." Men in their ignorance of the true atomic nature of death are struggling over *corpora* that will simply dissolve into the anonymous atoms of the world. As to the general mood of this development, how death affects us, and the dissolution of all things at the end, I think it is very hard to get away from that. Book 6 as we have it is roughly the same length as the other books, so it could not have gone on for too much more.

Wiseman: I agree with that. I think you're right about Books 5 and 6 belonging together, and at the beginning of 5 he gives a contents list of the two books together. What worries me is the idea that we end with this really appalling passage. If there is a message of hope, it is only implicit, which is very unlike him.

Segal: Scholars will probably never completely agree about elements like the anti-Epicureanism and the pessimism of Lucretius, the conflict between between vitalism and pessimism in the poem and so on. This may represent a conflict within the mind of Lucretius that never gets resolved, or it may represent a conflict that he sees as the basic issue of the universe, the battle between life and death that I think to some extent does organize the poem. I do think (and perhaps this is where my psychological approach may be of help) that this emphasis on the fear of death, and its particular manifestation in boundary anxiety, is an aspect of the therapy of the poem. Where Lucretius' psychotherapy lies is in making us aware of the fear of death, of bringing into the light those things which have been hidden in darkness, as he says, so that if we can actually get out and see what it is that we fear, we are really helped and improved. It is in that sense that this ending may be the right one.

Skinner: I wonder if we could apply one more category of analysis to your model. It is a brilliant model, but I missed any reference to gender in all of this. It seems to me that, in antiquity, by definition the permeable or the penetrable body is the female body, and the male body is also by definition that which penetrates but is not penetrated. In the Hippocratic corpus you have the explicit comparison of the woman to the earth. Both are porous, both absorb liquids. Given that, it would seem to me that the Lucretian argument renders every human body pathic, vulnerable, and passive. Given the horror of sexual violation implicit in ancient masculinity, this is yet another dimension on top of all these other anxieties we are talking about.

Segal: Lucretius is perhaps more aware than many ancient poets are of a kind of unisex world, in that the female body is not the one that's penetrated, but it is the one that, in the image of Venus that he uses, is *circumfusa*, surrounding. And that, of course, goes back to other ancient cosmogonies, both Greek and from elsewhere in the ancient world. He insists on the equality of male and female sexual pleasure in the end of Book 4. The mutual interpenetration of the lovers is both male and female. The language he uses is that they both wish to fuse together. On the other hand, in the famous passage at the end of Book 4 he does present something of the more stereotypic view, where the man is outside, wants to get in, and if he should once get inside those doors and got one whiff of what was going on, he would run outside as fast as possible and never come back. In his philosophical view Lucretius does get beyond this simple dichotomy of male as the penetrator and the female as a passive figure. This makes one think of the *Magna Mater* as well. But this is an area that I have not explored, and it would be very interesting to pursue it.

OVIDIAN SCHOLARSHIP: SOME TRENDS AND PERSPECTIVES

"It is harder to work to interpret interpretations than to interpret things." This dictum of Michel de Montaigne has not been belied ever since the sixteenth century; in our days, Umberto Eco wrote a novel on the problem of various interpretations (*Foucault's Pendulum*). If—according to Augustine— our world is a world of signs, there is small choice; we have to interpret them or resign. Interpretation, then, is part of the human condition.

I do not wish to give an exhaustive report on Ovidian scholarship: instead of talking of books we all use every day I would like to confine this paper to a very small number of recent studies on the *Metamorphoses*—most of them German—which are probably less well known. They illustrate, however, the merits and limits of a number of approaches to Ovidian texts and to Roman poetry in general. I will proceed from more general subjects to more specific ones: from history, *Zeitstil*, structure, and poetology, viewed either within the text or on a comparative scale, to metrics, grammar, and rhetoric.

As for political Augustanism, it requires either a very long or a very short discussion. The fact that Brooks Otis spent many years on reworking this subject several times—each time with a completely different result—is rather discouraging, and this impression does not seem to have been substantially changed by a more recent attempt of a Swedish scholar to find traces of a critical attitude of Ovid towards Augustus throughout the *Metamorphoses*.[1] Words are ambiguous, and under a more or less authoritarian regime ambiguity itself is part of the pleasure for the readers. Ronald Syme—a master of ambiguity himself—speaks of Ovid's "malicious frivolity or even muted defiance."[2] I would not venture to go further than that. Everything would be spoiled if we tried to change the skilful balance of words and ideas created by the poet into an unequivocal political utterance. Should we really condemn the poet to the role of a suspected person and ourselves to the role of inquisitive policemen? Elaine Fantham rightly said that for Ovid—who was not a modern democrat—Augustan themes were "a challenge to his

---

1   S. Lundström, *Ovids Metamorphosen und die Politik des Kaisers* (Uppsala 1980).
2   R. Syme, *History in Ovid* (Oxford 1978) 190.

professional versatility, not a threat to his private integrity,"[3] and Hartmut Froesch has perceptively concluded that—given the persistence of literary genres—labels such as propaganda, résistance, protest or opposition are inappropriate.[4]

A literary text is not necessarily a personal confession. "The poet, he nothing affirmeth" Philip Sidney said in the sixteenth century. In our days Iser went still further saying that a literary text cannot refer to realities immediately, only to patterns of reality,[5] an idea either too little known or too well known among historians of literature. Whenever they have to say something about an author's life they scrutinize the texts for facts and often finally find they have almost nothing to say.

Nonetheless it would be wrong to give up all hope to find the historical truth. It is still a fascinating task to reconstruct at least the patterns of reality which meant something to our authors and readers. And we ought to relate those patterns to all that we know from other sources about our author's times. Let us not dismiss Ronald Syme's book on *History in Ovid* as "more history than Ovid" (Sir Ronald's own words) but be grateful to him for competent guidance concerning such important subjects as patronage of letters, poetry and government, legislation and morals and, last but not least, Ovid's friends. Sometimes we tend to forget that Roman authors did not write for some anonymous public but for real people they knew.

The limits of Ovid's works as a historical source have been traced impressively by A. Podossinov who showed how much in them is due not to observation but to literary clichés.[6] Thus history itself compels us not to neglect a strictly literary interpretation. In order to understand writers and books, art and artists within their epochs we have to find out what is traditional and what is new about their works. In a recent Freiburg dissertation Martin Glatt affirmed that the Roman elegists construct a world of their own quite aloof from the Augustan state.[7] If, according to Adorno, artists by creating works of art show a sort of "negative capability," it might be tempting to use

---

3   E. Fantham, "Sexual Comedy in Ovid's *Fasti*: Sources and Motivation," *HSCP* 87 (1983) 185-216, esp. 210.
4   H. Froesch, *Dichter und Staatsmacht. Vergil, Horaz, Ovid und Augustus* (Frankfurt 1984) 5.
5   W. Iser, *Der Akt des Lesens* (München 1976) 118.
6   A. Podossinov, *Ovid's Dichtung als Quelle für die Geschichte des Schwarzmeergebiets* (Konstanz 1987).
7   *Die "andere Welt" der römischen Elegiker. Das Persönliche in der Liebesdichtung* (Diss. Freiburg 1990).

Glatt's view of the Roman elegists as an example. This approach helps to discover the innovative aspects of elegy. However, the elegiac poets would not be able to communicate with their reading public if they did not use traditional language: this conventional aspect can be grasped better by the reception theory of Jauss. Either theory is incomplete: negativity alone can hardly explain communication, whereas a receptionist view alone can hardly explain what is beyond convention in art, though as a foil it helps to evidence indirectly what is new in a text. And even in our elegiac poets negativity itself is not perfect: Tibullus frankly admits that he cannot escape the necessity of doing military service and earning money, whereas Propertius initially is more consistent but later on abandons elegiac love and love poetry. The sincerity of his conversion to Augustanism is disputed. In my opinion, it is hard to assess his sincerity since we do not have external evidence such as private letters. As for Ovid, he might be a good candidate for Adorno, but is he not all too communicative? Almost everyone agrees that he was not serious about anything except poetry. I would warn against even such an exclusive statement. Ovid as a person is elusive; we can study only his poetic *persona* in the context of each of his works. It is a truism that he cared for poetry, but it would be foolhardy to deny that he might have cared for love which is an all-pervading theme in his oeuvre.[8]

More promising are attempts to define Ovid's Augustanism in terms of "style of the époch" (*Zeitstil*). Karl Galinsky has compared the elusive structure of the *Metamorphoses* to the structure of mural paintings of the same period.[9] The methodical advantages are evident: art is compared to art and structural principles to structural principles. Being based on commensurable facts the result is convincing. Both the mural painting in question and the *Metamorphoses* exhibit an unreal and phantastic architecture as far away from the *Aeneid* as is Arachne's Hellenistic tapestry from Minerva's *augusta gravitas*. This is in tune with the fact that Ovid in the *Metamorphoses* follows the Hellenistic mainstream of the historical development of literature, whereas in other poets—some of them perhaps more strictly "Augustan" than Ovid— there is a reaction which creates a new form of classicism; yet it is equally true that the "classical" aspects of Ovid's works have often been underrated.

---

8   For love as a theme in the *Metamorphoses* see B. Otis, *Ovid as an Epic Poet*, 2nd ed. (Cambridge 1970) *passim* and E. Fantham, "Ovid's Ceyx and Alcyone: The Metamorphosis of a Myth," *Phoenix* 33 (1979) 330-345, esp. 330.
9   K. Galinsky, *Ovid's Metamorphoses. An Introduction to the Basic Aspects* (Oxford 1975) 83 f.; for his stylistic closeness to Augustan standards: K. Galinsky, "Was Ovid a Silver Latin Poet?" *ICS* 14 (1989) 69-89.

Generally speaking, there has been too little interaction between historians of literature and archaeologists. Especially in the field of *Zeitstil* there is much to be learned from the historians of art, who have made much progress also in defining the specific style and character of other epochs (e.g., the ages of Nero, Domitian, Constantine, Justinian).

Comparative sociology of art might be equally helpful to locate the artist's position within the society of his days. When Auguste Rodin creates a big public monument representing a kiss of a loving couple he acts like Ovid, who in the venerable attire of epic poetry speaks of private love affairs. Both artists live in societies that have lost belief in religion but still believe in love, art and, to some degree, the divine genius of the artist.

Similarly, with respect to transgression of boundaries, we may mention that both Rodin and Ovid defy the limits of their respective arts.[10] Rodin consciously enriches sculpture, which by nature is spatial, to create the illusion of metamorphosis, movement, and time: some of his figures which have been left on purpose in a state of *inachevé* seem to grow out of the raw material, others seem to move because their arms are shown at a slightly different moment than their legs, others suggest the lapse of time through the contrast between the public's expectations (*la belle Heaulmière*, a beautiful young woman) and the old age and ugliness of the figure (*celle qui fut la belle Heaulmière*).[11] Conversely, Ovid tends to bestow on poetry, which by nature is a diachronic process, an almost sculptural precision of design and vision (which is new in Latin epic). In their ability to transcend the limits of their respective arts both Rodin and Ovid are reminiscent of Orpheus who stops rivers and makes rocks and trees move. Despite this primeval patron their idea of an art, which by nature is opposed to "purism," presupposes late and sophisticated societies knowing the laws of genres—otherwise there would be no point in breaking them. (There are, of course, just as many differences between the two artists—social, cultural, ideological—but that would be the subject of another paper).

In the following remarks I would like to dwell more on the wonderful fluency of Ovid's poetry than on its "sculptural" aspects. This leads us to the problem of structure, a field in which, generally speaking, scholarship has paid more heed to overall concepts than to details. Just think of Ludwig's division

[10] M. von Albrecht, *Rom: Spiegel Europas* (Heidelberg 1988) ch. 13: "Metamorphose in Raum und Zeit: Vergleichende Untersuchungen zu Ovid und Rodin" (pp. 517-568).
[11] Similarly Ovid has an aged Helen look into the mirror and wonder why she had been raped twice (*Met.* 15.232f.).

of the *Metamorphoses* into twelve major parts (*"Grossteile"*) or Brooks Otis'
panel structure. Doubtless there is some merit to their observations. I think
the structure of Books 1 and 2 as well as the following Cadmus section has
been firmly established; it is also evident that the Orpheus section has been
planned very carefully. On the other hand, there are some strange lacunae in
Ovidian scholarship: for all the care lavished on sections and major parts, the
real division of the work into fifteen books has been amazingly neglected,
though Ovid himself explicitly drew his readers' attention to the fact that there
are *ter quinque uolumina* (*Trist.* 3.14.19). Studies of single books of the
Metamorphoses have been rare. There are old contributions by students of the
great Latinists Friedrich Leo and Eduard Norden,[12] but Richard Heinze—
unsurpassed Vergilianist and slightly less felicitous Ovidianist—gave a
different direction to Ovidian studies.[13] Strangely enough, but not
surprisingly, Bömer's monumental commentary is particularly unhelpful in
this regard.

In recent years, scholars have become increasingly aware of the
importance of single books: Stephen Hinds has written an inspiring study on a
considerable part of Book 5 and—in a forthcoming Heidelberg dissertation—
Alexandra Bartenbach examines Books 5, 10 and 15. She wanted to consider
each of these books by itself and did not presume to establish strict parallels
between them. I think nobody would expect to find in the *Metamorphoses*
symmetries comparable to those evident in the *Aeneid*. With these important
reservations we may mention some similarities of form and content, which are
peculiar to these three books, and even some parallels as to the transgression of
boundaries of books. Each of them contains an unusually long section spoken
by a single person, a professional speaker: the narrative of the Muse in Book
5, the song of Orpheus in Book 10, and the speech of Pythagoras in Book 15.
First the goddess speaks, then her inspired son, the poet, finally the
philosopher. Each of these books is followed by an epilogue which is on an

---

12   H. Peters, *Symbola ad Ovidii artem epicam cognoscendam*, Diss. Göttingen 1908
(student of F. Leo); A. Rohde, *De Ovidi arte epica capita duo*, Diss. Berlin 1929 (student of E.
Norden). Both books were reprinted together with G. Lafaye, *Les Métamorphoses d'Ovide et
leurs modèles grecs* (Paris 1904 and Hildesheim 1971); a good interpretation is H.B.
Guthmüller's *Beobachtungen zum Aufbau der Metamorphosen Ovids* (Diss. Marburg 1964
supervised by C. Becker.)
13   The influence of his ideas on epic and elegiac narrative (*Ovids elegische Erzählung*,
Leipzig 1919) is still considerable: see the books of S. Hinds and P.E. Knox listed in the
bibliography. The fact that Ovid thinks less of separating the genres than of enriching them
from one another had been seen as early as 1924 by Wilhelm Kroll in his admirable *Studien zur
römischen Literatur* (Stuttgart 1924) 202-224 ("Die Kreuzung der Gattungen") esp. 215f.

artist's death: Arachne's death 6, 1 ff.; Orpheus' death 11, 1 ff. and Ovid himself defying death in his epilogue to Book 15. The Muses are mentioned only in these three books. Stephen Hinds had already pointed out that Book 5 is referred to in Book 10 and that Ovid's Orpheus, as it were, has "read" Book 5. Hinds correctly spoke of Ovid's self-conscious Muse. The relationship between Ovid's personal epilogue and the other two "epilogues" is one of increasing explicitness. Karl Galinsky had observed a similar relationship between the quasi-scientific speech of Pythagoras in Book 15 and the mythological parts of the poem (*Ovid's Metamorphoses* 104-107).

In this context, Charles Segal's idea that the Orpheus myth is the myth of the poet deserves attention. For the Eurydice narrative in Book 10 I find it difficult to accept this interpretation, since Orpheus is represented by Ovid as a lover and the love theme is made explicit by key words and other means, as we shall see later.[14] Yet the narrative opening of Book 11 (which is in fact the "epilogue" to Book 10) describing Orpheus' death is different. Here Orpheus is clearly seen as a poet. The parallel with Arachne (whose tapestry has frequently been interpreted as foreshadowing some aspects of the *Metamorphoses*) and with Ovid's personal epilogue suggests a strong possibility that the Orpheus narrative in Book 11 is to be read in a poetological context.[15] I think Mrs. Bartenbach has made a rather convincing plea for her case without forcing the texts and without perverting the fluency of Ovidian art into a rigid geometric scheme.

The study of single books has been done successfully for the *Aeneid* and the *Georgics*. Ovid's case is different. His books obey other rules, but they are conceived as reading units, and we ought not to neglect this fact. As I said long ago,[16] the interrelations between Ovid's transitional formulas, different types of thematic connections, and book limits have to be studied anew. I would encourage detailed interpretations of and literary commentaries on single books, because only then can we proceed to a comparative analysis of the

---

[14] Orpheus in Book 10 is a lover and an orator. I would not think he is intentionally depicted as a bad orator, since his speech is shown to be effective. Within the narrative there is a continuous shift of emphasis: distance and irony prevail at the beginning and ending of the Eurydice narrative, as pathos does in the center. The change of focus between Book 10 and 11 may be compared to Tacitus and Suetonius who in various chapters portray the same persons differently: a typically Roman "additive" or "mosaic" style.

[15] Boccaccio turns the tale of Orpheus' head rescued by Apollo into an allegory of the posthumous fame of the poet; see C. Segal, "Orpheus, Agamemnon, and the Anxiety of Influence", *CML* 9 (1989) 291-298, esp. 298. Did Boccaccio think of the epilogue of Book 15 as parallel?

[16] *Gnomon* 37 (1965) 771-774, esp. 774.

structure of single books and perhaps to a better understanding of the work as a whole. In this area almost everything still has to be done. It may be that this desideratum applies also to some other Latin epic poets.

In this context I would like to mention studies concerning *Nachleben*; not only are they a help for the understanding of modern texts but also an additional tool for the interpretation of classical texts. Aside from literary reception aesthetics, an interesting and still almost unexplored field is a certain type of Renaissance and Baroque illustrations for the *Metamorphoses*. They represent, in a single picture, the contents of entire books, thus, in different ways, projecting time into space. In a forthcoming article I hope to show the relevance of this type of illustration to our understanding of Ovidian book structure. It is telling that after the middle of the eighteenth century this type was abandoned. In his influential translation, Johann Heinrich Voss cut the *Metamorphoses* into single epyllia. Rationalistic and romantic readers concentrated on single stories, so did the illustrators, and so, as a result, did many scholars.

Let me give another example of how we can usefully apply interpretive methods from other areas of art and literature. There is a new way of evidencing metrical facts which I learned from Russian symbolism. In a Heidelberg dissertation, Gabriele Möhler found a useful way of making visible an aspect of the metrical infrastructure—or, if you prefer, the beautiful surface—of dactylic texts: the Möhler graphs. In classics this is a completely new use of a method invented by a Russian symbolist poet, Andrey Byely, who as early as 1913 in his book on *Symbolism* found a graphic means of exactly representing and comparing the use of a certain metre by several Russian poets. Some years ago, I had tried to apply this method to a classical text (in an article on an epistle of Horace). The advantage of the graphs is that the metrical facts are not isolated (as happens in both impressionistic interpretation and abstract statistics), but visualized in their continuous flow as they reach the ear. Thus, for the first time in classical metrics, it becomes easy to observe the musical infrastructure of a text in its entirety. By paying close attention to the succession of such forms we are able to continue and develop some lines of research opened up by the important studies of G.E. Duckworth. In her graphs, Gabriele Möhler draws lines from one spondee to the next one. The resulting figures are different for each poet and characteristic of each of them. The Möhler graphs, first, can serve as a tool for authenticity criticism (she proved that the *Ilias Latina* cannot be by Silius Italicus). Secondly, the graphs can serve as a means of interpretation. Unfortunately, Gabriele Möhler, who concentrated on the mathematical and statistical side—and through random tests proved that the resulting figures are not the product of mere chance—has not worked out the interpretative aspect. I will try to take some first steps in this direction.[17]

In my opinion, the Möhler graphs enable us to grasp the text as a process without any premature "logocentrism." One rhythm follows another without any semantic reference: a marvellous dance, a real deconstructionist theater unspoiled by words and meanings. The bad message to a good deconstructionist however, is that even so you do not get rid of the individual author: each rhythmic pattern, like a fingerprint, is typical of a single poet. On the other hand, if you do not suffer from logophobia but from *philologia* and try to watch your human rights, you may feel tempted to search for convergences between *logos* and rhythm, text and meaning. Let us start from studying all the occurrences of some especially characteristic metrical patterns in a given text.

The extremely high percentage of dactyls in Ovid's hexameters determines the fact that the continuity of the graph is relatively often interrupted by purely dactylic verses. This type *dddd*, which is rather frequent in Homer, is shunned by most of the Latin poets. It gives to Ovidian texts their specific touch of lightness and fast movement. In the Orpheus story (*Met.* 10.1ff.) the type *dddd* occurs for the first time in line 2, showing the swift walk of the god Hymenaeus through the air. The next instance is Orpheus' travel to Persephone through the host of bodiless souls.

Lightness and swiftness, however, do not imply lack of meaning: when speaking of the god of love and his power, Orpheus uses a sequence of two *dddd* lines which at a distance of one line is followed by a third one (26-29). Equally, in line 61 the theme of love is expressed in a *dddd* line as is Orpheus' sorrow in 75. It seems worth mentioning that the important theme of love in these lines is accompanied not by pathetic spondees,[18] but by light dactyls. Ovid uses this kind of parlando (*dddd*) for his own and Orpheus' comments, as he does for a transitional line (such as 64). Hence, in the use of *dddd* in thematic contexts there is some understatement typical of Ovid.

---

[17]   I am aware of the fact that the study of dactyls and spondees ought to be complemented by an analysis of other metrical phenomena and that convergences or contrasts between different types of analysis would be more telling (cf. my article on Horace, *Epist.* 1.4, quoted in the bibliography.)

[18]   The ancients assigned to the spondee the character of *gravitas* (Cic., *Orat.* 216; Iambl., *vit. Pyth.* 112).

The opposite type, a ponderous sequence of four spondees (*ssss*), is rather rare in Ovid. Its use is purposeful. In line 5 it heavily stresses the important fact that there was no joy and no good omen at Orpheus' marriage. In line 12 the four spondees dwell on Orpheus' plaint for Eurydice.

It is especially interesting to note that a type which is only slightly less heavy (*dsss*) has a special function in the Orpheus narrative of book 10. In the first ten lines it occurs no less than three times as an intentionally monotonous and weighty ending of sentence and paragraph (in line 5 we get *ssss* in the same function). The rhythmical pattern *dsss* will come back in the bard's fruitless call in lines 11 and 41. In 10.3 Orpheus invites Hymenaeus in vain in this rhythm, and in line 7 the torch is shaken unsuccessfully and does not come to a burn. In line 10 the same rhythm accompanies Eurydice's death. The analogy between the foreboding and the fulfillment is stressed by the obsessive use of the same rhythm. In the following segment, the type *dsss* keeps this leitmotif character: in Orpheus' speech we get three continuous *dsss* lines when he speaks of Eurydice's death. Thus lines 22-24 look back to line 10. Equally, when Ovid speaks of Orpheus' successful singing (line 40) there is an almost ironic rhythmic parallel to line 3 when Orpheus had sung in vain. The next time the *dsss* pattern comes back at Eurydice's appearance (line 49). Here Ovid explains the precise meaning of the rhythmical leitmotif by speaking of her slow pace caused by the wound. The last instance of *dsss* is especially telling: we get two lines of this type (58-59), when Orpheus vainly tries to embrace Eurydice. Some critics have felt that the name of Eurydice is not used frequently enough by Orpheus in this text. Our rhythmical analysis shows that the Eurydice motif, though sparingly used in the text, is clearly articulated by Ovid in the rhythmical accompaniment.

Another feature which can be easily detected in graph is the fact that Ovid prefers to begin his lines with a dactyl. At the moment, however, when Orpheus through his song changes the laws of the world (Ixion's wheel stops, Sisyphus sits on his rock, and the Eumenides weep) we get three continuous lines beginning with spondees (41-43), followed by another one two lines later (45). So the reversal of laws is mirrored in a reversal of rhythm.

These examples may suffice to show that it is not true that the Ovidian hexameter is stereotyped and mechanical. The Möhler graphs give a practical guide how to overcome both—interpretative impressionism and statistical boredom—by means of a consequent "structuralization" of metrics, i.e., regarding each line in its specific context as part of a metrical continuum. This continuum follows musical and rhythmical laws of its own. It is important to note that metrics or rhythmics most frequently do not give a strictly onomatopoetic or symbolical image of the text. More appropriate is the notion of "accompaniment." As in a piece of vocal music, the accompaniment usually does not imitate the text slavishly but accompanies it following its own laws. Yet there are convergences, and the Möhler graphs make it easier to grasp and exploit them for a more precise understanding of the poet's intentions. For the first time, the Möhler graphs convey a palpable picture of the rhythmical flow of a text. This may facilitate a more adequate recognition that texts are not spatial phenomena but processes in time: they make visible the speed, elegance, and fluency of Ovid's verse.

Finally, some short remarks on two of my favorite concerns: the relevance of syntax and rhetoric to literary studies.

In 1959, when there was no talk yet of the "implied reader," I tried to capture an aspect of the relationship between author and reader by doing some stylistic research. I studied the literary function of parenthesis in Ovid[19] in order to understand better how the poet guides his reader's attention by remarks which psychologically prepare him for unexpected events or ironically turn the reader into the author's accomplice by having him share his disbelief in silly old stories. Moreover, a parenthesis might retrospectively comment on some strange aspect of a story, e.g., on Orpheus' motives for not touching women any more (*seu quod male cesserat illi, siue fidem dederat, Met.* 10.80f.) or on the fires caused by Phaethon: the fires gave light by night, and so, Ovid concludes edifyingly, "there was some good to that evil" (*Met.* 2.332). These comments deflate pathos and make the reader keep his distance from the events. Explicit authorial comments may provide an interpretation, if not always without irony: despite the moralizing warnings he pronounces before the Byblis and the Myrrha story, Ovid does not expect young girls to follow his advice and stop reading. It is worthwhile studying the syntactic form of such authorial comments and their position within a sentence or the narrative. Placed at the beginning, they point out the leading passion of the story or arouse expectations; in the middle of the action, they often serve to protract suspense; and when placed at the end, they unmask pathos and create a certain distance. Parenthesis is a typically Ovidian transgression of boundaries: a phenomenon on the borderline between syntax of sentences and syntax of texts.

---

[19] *Die Parenthese in Ovids Metamorphosen und ihre dichterische Funktion* (Hildesheim 1963).

A more direct means of guiding the reader's attention is the conscious use of narrative tenses. In this area we can learn much from linguistics as developed in the departments of modern languages. Although Harald Weinrich's book *Tempus* in its details does not completely accord with the linguistic facts exhibited in Latin texts, I have found its categories very helpful for an analysis of narrative structures in Latin texts.[20] Especially the variation between perfect and historical present (the latter is the "normal" narrative tense in Latin epic—a fact noticed by G. Pasquali,[21] but frequently ignored) and other strategies (secondary clauses, participles) allows the author to view the action in different perspectives and create a kind of "scenic" narrative which gives the impression of a multiple frame and the illusion of a three-dimensional stage. This type of narrative—a product of a calculated interaction between narrative fluency and syntactic framework—is also observable in Livy, whereas it is still absent from the pre-classical Claudius Quadrigarius. In its Ovidian and Livian form it is part of the style of the Augustan epoch. Here the results of linguistic research converge with the study of *Zeitstil*. I was glad to see that my attempts were accepted by Anton Scherer in his *Lateinische Syntax* (Heidelberg 1980) and felicitously labelled as "text syntax" (*Textsyntax*). I think classicists might find it exciting to study not only the spirit, but also the body of our texts and exploit language and style for the purpose of literary interpretation; I welcome the steps done in this direction by J.B. Solodow[22] and others.

Another field which seems promising to me is rhetoric. Since about 1900 the neglect of rhetoric and Latin composition in European schools has produced ignorance of how effective speeches are constructed, a neglect which made people vulnerable to dictators and their eloquent propagandists. In practical teaching this loss of active linguistic and rhetorical competence in Latin—a training which had been the basis of independent thinking since the Renaissance[23]—was not replaced by a comparable amount of theoretical

---

20   *Römische Poesie* (Heidelberg 1977) *passim*; forthcoming: *Studies in Roman Epic*; cf. also: *Masters of Roman Prose*, *passim*.
21   "Ennio e Virgilio" (1915), rev. repr. in: *Vecchie e nuove pagine stravaganti di un filologo* (Florence 1952) 285-307, esp. 296: "In Ennio l'azione principale era narrata sempre al presente"; for Vergil: M. von Albrecht, "Zu Vergils Erzähltechnik. Beobachtungen zum Tempusgebrauch in der Aeneis," *Glotta* 48 (1970) 219-229.
22   "*Raucae, tua cura, palumbes*: A Study of a Poetic Word Order, "*HSCP* 90 (1986) 129-153.
23   Through Latin grammar students learn how to learn, how to work methodically and distinguish what they know from what they do not know. This is a basis for independent

hermeneutic insight (which would have been a real step forward). In late antiquity, at a historical turning point, Augustine, in his *De doctrina Christiana*, had converted what had been mainly an art of writing (rhetoric) into an art of reading (hermeneutics) based on a general doctrine of signs (*De magistro*). Fortunately, in our days, the rediscovery of rhetoric has created among classicists a new awareness of how Latin texts were made. It has considerably furthered literary interpretation, especially through the refined study of generic composition.

To show the interaction of narrative, epic genre, and rhetoric let me dwell for a moment on a literary device: the epic simile.[24] In Ovid, the treatment of antithesis in the epic simile—just think of "fear and hope" (*Met .* 1.539)—is strongly influenced by rhetoric as is the very use of the simile. It guides the reader's attention in different ways according to its position in the narrative: (1) At the beginning of the narrative it underlines what will be the leading passion in the story: Apollo's falling in love with Daphne is illustrated by a fire simile (*Met.* 1.492ff.). (2) Before the turning point of a story a simile helps to enhance the reader's suspense: Apollo pursues Daphne like a hunting dog. The graphic picture of the persecution puts off the decisive event and creates suspense (1.533ff.). (3) A third place where similes are frequently found is the explanation of the final metamorphosis: thus, in the Pyramus story of the image of a jet springing forth from a small hole in a water tube helps to explain why the fruits on a high tree get the color of Pyramus' blood (4.122ff.). Consequently, some functions of the simile appeal to the reader's cognitive faculties (marking important points of the narrative and helping to grasp the principal emotion of the story) or they are pseudointellectual: making the reader believe the absurd metamorphosis. Other functions are emotional—such as prorogating suspense in the middle of the narrative—or anti-emotional: dissolving pathos through irony, creating some distance at the end of the story. On a larger scale, then, the Ovidian simile fulfills interpretative functions comparable to those of parenthesis. To Ovid, it is an intellectually and emotionally stimulating component of epic narrative which establishes contacts between author and reader: despite its epic origin, it obtains rhetorical power.

---

thought: grammar and rhetoric have a liberating effect (and justly were the basis for the *artes liberales*); therefore learning Latin ought to be a human right.

[24] "Zur Funktion der Gleichnisse in Ovids *Metamorphosen,*" in: *Studien zum antiken Epos*, Festschrift F. Dirlmeier and V. Pöschl (Meisenheim 1976) 280-290.

Another crossroads of poetic and rhetorical traditions is allegory. Ovid's frequent use of it shows that he does not want us to take his texts at face value. While he consciously plays on allegory, he turns it from a hermeneutic technique into a poetic one, from a method of reception into one of creation. By so doing, he prepares of the more systematic exploitation of this kind of rhetorical invention in late antiquity. The illustrative richness of brilliant descriptions such as the House of Fama (*Met.* 12.39ff.) or the House of Sleep (*Met.* 11.591ff.) prove that rhetoric did not impair his poetic genius but liberated it. In such cases he expects his readers to undo mentally the surrealistic *mixtum compositum* he presents to them and to enjoy acute reading as he had enjoyed acute writing.

By a careful analysis of style and literary technique we can hope to grasp the interaction between author and reader; in this I agree with Iser. It is true that classical scholars had done this kind of research long before Iser gave it theoretic formulation, but they will go on doing it now with fuller awareness of what they do and they will now be able to tell why careful analysis of the original and special attention an author pays to details of style and literary technique is essential to the understanding of texts.

Interpretive research on given texts is a rich and very complex field. It has to take into account text syntax, rhetoric, and generic composition. It might also be furthered by modern studies on the structure of narrative,[25] fairy tale[26] and myth, if we use those methods to understand our texts and not just use the texts to illustrate our methods. Yet there are still more elementary needs: there is for instance no comprehensive modern work on Ovid and Callimachus and none on Ovid and Homer. Both these subjects despite their seemingly modest starting point would answer important questions: they would shed light on important types of texts such as dialogue with the Muse, hymn, prayer, battle scene, assembly of gods, and others.

It might be appropriate to insert here a short excursus on teaching. I am glad that Fred Ahl alluded to reading Latin aloud and acting, which are good Texan traditions; I gratefully attended Gareth Morgan's noon readings of major Greek and Latin authors in the original. I liked G.B. Conte's idea of "dismantling" an ancient text and then composing it anew. It might be an enjoyable exercise for students to apply the structures and methods of a

---

[25]   Cf. my article "Le figlie di Anio" in: *Atti del Convegno internazionale "Letterature classiche e narratologia,"* (Brindisi) 105-115.
[26]   This problem was treated by the Russian classicist N. Vulikh and is the subject of a forthcoming Heidelberg dissertation by C. Endlich; cf. also *Rom: Spiegel Europas* 166 f.

Tacitean prologue to modern events or use a Ciceronian speech to prove the contrary of what Cicero meant to say: thus they will grasp immediately the power of the literary devices involved. An easy task for beginners is bringing the words of an Ovidian line into the right order. As G.B. Vico put it: you only can understand what you are able to do yourself, albeit on a modest scale. Some active mastery of Latin is not an end in itself, but, if combined with a solid interpretive training, it may produce faster and more efficient original reading, because the student gets an awareness of structures, connectors, and markers. Active linguistic competence united with hermeneutic insight would make a reader of Latin texts feel like a traveller with a good map in hand.

To sum up: methods and theories are tools, and if the use of tools is not an exclusively human privilege, the creation of new tools certainly is. Let us therefore not scorn the tools some of our colleagues created for the benefit of our progress. On the other hand, tools are not made to be collected or worshipped, but to be used. They are not an end in themselves but, as the Greek word *methodos* says, ways to get something: any method is as good as the results you obtain by using it. Each method must be controlled by others, and especially when their results converge we may feel that we are on the right track. I think our understanding of classical texts ought not to stay at a pre-theoretical stage. Rather, it ought to go through a theoretical stage and finally arrive at a phenomenological one. To our understanding—as *philologoi*—the *logos* is nothing outside history and, I may add, nothing outside language. This is why in my opinion language in its impact on literature deserves to be studied as thoroughly and as methodically and as judiciously as possible.

SHORT BIBLIOGRAPHY

M. von Albrecht, *Masters of Roman Prose*, translated by Neil Adkin, (Liverpool 1989).

_____*Die Parenthese in Ovids Metamorphosen* (Würzburg and Hildesheim 1963).

_____*Römische Poesie* (Heidelberg 1976).

_____*Rom: Spiegel Europas* (Heidelberg 1988).

A. Bartenbach, *Der Künstler im Widerschein seiner Kunst. Interpretationen zu Buch 5, 10 und 15 von Ovids Metamorphosen* (Frankfurt and New York 1990)

G.E. Duckworth, *Vergil and Classical Hexameter Poetry. A Study in Metrical Variety* (Ann Arbor 1969).

J. Derrida, *L'écriture et la différence* (Paris 1967).

G.K. Galinsky, *Ovid's Metamorphoses. An Introduction to the Basic Aspects* (Oxford 1975).

_____ "Was Ovid a Silver Latin Poet?" *ICS* 14 (1989) 69-89.

S. Hinds, *The Metamorphosis of Persephone. Ovid and the Self-Conscious Muse* (Cambridge 1987).

W. Iser, *Der Akt des Lesens. Theorie ästhetischer Wirkung* (Munich 1976).

H.R. Jauss, *Ästhetische Erfahrung und literarische Hermeneutik (Munich 1977).*

P.E. Knox, *Ovid's Metamorphoses and the Traditions of Augustan Poetry* (Cambridge 1986).

W. Ludwig, *Struktur und Einheit in Ovids Metamorphosen* (Berlin 1965).

S. Lundström, *Ovids Metamorphosen und die Politik des Kaisers* (Uppsala 1980).

G. Möhler, *Hexameterstudien zu Lukrez, Vergil, Horaz, Ovid, Lukan, Silius Italicus und der Ilias Latina* (Frankfurt and New York 1989). (=*Studien zur Klassischen Philologie* 35); cf. also: M. v. Albrecht, "Horazens Brief an Albius. Versuch einer metrischen Analyse und Interpretation," *RhM* 114 (1971) 193-209.

B. Otis, "Ovid and the Augustans," *TAPA* 69 (1938) 188-229.

H. Peters, *Symbola ad Ovidi artem epicam cognoscendam*, Diss. Leipzig 1903.

A. Scherer, *Lateinische Syntax*, Heidelberg 1980.

Ch. Segal, *Orpheus. The Myth of the Poet* (Baltimore and London 1989).

R. Syme, *History in Ovid* (Oxford 1978).

H. Weinrich, *Tempus. Besprochene und erzählte Welt* (Stuttgart 1964).

STRENGTHS AND WEAKNESSES OF CURRENT OVIDIAN CRITICISM
Response to Michael von Albrecht

A respondent must be forgiven for hoping that his or her rhetorical counterpart will be unreasonable or extremist. But how can I take issue with Michael von Albrecht, either with his brilliant and wideranging analogies from other arts and periods, or with any of the proper scholarly approaches that he has described so clearly to us? I wish I shared his learning: I hope I share his traditional values and respect for the ancient poet's craft that sees the poet's own *corpus* as the best source of understanding of the individual disputed text.

I would like to start with some misgivings about our continuing concern with the overall structure of the *Metamorphoses,* which has generated so many competing analyses and diagrammatic schemes. Of these one of the most modest and persuasive has been developed by Rudolph Rieks[1] and by Michael himself, taking up Ovid's own description of *ter quinque libelli.* They have offered persuasive arguments that Ovid, like Livy, composed in pentads, which he has marked by special features of the fifth, tenth and fifteenth books. These are the extended discourses by professional exponents, the Muse, the poet and the philosopher. But contrast, for example, R. Coleman's study[2] or most recently Anna Crabbe's fair and careful analysis.[3] Using a different methodology, she argues for the centrality of Book 8 by moving from analysis of the book itself to explication backward and forward, demonstrating symmetrical lay-outs in books 7 and 9, although she herself has to recognize Ovid's plurality of articulation: "The structure of Book 7 is at once bi- and tripartite" (2302). How then shall we make any significant progress given such genuine flexibility of form? How should the critic divide the units of action? By change of scene? Of personnel? Of dynasty? Of myth or mythical source? When Crabbe, a scrupulous scholar, moves to comparable patterning in the first and fifteenth books her chiastic symmetries are confined to minimal units, and she is more convincing in presenting the affinities between the sky-ride of Phaethon in Book 2 and the flight of Icarus that opens Book 8 as evidence counter to her structural scheme.

1   "Zum Aufbau von Ovids Metamorphosen," *Würzburger Jahrbücher* 6 (1980) 85-103.
2   "Structure and Intention in the *Metamorphoses,*" *CQ* NS 21 (1971) 461-77.
3   "Structure and Content in Ovid's *Metamorphoses,*" ANRW II.31,4 (1981) 2274-2327.

What the reader or listener notices is recurrence of narrative patterns, each bringing with it expectations engendered by the last version, and subtly shifting—to defeat his expectations. This may in the end be a better key to construing the quasi-historical forward movement of the poem, progressively blending the fantasy of episodes of transformation with the more naturalistic narrative of familiar heroic legend: from the monsters and magic that surround Perseus in 4-5 through Theseus in Books 7-8 and Hercules (Book 9) to recur with increasing incongruity as the narrative incorporates the Homeric cycle and escorts the westward voyages of Odysseus and Aeneas.

Instead of renewing the search for a grand design I see more hope of appreciating Ovid's invention and organization in one of the following approaches: first, taking a cue from some brilliant observations of Alessandro Barchiesi,[4] we can focus on Ovid's ingenuity in linking previously unconnected myths, creating synchronizations or intermediaries like Macareus in *Met.* 14 to bond the narratives. There is also much still to be done in tracing how Ovid exploits allusion to conflate rival versions of a single myth: this is one aspect of Hinds *The Metamorphosis of Persephone*[5] that wins my admiration—when for example the swans of Cayster near Asian Nysa are transferred to lake Pergus near Sicilian Enna as a trace of the original Persephone legend.[6] This kind of work has also been the special contribution of David Ross[7] and Richard Thomas[8] to the study of Virgil, though they may sometimes lose sight of a Virgil's Roman models or narrative direction, distracted by a shattered fragment of Parthenius or the notorious gadfly that simultaneously evokes the Io sagas of Calvus, Aeschylus, and Apollonius.

Certainly the student should consider the internal organization of the books that Ovid himself marked off. But if he wants to work on the larger scale, I believe he should trace two complementary aspects of Ovid's narrative chain: *continuity*, as maintained, for example through the erotic career of Apollo or the dynasty of Peleus, and *recurrence*, in mythical actions, e.g., combat with the shapeshifters Achelous, Thetis and Periclymenos, or acts of divine favour to unite loving couples, or the deaths by transformation of rejected and passionate women. Only through analysis of divergence in

---

4   *Materiali e Discussioni* 16 (1986) 82-92.
5   Cambridge 1987.
6   *Ibid.* 26-27.
7   *Virgil's Elements* (Princeton 1986).
8   See *A Commentary on the Georgics of Vergil,* vols. I and II (Cambridge 1988), and the articles cited in his bibliography.

recurring themes, studying the variations in tone and form and their impact on Ovid's audience, will we be able to represent the cumulative effect of this *perpetuum carmen*, or better *perpetuum mutabile*.[9]

Is there a place here for hermeneutics? Certainly structuralist (as opposed to structural) analysis can contribute, provided the codes adopted fit the way in which the poet originally shaped his episode and the critic does not force a match between disparate forms. Thus a gender-based analysis is appropriate to Iphis and Ianthe, or the tale of Salmacis and Hermaphroditus— and we will shortly have such a study from Georgia Nugent. When the poet operates with the polarities of mortal man and immortal god, or man and beast as in the transformation of Chiron's daughter Ocyrhoe, or the *Liebestod* of Cyllarus and Hylonome, or when he exploits the divisions of *tria regna* in the change of man to bird or sea-god, constructing interpretation around these categories may uncover and explain anomalies, but in general Ovid seems to privilege obvious bonds like sexual love or kinship.

Although Michael barely mentioned genre-based criticism in his listing, his praise for Hinds' new book surely implies recognition that the post-Heinzian issue of *elegische* versus *epische Erzählung* deserves the attention it has attracted. I would hope that he also found much to approve of in the generic arguments of Peter Knox.[10] Knox's *Ovid's Metamorphoses and the Tradition of Augustan Poetry* adopts a series of approaches to illustrate the persistence of elegiac technique from Ovid's erotic poetry into his narrative epic, whether in scale of episode, choice of diction, compression or ellipse of dialogue, or the sheer chop and change of Hellenistic narrative. Familiar myths are recalled, rather than retold, and the ostensibly simple account is mined with subsurface allusion and correction of predecessors.

Ovidian elegy in the wider context of Roman love elegy is currently the subject of radical and, to my mind, damaging reinterpretation, and the recent articles of Maria Wyke and book of Paul Veyne[11] seem to have deconstructed

[9]   I owe the final formulation of this approach to discussion with Stephen Wheeler of Princeton University.
[10]   *Ovid's Metamorphoses and the Traditions of Augustan Poetry*, Camb. Phil. Soc. Suppl. 11 (Cambridge 1986), most recently reviewed by Hinds, *CP* 84 (1989) 266-71. Note esp. 270, a key excursus on *perpetuum carmen* and the problem of epic versus elegiac in the prologue of Callimachus' *Aitia*.
[11]   For Wyke, see "Written Women: Propertius' *scripta puella*" *JRS* 77 (1987) 47-61; Paul Veyne's *Elégie érotique romaine*, has recently been translated as *Roman Erotic Elegy: Love, Poetry and the West* (Chicago 1988). Both authors use the acknowledged fictionality of the women to justify treating Roman elegy almost exclusively as the poet's representation of himself and his artistic *parti pris*.

the artistry along with the woman and the world. I can only hope that Gian Biagio Conte's voice of reason will be heard over their protestations: "The fact that in the dialectics of life/literature, reality/fiction the elegists place themselves on the side of literature does not mean that life is considered an epiphenomenon or a shadow of literature, but only that reality, to find a possible expression, necessarily enters into the language of literature. . . the literary conventions of elegy are the grammar of this discourse, the form of a content whose substance is precisely the life experience of the lover poet."[12]

But if Gian Biagio Conte rightly warned us yesterday that *die Kreuzung der Gattungen* cannot resolve the complexities of poems such as *Eclogues* 6 and 10, there is still a need to investigate generic features as part of the attempt to understand Ovid's other great *Kollektivgedicht*, the *Fasti*. Yes, Callimachus is marked as the dominant model by the elegiac meter and programmatic announcement of *tempora cum causis*, but since Propertius avoided any semblance of continuity in the *Aitia* of his fourth book, and so little has survived of the link passages in Callimachus' *Aitia*, the discontinuous continuities of the *Fasti* are for us a new kind of poetic achievement. Here I found Carlo Santini's papers, especially his study of the role of Aratean astronomical entries to articulate the aetiological episodes, to be helpful in explaining the organization of the poem,precisely because he identifies traces of the submerged genre.[13] I hope Michael would agree that didactic, a genre unrecognized by contemporary Romans, is the most ambiguous and therefore the severest test of the utility of generic theory; here is the greatest indeterminacy and the boldest innovation.

If I may, I would like to broaden the discussion by remarking on some limitations of contemporary criticism and teaching of Roman poetry. Why, I wonder, is the study of Latin literature increasingly concentrated on the two great narrative poems from the beginning and end of the Augustan age? Of course both epics deserve our lasting devotion, offering rewards to both the first time reader and the persistent student clutching at Servius, or at Bömer, our modern Servius. Certainly each poem retains enough of its color even in translation to attract the Great Books Class on its way from Greek Tragedy to Dante, or perhaps Augustine. In contrast, Lucretius, Horace, Cicero, the great historians or, say, Lucan, make demands on the reader's knowledge of antiquity for which most students are ill equipped. But the dominance of these

---

12   "Love without Elegy: the *Remedia Amoris* and the Logic of a Genre," *Poetics Today*, 10.3 (1989) 451-2 n.16.
13   "Motivi astronomici e moduli didattici nei "Fasti" di Ovidio," *GIF* 27 (1975) 1-26.

two texts persists in graduate school in the writing of theses and the publishing of articles and monographs. I would suggest that the fault lies with our common schooling in modern narrative fiction. As Peter Wiseman suggested, preoccupation with the novel shapes the questions we ask and the expectations with which we approach an ancient text. Turning to Latin literature, the student can apply his critical procedures only to the epic or the novel—but Petronius is incomplete and Apuleius ornate and difficult in diction; and so this age has produced Winkler's brilliant narratological study of Apuleius, and a series of challenging books on the *Aeneid* and *Metamorphoses*.

There are two corollaries of this narrow, if stereoscopic view. The first is the inevitable resort—and I shall resort to it myself shortly—to comparing and contrasting Ovid as not-Virgil with Virgil (less often) as not-Ovid: this leads us to privilege the episodes that we perceive as being most Virgilian in the *Aeneid* and deprecate as too "Ovidian" Virgil's love of fantasy and his reluctance to leave the Apollonian sea-scape for the urgencies of battle in Latium. In the same way scholars now play down the elements of genuine pathos in Ovid's *Metamorphoses* that Brooks Otis cherished, such as the death of the innocent Dryope or the sufferings of Hecuba. It has proved far more fruitful in recent years to consider both poets in the light of post-Augustan developments; there is much of the "baroque" in Virgil, and I was glad to see that Karl Galinsky had taken up the approach of both Gordon Williams and Stephen Hinds to consider Ovid in terms of Silver Latin poetry.[14]

The second corollary is the quest for structure, which I have already regretted, one of misapplied methods rather than inappropriate value judgements. I am sure our host, as author of one of the best introductions to the *Metamorphoses*, will agree that one cannot "cover" the diversity of Ovid, and criticism that attempts to be comprehensive will end in panic or dementia. We need a closer focus on the tale as it is told, the kind of work we have learned to expect from E.J. Kenney and his pupils, who now in turn are bringing forward young Canadian and American university teachers. Our first care should go to Ovid's words: their choice, their arrangement, and their interplay of echo and allusion.

In privileging Ovid's language I do not want to neglect the relatively unexplored field of versification. Metrical patterns can carry generic

---

14   For inclusion of Ovid as a precursor to Silver Latin poetry see Williams, *Change and Decline* (Berkeley 1978) and Hinds, "Generalizing about Ovid" in *The Imperial Muse*, ed. A.J. Boyle (Victoria, Australia 1988). G.K. Galinsky provides formal and stylistic illustration in "Was Ovid a Silver Latin Poet?," *ICS* 14 (1989) 69-89.

overtones, as Knox has shown in tracing the persistence of the elegiac fourth-foot trochaic caesura not only in Ovid's later "serious" elegy but also in the *Metamorphoses*.[15] But if Frau Möhler's imaged sequences of dactyls and spondees are a precious tool for determining the paternity of the *Ilias Latina*, they seem more subjective in Michael's association of individual lines with mood or content. He did not mention the additional factors, the complex interplay of sense and metrical units, hiatus, heterodyne word-forms and the multiple components of rhythm, so clearly illustrated in Michael's own brief study of a Horatian Epistle.[16] Thus when Michael called *Met.* 10.40 (*talia dicentem nervosque ad verba moventem*) an "almost ironic" echo of the rhythm of 10.3 (*tendit et Orphea nequiquam voce vocatur*), I suspect that irony has been invoked, as it often is, to smooth out an anomaly. What most readers hear in 10.40 is the internal rhyming of the two unfulfilled present participles that will be repeated again at 10.72-3 (*orantem frustraque iterum transire volentem*). There is a parallel use of the less noticeable nominative participles in 10.58. This is Virgil's audible graph of frustration, found in *Georgics* 4.501-2 (*prensantem nequiquam umbras et multa volentem/dicere*) as it will most famously recur in Aeneas' farewell to Dido.[17]

The beginning of Ovid's Orpheus narrative raises larger questions. And since these could involve no less than three of my fellows in discussion it would be a pity to pass them by. We have all come to think of the myth of Orpheus as the myth of the poet, especially since the valuable discussion by Bill Anderson[18] and Charles Segal's recent consideration of his previous articles on this theme.[19] Anderson showed how much a reader's appreciation of Ovid's negative presentation is sharpened by comparison with his preeminent model. Reacting against the supremacy of his predecessor Ovid shuns Virgilian pathos, but uses echoes and half-echoes of Virgil to highlight points of divergence, constructing a speech for Orpheus where Virgil left it unreported, and implicitly reproaching the older poet for the few words of complaint he gave to Eurydice at the fatal moment when Orpheus looked back; of course she did not complain: *quid enim nisi se quereretur amatam?* (10.61).

---

15   Knox, *Ovid's Metamorphoses*, Appendix I 84-87.
16   "Horazens Brief an Albius," *RhMus* 114 (1971) 193-209
17   *Aen.* 4.390-91: *linquens multa metu cunctantem et multa parantem/dicere.*
18   "The Orpheus of Vergil and Ovid" in *Orpheus: the Metamorphoses of a Myth,* ed. J. Warden (Toronto 1982).
19   C.P. Segal, *Orpheus: the Myth of the Poet* (Baltimore 1989) 73-94.

I share Michael von Albrecht's reservations about Ovid's presentation of Orpheus in the underworld, but despite his interesting suggestion that Ovid is deliberately beginning his account in a low key before intensifying the emotional content, I feel compelled to read negatively both Orpheus' behavior in Hades and his poetic prologue in the following scene. While love overcomes his gift of poetry in Virgil's narrative, reducing his song to the single name of his lost wife, in Ovid's account Orpheus is not even a convincing lover, but a *causidicus*, and a dull one. His petition to the rulers of Hades is a veritable Beckmesser's song, absolutely incongruous with the lyre which we are told accompanies it. Similarly, the poem with which Orpheus begins his one-man recital for the trees, birds and beasts is self-consciously professional. Not only has he heard the song of his mother Calliope in book 5: his opening *ab Iove, Musa parens. . . carmina nostra move* echoes the now hackneyed theme of Aratus. The modest presentation of his program as a sort of dessert, *leviore lyra*, after the sterner stuff of his main course, is not only a rhapsode's cliché, but plays another programmatic game.[20] It is Ovid, not Orpheus, who has already sung a lay of the gigantomachy, in all of twelve lines (*Met.* 1.151-62). Not surprisingly interpreters recall the function of both Zeus and the gigantomachy in Augustan panegyric. Orpheus is making Ovid's excuses for him, but his eight-line poem evokes not true art but the career performer.

Have we become too obsessed by meta-poetics? If poets were entirely or predominantly concerned with their own creativity, such narcissism would turn away readers. We as critics have done much to devalue the poets we recommend to our students by our insistence on reading them in terms of their poetical apparatus. Not only do academic critics harp on the geography of Parnassus, untrodden paths and crystal springs, the fine-spun song, and the laurel or wand of honor, where such overt symbols cluster in programmatic passages, but they seize on every slender epithet, or hint of water, even taking such descriptive details as the swans of Lake Pergus, which function as an allusion to the Homeric location of the rape of Persephone, as a symbol and reflection of the poet's song.

Alongside modern concern with meta-poetics comes that other subtext, the hunt for political ideology. Perhaps because we grew up in the shadow of Syme's *Roman Revolution* in which the Augustan poets served "The Organization of Opinion," or perhaps because we are burdened with disillusionment about contemporary leaders and their ill-disguised imperialism,

---

20   Detected by Knox, *Ovid's Metamorphoses* 50.

the scholars of this continent have become obsessed with Augustanism as a problematic varnish that must be stripped from the text to reveal the liberal democracy of our poets, and free them from the dishonor of believing in Rome and its empire, or failing to declare their dissent. Respecting and loving Virgil we exonerate him by discovering pervasive pessimism[21] and overhearing further voices[22] that cancel every exhortation (*tu regere imperio populos Romane memento*—but don't go near the water) so that Aeneas can either be honored for disillusionment or dismissed as flawed. It has taken the extraordinary achievement of Philip Hardie's study of cosmic allegory in the *Aeneid*[23] to demonstrate the inspired tropes by which Virgil implies the greatness of his ancient and his modern hero—and his empire.

Sceptics find Ovid easier to handle. Sure that he cannot have respected an aging establishment, they credit him with blatant mockery of his Princeps as if Augustus were too stupid to recognize such malice. Once again we owe a shrewder formulation to Stephen Hinds; he argues that the poet calculated his panegyric to be read respectfully by the orthodox but to leave pleasantly subversive associations in the minds of the dissenting.[24] Thus Ovid's Palatine Jupiter with his Tacitean Senate of yes-gods uses the means so brilliantly analyzed by E.J. Bernbeck[25] to discredit the ruler of the gods and obliquely his earthly counterpart. Or, to take a symbol common to Virgil and Ovid: the serpent which, as Hardie has shown,[26] conveys the horror or the awe of divine power in the *Aeneid* becomes an absurdity when Ovid depicts the gliding serenity of the snake god Aesculapius *en voyage* from Epidaurus to Rome. Despite the timely return to his *species caelestis* this godhead venerated by the sons of Aeneas[27] is an undignified precedent for Julius and Augustus Caesar who follow so closely on his tail.

---

21   See M.C.J. Putnam, *The Poetry of Vergil's Aeneid* (Cambridge, Mass. 1965), W.R. Johnson, *Darkness Visible: a Study of Vergil's Aeneid* (Berkeley 1976) and what is often called "the Harvard School."
22   R.O.A.M. Lyne, *Further Voices in Vergil's Aeneid* (Oxford 1987).
23   *Vergil's Aeneid: Cosmos and Imperium* (Oxford 1986).
24   "Generalizing about Ovid" 23-31. For a discussion of such political equivocation in prose and verse compare F.M. Ahl, "The Art of Safe Criticism in Greece and Rome," *AJP* 105 (1984) 174-209.
25   *Beobachtungen zur Darstellungsart in Ovid's Metamorphosen. Zetemata* 43 (Munich 1967).
26   See also Putnam, *The Poetry of Virgil's Aeneid*, passim (index s.v. "serpent" p. 237).
27   *Met.* 15.680-82: *quisquis adest visum venerantur numen, et omnes* / ... / *Aeneadae praestant et mente et voce favorem.*

In our academic climate it is unfashionable to be empiricist, like an emperor who refuses to buy new clothes. Perhaps his old clothes were of better quality and a more comfortable fit, but this is no reason to refuse all new clothes even if some may prove transparent or unbecoming when put on. In his illuminating history of our profession,[28] Gerald Graff rightly warns conservatives like myself that we differ from the new theorists only in not having realized and systematized our presuppositions. The literary interpreter who has not asked himself—or herself—what his critical principles and values are may well be threadbare. But if he cannot bring himself to put on the new methodology, he can at least try to find merit in other critics' approaches to the text.

I must confess that preparing for this colloquium has left me troubled by my own unadaptability. It is the empiricist's failing to treat a lyric like a prose text, a work of poetry like a document. Of course we should not expect a witness's truth from our poets,[29] but it is as much an offence against them to blur their delicacy with overinterpretation.

With his usual modesty and good sense Michael has offered in his survey of current approaches to *Metamorphoses* a variety of careful techniques that can and should be applied to prepare a secure understanding of a Roman poetic text. If they seem only preliminaries to the more exciting application of critical theory, they are still essential preliminaries that will protect the aspiring scholar from the hazards of subjectivity. It is timely and salutary to have them brought to mind.

---

[28] *Professing Literature: An Institutional History* (Chicago 1987). See especially ch. 15.
[29] Ovid made this quite clear (*Am.* 3.12.19): *nec tamen ut testes mos est audire poetas*, and *ibid.* 41-42: *exit in immensum fecunda licentia vatum/obligat historica nec sua verba fide.*

THE DEATH OF PLEASURE: LITERARY CRITICS IN TECHNOLOGICAL SOCIETIES

nos utinam vani

Pleasures in their kinds are varied and many, some good, some bad, or indifferent, depending on one's points of view or—to use a more draconian formulation—on the degree to which they manifest themselves as merely repetitive, obsessive, addictive, or otherwise worthless, boring or destructive. In a not dissimilar way—and again Aristotle's *ho peri ton kath' hekasta logos* marks the necessary distinctions—we may, theoretically, reckon technological societies as being sane, insane, or mediocre, depending on the degree to which they not only foster and promote real prosperity but also encourage everyone's lifelong, personal education (*Bildung*) and the collectivity's genuine harmony-in-discord. For the purposes of this paper, however, I am going to ignore the realities of these wide and complex spectrums (there are no comforting bipolarities in these matters) and to treat both pleasures and technological societies as if they were simple, unified actualities. I could claim that I take this shortcut because the exigencies of time and space require me to do so, but that excuse would be, though true enough in a sense, something more than a fib. I forgo an adequate analysis of these terms, crucial though they may be to my argument, because I am not a philosopher, but a literary critic—that is to say, in the context of a certain kind of technological society (this one, ours), a sophist, a rhetorician, a school-master—a literary critic who is trying to understand what it is I have been trying to do in (with? for? to?) Ancient Latin Literature for these last three decades and what it is I think that the new generation of literary critics will be likely to busy itself with, or perhaps ought to be busying itself with, when my generation—*et donati iam rude*—totters off to our nursing homes, and as what we used to call The Classics, in a yet more humble disguise (one designed by Euripides perhaps), tries to sneak its way into the next century and the next millenium. In this situation of discourse (that of yet another desperate sophist with his back to the wall), I am not about to offer you philosophical definitions of my major terms and must rather content myself with a *bricolage* of clichés.

In the context of my argument, pleasure is delight, the delight one feels in reading literary texts. Now this delight is, in my eyes, in fact fairly simple:

it is, ideally and often really, sensual, thrilling; it is (as Barthes pleasantly reminds us) something almost sexual in its power to overwhelm our nervous systems with its surges of sounds and images and complexly verbal implosions (by verbal here, I mean, at once, lexical, logical, figural, emotive, intellectual, that place where, beyond sound and image, connotations and denotations, "public images of sentiment" and merely personal *opiniones* collide and coruscate). Reading poems should be a delicious experience—lips, tongues and ears tingling, mice dancing up and down one's spine, the top of Emily's head coming off, Housman's beard bristling when, as he shaves, a particularly sumptuous trochaic verse pops into his memory: all that kind of thing. That (perhaps archaic or primitive) physical pleasure is what I most look for in a poem (long or short, high or low), and I must confess that at my age this experience is rather rarer than it was at earlier times in life, but that's all right: it is still frequent enough, and I still have my memories of the first time I looked into Keats or Millay or Whitman, into Spenser or Milton or Ovid, into Horace or Cavafy or Mallarmé, or Herbert, or Yeats. So, I am not inclined to alter my personal definition of poetry, or the expectations of poetic pleasure that I have, merely because much of the carnal equipment I bring to the taking of this delight is perhaps a bit faded and jaded—and certainly more than a bit diminished by the passage of my years. For strong memory and an occasional surprise still insist to me that such violent sweetness is of the essence for the reading of a poem.

Nevertheless, I'm more than willing to allow the legitimacy of other sorts of poetic reading pleasures. I agree with Dinesen's description of the functions of art: that it gives diversion to the rich and solace to the poor. These functions, it seems to me, have always been very crucial in the making and using of poetry, and ones that color the meaning of poetic pleasure in special ways. Diversion and solace, as any good if unorthodox Epicurean knows, are as primary in pleasure's spectrum as the more carnal pleasure I began with. Finally, if I may be permitted to sneak Aristotle in through the back door, I might as well be forthright here at the outset and admit that I am not a pure voluptuary and that I believe that, mingled with poetry's sensual pleasures, interdependent with them, inextricable from them, are other pleasures, not least among them being that specially peripatetic one, our pleasure in coming to know or to recognize something, either something we thought we had known but had not really known, or something we had not the had the slightest notion of, till poetry revealed it (*Poetics 1448b, Rhetoric 1410b*): in both cases, a pleasure that is at once carnal and intellectual stimulates and liberates our imaginations, and when imagination connects the new configuration of words to the new perception of things, what results (it may be a form of enchantment or disenchantment, depending on our previous state of being and feeling), what happens in our bowels and our spine and our nerves and our brain, is pleasure.

Learning tends to be, in various ways and for various reasons, pleasurable, and for many of us learning from poems (or novels or movies or pop songs) tends to be doubly pleasurable, to flesh and spirit equally, to mind and heart simultaneously—that harmony, that interdependence of our faculties seems to me of the essence for this enjoyment, for these literary pleasures. But as Barthes insists and Aristotle, were he not something of a prude, would agree, without the *sensual* urge for the satisfaction of the senses, the mind's and the spirit's pleasures, unsummoned by the sensual imagination, would not exist. Delighted cognition would no more exist than would the pleasure of solace or diversion, and so it is the carnal pleasure in reading poems aloud, the heard voice's evoking images and sounds and meanings, that I emphasize. And this pleasure has much less to do with that cunning honey smeared on the rim of the medicinal cup (but what child was ever twice fooled by that ruse?) than it does with the slow and imperceptible nurture that Valéry assures us we forget that we ingest, so intent we are on sucking the sweetness from the orange.[1]

And technological societies, what of them in this context? (But of course, they *are* the context of our discourse because we are in one of them, we teach in what was, until very recently, the absolute paradigm for them.) In his splendid and to my taste most important book *The Pleasure of the Text*, Roland Barthes has this to say: "One out of every two Frenchmen, it appears, does not read; half of France is deprived—deprives itself of the pleasure of the text. Now this national disgrace is never deplored except from a humanistic point of view, as though by ignoring books the French were merely forgoing some moral good, some noble value. It would be better to write the grim, stupid, tragic history of all the pleasures which societies object to or renounce: there is an obscurantism of pleasure."[2] This opening paragraph of this *pensée* *("Obscurantisme")* moves in its final sentence from a particular (France) to a universal—to something wrong in the human condition itself. In the second and concluding paragraph, however, Barthes returns to France, without this time naming it: ". . . the foreclosure of pleasure (and even more of bliss)" characterizes "a society ridden by two moralities: the majority one, of platitude; the minority one, of rigor (political and/or scientific). As if the notion of pleasure no longer pleases anyone. Our society appears to be both

staid and violent; in any event: frigid."³ In Barthes' view, what I am calling
the death of pleasure may have been taking place in France (or mainly in
France) as he wrote, but it seems to me that his observations suit most, if not
all, contemporary societies that our current technologies have made at once
rigid and frigid and that are therefore incompatible with genuine pleasure in
general and with genuine literary pleasure in particular.

I distinguish genuine pleasure (the kind that Barthes says no one is any
longer pleased by), from another, unreal variety of pleasure that bureaucrats,
that is to say the technocrats who administer technological societies, have no
objection to: mechanical pleasures, electronic, mass-produced pleasures which
are easily controlled and which both promote consumerism and conformity and
induce temporary oblivion in the people whose labor fuels the elaborate
mechanisms that the technocrats invent, reinvent and manipulate: it is only
prudent and good management to make sure that the workers are not ruined by
their work, that they are refreshed and recreated for the sake of an ever
greater, ever improving efficiency, that their attention is frequently and
forcefully distracted from their work so that they will not notice there is no
genuine purpose to what they are doing. (In passing let me say that I am not
claiming that electronic poetry, produced for the masses, must by definition be
low, vulgar, and unreal. Such a definition would ridiculously exclude, for
example, Tina Turner and Willie Nelson, not to mention Tracy Chapman.
Here I am only concerned with what motivates the technocrats to tolerate what
they take to be useful and innocuous pleasures of this sort.)⁴ I am here making
use of Jacques Ellul's definition of a technological society: "Our civilization
(he doesn't mean France alone) is first and foremost a civilization of means; in
the reality of modern life, the means it would seem are more important than
the ends";⁵ in such a civilization, "technique has taken substance, has become a
reality in itself. It is no longer a means and an intermediary. It is an object in
itself, an independent reality . . ."⁶ Or, to put it another way, if the
technological society has any purpose it is autotelic, it wants, so to speak, only
more of itself, it wants (that is to say, its rulers, the technocrats want) more
efficiency from its means, it wants more and better means to more and better
means; what it has suppressed, what it does not want to think of (and wants its
workers not to think of) is any notion of ends, of what the work is for, of what
the means are to.⁷ For if the technocrats and the workers should begin to
think of what they were doing all this for, they would have to change their
lives (and reorder their priorities and dismantle their mechanisms and their
bureaus—to the technocrat this process is the equivalent of suicide).

All societies are in large measure held together by shared conventions (codes, models, patterns of clichés) which Barthes chooses to call the morality of platitude, but some societies have pleasure nearer their center than do others; the morality of platitude is, in some societies, little more than a benevolent hypocrisy that freely allows what it claims to disallow.[8] More formidable and more sinister, partly because it can always lay claim to God or reason or necessity as its source, is the morality of discipline (*rigueur* as Barthes calls it), which mobilizes everyone in the name of efficiency and goal and uniformity. Here sin (along with pleasure, of course) is rejected not so much because it is wicked as because it is wasteful; like its twin (pleasure) it squanders energies that are needed for the performance of the common chores. The morality of platitude is not really incompatible with literary or other pleasures; but the morality of *rigueur* and efficiency, of means, of technology, is totally incompatible with any and every pleasure, not least with poetic pleasure, since it is poetry that coaxes us to learn to enjoy our imaginations— an activity, a skill, a passion, that a technological society cannot afford to let flourish.

I am not trying here to revive Snow's old fallacy of the two cultures in a new guise, changing *scientific* to *technological* (which is actually the term he ought to have used) and changing *humanistic* to *poetically hedonistic*.[9] Nor am I engaged in restating the terms of the old conflict between the aims and methods of rival notions of education, the professional and the liberal (but clearly, I *am* rehearsing the old *agon*, defined by Gerald Graff in his *Professing Literature*, between the specialist and the generalist). I am trying to imagine how our students and their students are going to function in—to survive in, would perhaps be a better and not too strong way of putting it—a society that is already overwhelmingly technological in its values and in the codes of living and thinking that shape and control it and that shows no signs, as far as I can tell, of reversing that pattern. As things are and seem likely to continue to be (but a worsening is not impossible), a few of our students may well end up devoting a considerable portion of their time to writing about the literary texts of ancient Rome, and some of these will doubtless devote some of their time to shaping (or rehashing) theories about the production and consumption of ancient Roman literature. But most of our students are going to be teaching *their* students how to read Latin, and to some few students, how to read ancient Latin literary texts.

To do this they will need much less in the way of theory about what literature (any literature) is and how it works than they will need experience in seeing, in being able to see, the surface of the text. As Hofmannsthal insisted, the depth is buried on the surface, and (this is what his epigram implies) the surface, because of its deceptive easiness and elusive transparencies, is hard to see.[10] Hard enough in one's own language, harder in a foreign language for all sorts of reasons. How about in a dead language? Well, we know it is not impossible in the poems of a dead language to find the surface and the fun, to yield oneself to the pleasures of those texts and their surfaces. Not impossible, but difficult, especially for newcomers. I remind you, again, that we are teaching students to teach students how to read the surface of poems in a dead language; we are not, we better not be, primarily engaged in teaching students to become theorists who will be primarily engaged in, technologically speaking, producing more theorists.

What is irritating about an excess of literary theory in a technological society (and it is a natural but fatal error to want more and new techniques in literary study when one sees such a proliferation of techniques in the more successful disciplines around one's own) is that, particularly for the novice hedonist in his and her first encounter with the pleasures of literary surfaces, especially those in dead languages (and this holds true of course for Shakespeare no less than for Seneca), there are already more than sufficient obstacles to delight in the various allegorizers who require that the surface be plunged through and the depths found and measured and explored and explained and, by a dreadful alchemy, the poetry be turned into prose and that prose have the poet's opinions about ethics, theology and politics and what have you extracted from it (and we are all of us worse than snake-oil salespersons with our shrill advertisements of The True Meaning). If we insist on prioritizing the mysteries of the depths over the pleasures of the surface, and then come to rank even the treasures of the depths beneath the aporia of literature and language, we have given pleasure the kiss of death. For in the theories above and beyond allegory (the poem's metaphysical or moral meanings) it is revealed that the pleasures of the poem and its plenitude of meanings are equally illusory, that the only realities are those of Writing Itself and of its endless and futile self-replications.

Teachers of literature have always found ways not to read poetry with their students, of course—that is to say, have always found ways to evade the terrors of poetic *jouissance* (or even of poetic *plaisir*). Very early on, for example, the Stoic allegorizers perverted our natural instinct for finding meanings in things (the pleasures of cognition) into the technique of allegory, but when they snatched Homer from the clutches of Plato, the cure, a single instance of *Schlimmbesserung*, turned out, not infrequently, to be worse than the disease. So, nearer to our own time, our 19th century *maiores*, partially to recoup the fading fortunes of the Classics as those of Science burgeoned, invented the Higher Criticism; when that could not shield students of Latin poems from the perils of pleasure, there was always some variety of *Realia* to do the trick or there were literary history or biographical criticism (the version of it that Forster calls "serious gossip") or various histories of manners, morals, and fashion. Somehow, through all the changes in styles and goals of pedagogy originating from within the pleasure of reading Latin poetry and all hostile challenges to it from without (for example, Christians who wanted to burn the Latin poetry books or white-out and reuse them for the lives of imaginary virgins; crazed logicians of the 13th or the 17th centuries who wanted the young to study only texts from which the mess of emotions had been ferociously pruned away; engineers and sociologists from the last century and this who, frightened of fantasy, shaped curricula for automatons)— somehow through all these hazards the pleasure of Latin poems managed to survive, sometimes feebly, sometimes vigorously. And I am fairly sure they will survive even the twin, formidable dangers (again from without and within) of a triumphant technological mentality and that cluster of attitudes toward literature, which, envying and aping their technological rivals, have proclaimed themselves "a science of literature."

The way to meet this latest double dilemma is, in my view, not to emphasize the pleasures of poetry less than before, but, on the contrary, to flaunt them extravagantly. There might well be some danger here that the technocrats who fund our schools (and pay our salaries) might become so irritated by our effrontery that they might simply close us down. If we insist that we are teachers of pleasure and are trying to teach young people to learn for themselves how to use their imaginations by seeing how this natural—but in our culture, unnatural—thing is done in poetry; if we steadfastly claim (without hiding behind the mask of humanism) that it is poetry and the pleasures of the imagination that shape and fix and transform much of the world's reality for humankind—if we do this they would not only stop paying our salaries, they would tar and feather us, they would hound us into the sewers or lock us up in asylums and throw away the key.

And they would do these things because, in fact, we have got them where it hurts. If we profess (we are professors after all) the truth of pleasure, we will have exposed what is most vulnerable in their vision of society: I mean the, for them, bitter truth that it is not technocrats who furnish human beings with wisdom and happiness, it is not various kinds of engineering that solve questions of manners and morals—is it poets who give us some of the courage and faith we need to live our lives richly and generously (they don't give us all that we need, for we also need what Socrates and Montaigne give us, what Manet and Rossini give us, what all the very ordinary people in Whitman's "A Song of Occupations" give us—but poets give us very much of what we need and need very much, not least of which is the freedom and exercise of our imaginations). The technocrats who give the orders for the pushing of the buttons that activate the machines we work in and live in are not displeased to learn that literature is about nothing but itself and that all the self-referential codes that propel poems have little or no reality in them and refer to no reality outside them, and they are delighted to see a proliferation of theories about language and literature distract incipient lovers of poetry from the enjoyment of poems and deliver them over to the dissection of poems and the construction of the laws of poems, to the science of literature. In palmier days for us hedonists, before the Gallic Juggernaut had complicated our struggles for poetic pleasure, the grandsires of our current technocrats were also content when teachers of poetry, again to ensure that pleasure should not rear its unlovely head except in very routine ways and in very controlled situations, concentrated on the moral meaning of poetry. And in any given year, under any given regime, the uses and the meaning of a poem, any poem that managed to retain its place in the canon, was somehow found to illustrate—for us the archetype here is still Matthew Arnold—the truths of the origins, the benevolence and the luminous destiny of the patriarchy.

These two versions of the metarhetorician, scientist of literature and moral allegorist, now function among us, here in America, without about equal vigor, and, though it is rumored that the scientific *littérateur* may now be fading on the other side of the Atlantic, he is likely to flourish here for quite a spell—we Americans tend to hold on to imported fashions long after their exporters have wearied of them and have discovered new toys. The allegorist, of course, we have always with us; indeed, as I hinted earlier, he is, for worse and for better, *in* all of us always, so there is not much use in worrying about him. Since the scientist of literature is the natural if unwitting ally of the technocrat, it is him I am especially concerned with.

So much for this extensive jeremiad! Suppose—what we must in any case suppose—that the worse does not happen if we stand up on our hind legs, without cap in hand, and demand that we be allowed to teach the pleasure of poetry as the *Camenae* intended that we should. Suppose that we refuse to don yet again the threadbare costumes of kindly humanist or stern textual critic or objective theorist or any other version of patriarchal school-master or marm that occurs to you. Free at last, how would we go about teaching poetic pleasure now? How would we begin to do it with students who had grown up on electronic, largely visual, barely verbal *frissons* (the various cheap but sometimes glorious thrills that the technopaths produce and distribute for their consumption)? How do we expect to persuade students to learn to enjoy themselves inside a poem when all they expect from us are prescriptions, caveats, megatheories, and intricate decodings of patriarchal ideology? How can we convince them that both they and we know enough about simple untechnological pleasures to be able to find them in poems that are not hearable on CDs or hearable/viewable on rock videos—find them in old, written, readable (hearable/viewable) poems, not just in dead languages like Shakespeare's or Byron's, but in really dead languages like Tibullus's or Juvenal's? Why should they trust us, used to deception and betrayal by the patriarchy as they are? Why should they not suspect just another trick?

I suggest that we could perhaps begin—and perhaps end—by teaching them to read, by showing them how reading is done. Again, I do not mean, by showing them how to get at *the* meaning of the poem or to discover the secret semiotic system that governs the autographologies of *ta semata*. I mean, reading the words on the page, learning to savor the surface of the text (that is, the poem), its sounds, the patterns of its syntax, the shimmer of its tropes and figures, the unique perspective on the world that its *parole* fabricates into what Auden called "a verbal contraption." I mean: what this voice, in this poem, sounds like, what it feels like to hear these sounds.

The heart of Latin poetry is its rhetoric. Beyond Greek poetry even, beyond even the later poetries that Latin poetry partly inspired, Latin poetry is nothing without that strange preoccupation with refining to high artifice ordinary emphases and ordinary narrative or structural movements of human speech that certain Greeks began to systematically study and whose discipline, rhetoric, after Isocrates and Alexander, became the center of Graeco-Roman education and found its ancient perfection in the Rome of the first century B.C. and the first century of A.D. We all know this about Latin poetry as well as we know our own names. We know it, we emphasize it sporadically, a little randomly. We caution our students (when we remember to) that they must never take their eyes off the rhetoric when reading Latin literature in general and Latin poetry in particular, and then we dash off, each on our own special hobbyhorse, in our own direction (thus teaching our students, in the most effective way, by example, what not to do).[11]   In short, we pay rhetoric devoted lip-service, but we mostly expect them to pick it up—this rigorous, intricate discipline!—for themselves, and we indicate, both in how we read in class and in what we write, that the rhetorical surface, though of course important, is not nearly as important as those precious depths and those more arcane and powerful hidden structures that lie even deeper than the depths. We give our students the impression that *ornatus* means ornament, though we know that it means weapon and structure and emphasis first, and that it means beauty or rather beautification only second. *Das Bekannte überhaupt ist darum, weil es bekannt ist, nicht erkannt.*[12]   Our students need to learn the meaning of *ornatus* for Latin literature and especially for Latin poetry, they need to learn to read rhetorically.   Not the way de Man or Lacan or Jacobson read rhetorically, but as Porson did, as Nietzsche and Wilamowitz did, as Gildersleeve did or Paul Shorey or Kirby Flower Smith.

Since we are all of us today essentially silent and solitary readers of the ordinary technological kind, how shall we go about thinking our way, imagining our way, back into understanding what that Latin rhetorical education was, how those people came to read as they did, how they came to want to read as they did?

We can begin by re-examining some first principles here. Even Barthes, who is rhetorically far more sophisticated than those of his colleagues who dabbled in rhetorical terminology, commits the usual error of supposing that ancient rhetorical theory was concerned solely or even chiefly with the writer, not with the reader (it is a mistake that fastens itself even on Brian Vickers in his admirable meditation on the history and meaning of classical rhetoric, *In Defense of Rhetoric*).[13]   He forgot that although our major rhetorical works, from Aristotle to Quintilian, may seem to be rhetorical manuals, part teach yourself how to write, part reference guides, what they contain, what they outline in great detail, are the things that were studied *ad nauseam* in school when their readers were children and young adults.   After they got past the basics, children learned to read by being saturated with the elements of rhetoric, by being required to read the texts aloud, by commenting on the syntactic and rhetorical surfaces of those texts, by being made to memorize vast portions of those texts and to sedulously ape their major rhetorical stratagems in, as it were, original compositions.   In short, they learned (some of them, maybe even many of them) all that rhetoric has to teach (which is considerable) by performing rhetorical masterpieces precisely, kinetically (Stanley Fish's word, I think), sensuously, by interpreting them (almost as a violinist interprets a sonata), and, not least, by listening to those texts while others performed them, while waiting for one's own turn to perform. And this they did, day after day, month after month, year after year. "I am artificial by nature," said the great Ravel, but any Latin or, for the matter, almost any Elizabethan poet could reverse that witty antithesis ("I am natural by artifice, that is, discipline frees me") and so define the degree to which, in this education, in this view of the world (for that is what it is in fact), freedom of instinct and artifice had fused into their grand interdependences. This liberation through artifice continued for Roman schoolboys until they had become consummate readers, readers who interpreted and performed and heard and shared literary texts with one another (when literary pleasures are mutual and communal one does not need the sort of interpretive literary criticism that the plight of the solitary silent reader has made all but inevitable). Then they were ready for their various careers.

Some of them would become teachers and writers and would thus continue to practice and refine what they had spent all their young lives learning; others would go into the government or the army or business and would, as occasion demanded, compose and deliver orations, or write formal letters, or secretly and sometimes not so secretly scribble verses, but these latter, usually rather semi-active rhetorians, whether they wrote little or much, would never forget how to read with precision and vividness (I mean, of course, those who had learned the discipline, not those who had somehow floated through it). Roman teachers of reading and rhetoric knew they were teaching some future orators and poets and historians the elements and some of the tricks of their future trades, but they also knew very well that all of the boys and young men they were guiding (and flogging) through this extraordinarily demanding intellectual discipline would not turn out to be major statesmen who needed to orate, or gifted poets and historians whose talents led them to make use of what they had learned in school in their work. If the main purpose of Roman education was to produce writers, it was wasteful, sadistic and even silly. But if its aim was to produce very effective readers—readers who could vigorously and critically participate in the act of communication as trained, disciplined listeners—then it was (making allowances for its dreadful indifference to the oppression of the illiterate) singularly successful.

We have not, of course, any hope of approximating this sort of success even if we wished to (and, of course, having other fish to fry, we do not). But perhaps we can make a gesture in that direction. Once we have emphasized the difficulties that our being trained as solitary, silent readers have put in the way of our learning to read rhetorically, we could begin by reminding ourselves that literary theory, like the various branches of classical philology itself, exists for the sake of the poems, not the poems for the sake of the literary theory. It is true that the poems can be used, in defiance of Heisenberg's principle, for the sake of creating theories or refining them, but nonetheless the theories thus invented and improved still exist for the sake of the poem, not vice versa. It is no less true that the enjoyment of Roman poetry depends on theory even as it does on the learning of the Latin language and on some degree of expertise in the various branches of classical philology. Nevertheless, theory and erudition *exist for the sake of the poems*, not poems for the sake of the theory or that of classical philology. If, pressured as we are by the demands of our technological society, we can yet retrieve some of this older notion, rhetoric's insistence that education is for living one's life—and not just as a speciously humanistic patriarchy prescribes that it be lived—and that the reading and the pleasures of poetry are part of that education; if, doing that, we can restore theory and philology and allegorization to their proper, I mean, their *ancillary* roles, perhaps we can then restore rhetoric to its rightful place in our teaching and learning how to read Roman poetry.

I think that in their first year, whatever else they take or do not take, graduate students might have a year's course in Classical Rhetoric. My current sketch for a version of it runs something like this: a reading of Barthes' *The Pleasure of the Text*, followed by a reading of Vickers' *In Defense of Rhetoric*, followed by Aristotle's *Rhetoric* and Cicero's *De oratore* and by as much Quintilian as one has time and patience and energy for. Those books and some frequent exercises in identifying and describing the operation of tropes and figures in some representative texts and in examining the parts of those texts, that is, the articulations of their parts, their structure in movement, the surfaces of their unfolding in literary, performative spacetime, would probably take up a year's hard work (but in discussing the rhythmic structures of a poem or a narrative or an oration one would want to make some space for cinematic narratology since that aspect of rhetoric has been entirely transformed by film and by our new habits of thinking in pictures).

Whether graduate students would like such a course or not, I do not know. Whether it would in fact make them better readers of Latin poetry, I cannot predict. But I think that it would make them much more aware (their rhetorical training is now commonly haphazard, inaccurate or all but non-existent) of what sort of world Roman poets wrote in, what sorts of pleasure

212   W.R. Johnson

their audiences could expect from them (having themselves been exquisitely
trained to recognize and to accept literary pleasures), and how they could go
about learning—imagining—those Roman pleasures for themselves. If having
done this, having learned to yield themselves up to and immerse themselves in
that ocean of verbal delight and cognitive pleasure, they should still want—for
temperament in such matters is all—to convert poetic experience into theories
of it or to use poems as grist for Realia's insatiable mills or to mutate poems
into moral prescriptions *allegorice*—if that is what they want to do with their
pleasures, more power to them. It ill suits a hedonist, as Buechner's Danton
reminds his Robespierre, to quibble with others' ways of having fun. But if
these readers of Roman poetry have *begun* their scrutinies with rhetoric and
pleasure, they will at least be starting their alchemical experiments with
genuine ingredients and that might improve their theories and their philologies
and even their allegories.

<hr>

NOTES

1   *"La pensée doit etre cachée dans les verse comme la vertue nutritive dans un fruit. Un
fruit est nourriture, mais il ne paraît que délice. On ne perçoit que du plaisir, mais on reçoit une
substance. L'enchantement voile cette nourriture insensible qu'il conduit."* Oeuvres, Tome II,
Pléiade (Paris 1960) 547-8. Only a California emigré could, when paraphrasing from memory,
convert Valéry's universal fruit into an orange.
2   (Paris 1973; trs. Richard Miller, New York 1975) 46 (pages refer to translation unless
otherwise specified). To say, in 1973, that one out of two Frenchmen reads sounds like a boast
to an American in 1990: here and now only two out of three adults *can* read much of anything.
Interesting, that in the corporate capitalist version of technological society the myth of universal
literacy should have been so vigorously maintained long after any real pursuit of the ideal of
universal literacy had been abandoned. The truth of the matter is that technocracies don't
want—only partly because they don't need—universal literacy; nor have they much interest in
continuing for humanistic literacy the specious reverence and grudging support that no longer
serve their purposes. For exact and passionate formulations of these questions, see Jonathan
Kozel, *Illiterate America* (New York 1985) 157-191.
3   46-7. Skinner bases her efforts to reduce my argument to nostalgic hankerings for
power and class privilege on Fitzgerald's attempts to do the same thing to Barthes' *Plaisir*.
Fitzgerald's peculiar way of converting Barthes' discussion of pleasure/bliss (two sides of the
same coin) into a panegyric on ecstacies which move beyond the merely elitist into a realm of
sybaritism that partakes in equal measure of the solipsistic and the arch-mandarin needs more
scrutiny than Skinner devotes to it. He quotes the first part of Barthes' own contrast of *plaisir
du texte* with *textes de jouissance* (51; original 82) as evidence of its author's contempt for what
Fitzgerald calls "a classical, bourgeois pleasure." Then, instead of quoting Barthes' description
of *textes de jouissance,* which Barthes immediately juxtaposes with his description of *plaisir du
texte,* Fitzgerald says: "By contrast, the text of *jouissance* produces a *loss* of ego-stability and
ruptures the plenitude of the classical text. Perhaps the most useful description of this kind of
text (usually modern) is in Barthes's *The Zero Degree of Literature*. . .". (85) If he feels that a
passage written twenty-two years before the one he's dealing with will accomplish his purposes
better than the contrast that Barthes himself provides in the passage in question, well and good;
yet I suspect that the earlier text, with its closing clause, "these poetic words exclude humanity,"
appealed to him in part because it offered him a path into the bourgeois/aristocratic antithesis (on

which his argument hangs) that is simply not available to him in the later passage of Barthes, which he suppresses. (Throughout, I retain Miller's *jouissance* = *bliss*, but I think *rapture* would be a closer approximation.) Barthes does in fact discuss class in respect of his dialectic of pleasure/bliss; at 38-9, meditating on the possibility of a "class eroticism," he rejects the claims of both the bourgeois and the People and briefly flirts with the idea that the mandarinate might hope for salvation in his voluptuous utopia. But mandarins, too, find those gates closed against them. It turns out that there are no aristocratic spendings or dyings (except maybe in aristocratic poetry); orgasms are ruthlessly egalitarian, coming is a classless activity. Because pleasure/bliss is something for the single self, it is beyond class and outside of society. It is joyfully anarchic (its closest poetic siblings perhaps are Yeats' *Meru* and *Lapis Lazuli*). It is a well known truth, of course, that the lower and upper classes share notorious capacities for vividly obscene language and for enjoying themselves immensely, while the middle classes . . .

What finally accounts for Fitzgerald's *Verschiebung* of the *jouissance* passage and his substitution for it of the structurally orthodox passage from a book that its author had outgrown we may never know, but one senses in the pages that surround this suppression some degree of irritation with Barthes, the traitor to the cause of the science of literature and to the elite who make up its literary technocracy. A not dissimilar pique is in evidence in Jonathan Culler's *Roland Barthes* (Oxford 1983) whenever he attempts to elucidate Barthes' inexplicable apostasy (15-17, 45, 99-100, 122; for "the science of literature," see 10, 68-9, 88-9). Doubtless, a founding father who forswore the science of literature with the panache that Barthes displays in *Pleasure* knew that eventually he would have to be abjured by the faithful as a failed hierophant, as a mere empiricist, a voluptuary, a human being. That is why, perhaps, in his witty inferno (63) he invents that funny and condign punishment for "obsessives;" why he warns us (57) of the two policemen always waiting to jump us whenever we utter the word "pleasure" (one of these cops, who is very class conscious, finds us hedonists idle, irreverent, frivolous); why he insists (52-84) *"Le text est (devrait être) cette personne disinvolte qui montre son derrière au Père Politique."* What most obviates Fitzgerald's efforts to grapple with Barthes' idea of pleasure/bliss is his failure to see its dialectical nature. For Barthes, all reading requires a "contradictory interplay of (cultural) pleasure and (non-cultural) bliss" (62-3); with each reading of each text, (and, in a certain way, at each moment of our lives) it is this interdependence—and countervailing—of stability and flux (shades of Empedocles!) that characterizes our texts and our reading of them no less than their contexts and ours. The "puritanism of" Fitzgerald's ideological analysis (84-5) reduces the Barthes of *Pleasure* to a sort of punk dandy (that is, he mistakes one of the self-narrator's droller disguises for the sincerest of the personae). For an elegant discussion of the dialectic of pleasure in *Pleasure*, see Mary Bittner Wiseman, *The Ecstacies of Roland Barthes* (London 1989) 101-5; see also Elizabeth Wright, *Psychoanalytic Criticism: Theory in Practice* (London 1984) 89. On the hazards to humanists of "old-fashioned notions about how 'findings' are 'established' in the harder sciences" see Clifford Geertz, *Works and Lives: The Anthropologist as Author* (Stanford 1988) 4 and passim; he is also superb on Barthes' concepts of personae, especially on his vast (and partially on-stage) wardrobe room: "ham actors and seducing selves," 90-93.

4   We should not ignore Barthes' own distinction (38) between "mass culture" and "the culture of the masses." The former is produced and distributed by corporations for mass consumption (as narcotic, harmless diversion); in the latter, individual artists still have some control over what they create and offer to their audiences and a certain reciprocity still prevails *despite corporate, technological efforts to control what the population enjoys.* For the effect of corporate technology on the art world, see Suzi Gublik, *Has Modernism Failed?* (London 1984) 52-3, 62, 66-70 and passim. For newer, current intrusions into the movie industry, see Mark Crispin Miller, "Hollywood the Ad," *The Atlantic Monthly* (April 1990) 157-191; for an older, conventional tyranny of corporate technology over the movies' artistic technology as exemplified in Filmland's "Octopus," see Dan E. Moldea, *Dark Victory: Ronald Reagan, MCA, and the Mob* (New York 1986) passim. For a powerful, fresh examination of the dismal story of television and technomania's role in it, see Mark Crispin Miller's *Boxed In: The Culture of TV* (Evanston 1988). For a welcome, if not entirely persuasive, discussion of how technological determinism and cultural pessimism might yet be defeated, see Raymond

Williams, "Culture and Technology," in his *The Politics of Modernism* (London 1989) 119-140.

5   *The Technological Society*, trans. John Wilkinson (New York 1964) 19.

6   63.

7   "To Cure Technophobia you Need a Good Psychologist." So reads a smarmy AT&T ad reproduced in Miller's *Boxed-In*, 303. Technophobic was the word for Lewis Mumford in the mass media during most of his career, but just how precise his analyses of our technological disorders were and remain becomes ever clearer as the consequences of unexamined and uncontrolled corporate technology reveal themselves. For the purposes of this essay, his classic statements on bad technology's corruption of higher education are in *The Myth of the Modern Machine: The Pentagon of Power* (vol. 2) (New York 1970) 181-5, 371-4. Everyone from George Bush to United Technology had a good time in 1984 making fun of Orwell's *1984* (Miller, *Boxed-In*, 309-11), but its images of evil political technology and its influence on the societies it touches continue to gather force and significance; as does the brilliant afterword that Erich Fromm wrote for a reissue of the book in 1961: see the New American Library edition, New York, 1981, 262-6, especially 266 and its discussion of Orwell's depiction of "the new form of managerial industrialism, in which man builds machines which act like men and develop men who act like machines"—that formulation, alas, is as valid today as it was when he wrote it, is as "modern as tomorrow," as the technocratic PR-men like to put it. See also: Rich Cowan, "Academia Un-Incorporated," *Z Magazine* February 1990, 47-52; Leonard Minsky and David Noble, "Corporate Takeover on Campus," *The Nation* October 30, 1989, 477, 494-6; David Noble, *America by Design: Science, Technology and the Rise of Corporate Capitalism* (Oxford 1977) passim and his "The Multinational University," *Z Magazine* April 1989, 17-23; David Harvey, *The Conditions of Post-Modernity* (Oxford: Blackwell 1989) 23, 31ff., 38, 45, 63-6, 155-6 and passim; Neil Postman, *Amusing Ourselves to Death: Public Discourse in the Age of Show Business* (New York 1985) 155-163; Mary Midgley, *Evolution as a Religion* (London 1985) 63-5, 141-6, 157.

8   See John J. Winkler, *The Constraints of Desire: The Anthropology of Sex and Gender in Ancient Greece* (New York 1990) 45-70.

9   Nabokov's version of the famous Snow fallacy may be the final word: "One of those 'Two Cultures' is really nothing but utilitarian technology; the other is B-grade novels, ideological fiction, popular art. Who cares if there exists a gap between such 'physics' and such 'humanities?'" *Strong Opinions* (New York 1973) 78.

10   *Das Buch der Freunde: Die Tiefe muss man verstecken. Wo? An die Oberfläche.*

11   As one of the very greatest of Latin poets reminds us: Juvenal 14.31ff., *velocius et citius nos/ corrumpunt vitiorum exempla domestica, magnis/ cum subeant animos auctoribus.*

12   Hegel, *Preface to the Phenomenology*, 2.3.

13   (Oxford 1989) 12.

LITERARY THEORISTS AT SECOND-RATE UNIVERSITIES
Response to Ralph Johnson

In what he himself terms a "jeremiad" (though, in keeping with the Latinate focus of this symposium, we might do better to call it a "philippic"), Ralph Johnson bleakly surveys the present intellectual climate in our profession. Taking the ideas adumbrated in Roland Barthes' *The Pleasure of the Text* as his point of departure, Johnson contends that the technological bent of modern society and the puritanic obsession with theory in academic circles are jointly responsible for a growing decline in the ability to experience pleasure—the sensual delights of reading, to begin with, and then, in more general terms, pleasure itself. That claim is a large one, and largely unsupported, even though it does rest on Barthes' dazzling analysis of the pleasure mechanism. Consequently, it poses a difficult tactical problem for a respondent. In the absence of available empirical data—a kind of scientific "pleasure index"—I can only fall back on my habitual method of dealing with a question, which is to have recourse, paradoxically enough, to the very theory Johnson condemns.

I adopt that approach, however, with a due acknowledgement of my own ideological bias, a bias that must necessarily put him and me at odds with one another. Johnson never quite defines what he means by that vague word "theory." That his chief target is the putative redundant *aporia* of deconstructionism, of "Writing writing Itself," seems obvious enough. In certain passages, though, he expresses the passionately felt conviction that pure, self-justifying textual pleasure is endangered by prying too deeply into the poem's latent ideological content.[1] In contrast, my own perspective upon ancient literature is that of a politically engaged feminist theorist. Through the interrelated activities of teaching and research I confront Greco-Roman culture

---

[1]   To be fair to Johnson, I will add that he now categorically denies any intent to attack feminist theory; deconstructionism, especially as practiced by some extremists, was, he affirms, his only target. But some of his remarks give a different—and apparently misleading—impression. At one point, for example, he demands, "how do we expect to persuade students to learn to enjoy themselves inside a poem when they expect from us only prescriptions, caveats, megatheories, and intricate decodings of patriarchal ideology?" Sensitized to the key word "patriarchal" (which, though it turns up frequently in Johnson's paper, is, like "theory," never defined), a feminist critic would readily conclude that such decodings of an ideology oppressive to her fall into the category of things opposed to literary enjoyment—which are, by definition, not good.

analytically, and that analytic process serves, in turn, as one vehicle of the feminist *praxis* that informs and governs my professional life.[2] To me, any critical position that assigns absolute priority to aesthetics over semiotics fails to come to grips with the way texts impact readers' concepts of reality and shape their beliefs. The question of the relative value to be placed on exposing and demystifying poetry's hidden social messages is, then, a primary locus of our disagreement.

Since reading, in my view, is a political act undertaken in classrooms (among other places), it must have pedagogical ramifications. Any divergence of opinion over its function and purpose, as they pertain to classical texts, will therefore bear upon corollary instructional disputes: the immediate, pragmatic [5] question of how Latin is to be taught in the future and the somewhat broader question of the role classical studies itself is to play within each segment of American higher education's recognized "two-tier system." Accordingly, I intend to address Johnson's arbitrary dismissal of theory in the light of class as well as gender difference. Armed with the self-consciousness that, according to David Konstan, defines the revisionist, or what I have elsewhere termed the "postclassicist," stance in Greco-Roman studies, I will explore the implications of Johnson's position first from a feminist perspective, and then from the standpoint of a faculty member at a Midwestern "land-grant" university with no degree program in classics—the type of institution in which class issues most intensely affect pedagogy.[3]

Before I take up those matters, though, let me apologize for my chauvinism in focusing so narrowly upon the peculiar concerns of classicists in my own country. Still, I hope that this glimpse of academic and pedagogical problems now preoccupying their American colleagues will perhaps be of some interest to our foreign guests. Likewise, I apologize to Johnson for transposing his discursive, lyrical prose into the logical mode within which I prefer to operate, a change that forced me to reconstruct some of his basic

---

2   Here I echo the exhortation of P.P. Schweickart: "Feminist criticism, we should remember, is a mode of *praxis*. The point is not merely to interpret the literature in various ways; the point is to *change the world*. We cannot afford to ignore the activity of reading, for it is here that literature is realized as *praxis*. Literature acts on the world by acting on its readers" ("Reading Ourselves: Toward a Feminist Theory of Reading," in E.A. Flynn and P.P. Schweickart, eds., *Gender and Reading: Essays on Readers, Texts, and Contexts* [Baltimore and London 1986] 39).
5
3   D. Konstan, "What Is New in the New Approaches to Classical Literature," in P. Culham and L. Edmunds, eds., *Classics: A Discipline and Profession in Crisis?* (Lanham 1989) 45-49; for "postclassicism," see M.B. Skinner, "Rescuing Creusa: New Methodological Approaches to Women in Antiquity," *Helios* 13.2 (1986) 4.

premises and, at certain points, to extend his conclusions a little. I hope I have not done violence to his train of thought; if I have, I expect I will hear about it shortly.

First, some general observations about the respective cognitive frameworks, the sets of epistemological presuppositions, to which Johnson and I subscribe—for there, too, I find fundamental differences between us. His term for the recent incursion of theory into classics is "the Gallic Juggernaut." There is a bumper sticker on that juggernaut: it says "THIS IS NOT A BUMPER STICKER." If those of us who attempt theoretical approaches have any one trait in common, it is the practice of carefully weighing the truth-claims of statements presenting themselves as categorical or absolute. Thus I cannot help but feel misgivings when Johnson categorically asserts that the immediate aesthetic experience of literature is intrinsically superior to the rational critique of its underlying assumptions. The contention is grounded upon a literal and personal application of Barthes' thoughts: according to Johnson, the physiological sensations accompanying the reading of poetry, as he himself has experienced them, share features in common with sexual pleasure, the ready touchstone of pleasure itself. Conversely, theory, being cerebral, is sterile. By a certain metonymic sleight-of-hand, inquiry into the concepts deployed in poetic discourse has become an automatic rejection of the body's transcendent truth, and so a denial, a death, of carnal enjoyment.

I think Johnson's idea of what constitutes an "authentic" textual encounter is far too limited. He is certainly entitled to accept the authority of his own sensations as primary; but it is not legitimate to elevate those sensations into a universal criterion of pleasure by which theory can be weighed and found wanting. His restricted notion of the reading experience undervalues the stimulation of engaging with the text intellectually—for me, the most exciting component of reader response. There is no place in his paradigm, moreover, for the ancillary, eccentric joys of scholarship, the ratiocinative delight of measuring a colleague's (and, most deliciously, a friend's) textual insights against your own.[4] Lastly, Johnson's contentions appeal to an age-old, and now recognizably dubious, epistemological opposition between mind and senses, privileging one over the other. Paradoxically, his inversion of the

---

[4]   Catullus would have appreciated the curious Callimachean pleasures of scholarly gamesmanship (50.1-3): *hesterno, Licini, die otiosi/multum lusimus in meis tabellis,/ut convenerat esse delicatos.* In that same poem he insinuates that a well-fought intellectual duel may have its own distinctive erotic undercurrents. A fascinating idea—but we will not explore it here.

traditional Aristotelian hierarchy of "male" reason over "female" body only makes the woman reader's situation *vis-à-vis* the text yet more problematic. For Johnson's ideal reader, his hero, is Barthes' anti-hero, "the reader of the text at the moment he takes his pleasure" (3).[5] Is that reader not male? And is the pleasure he takes not phallic—or, rather, phallogocentric?

I have now come up against a subject I was really hoping to sidestep, the question of how, as a feminist, I would deal with Barthes himself. It is not an easy question to answer, for in terms of gender and class ideology *The Pleasure of the Text* is a notoriously slippery document. On the one hand, Barthes' valorization of the body and its pleasures does resonate, seductively, with feminist theory—most notably with a cardinal tenet of French women writers, their controversial reappropriation of the concepts "body," "sexuality," "*jouissance*" for supposedly "feminine" modes of authorial discourse.[6] On the other hand, his figuration of the text as a source of gratification for a male subject inevitably raises the issue of gender objectification. While it is patently too crude to connect *The Pleasure of the Text* to the traditional masculinist fantasy of the book as mistress, there may be some trace of conventional symbolic constructs of womanhood ("woman" as metonym for fertility, reproduction, maternity and heterosexuality) even in Barthes' avowedly neutral, pointedly asexual eroticism.[7] To sum up my own cautious reaction, *The Pleasure of the Text* is not blatantly misogynistic; indeed, its degendered image of sexual enjoyment may contain something "potentially friendly to feminism," as Jane Gallop opines.[8] Nevertheless, it makes me nervous; seductiveness always does.

Barthes' concept of the relation between social class and textual pleasure is still more difficult to pin down, precisely because in bringing up this topic he himself deliberately obscures it. According to William Fitzgerald, *The*

---

[5]   All quotations from Barthes are taken from the English translation by R. Miller: R. Barthes, *The Pleasure of the Text* (New York 1975). Page references are given in my essay.
[6]   N. Schor, "Dreaming Dissymmetry: Barthes, Foucault, and Sexual Difference," in A. Jardine and P. Smith, eds., *Men in Feminism* (New York and London 1987) 98-110. One must add, however, that French neofeminism's identification of female textuality with female sexuality has not been well received on this side of the Atlantic.
[7]   S. Gubar, "'The Blank Page' and the Issues of Female Creativity," in E. Abel, ed., *Writing and Sexual Difference* (Chicago 1982) 76 forcibly inserts Barthes into a catalogue of writers and critics who "feminize" the text, ignoring the delicate homosexual nuances in his description of erotic desire. J. Gallop, "Feminist Criticism and the Pleasure of the Text," *North Dakota Quarterly* 54 (1986) 119-34 is, by contrast, much more tentative and judicious in pointing out possible traces of conventional gender stereotyping, and much more appreciative of Barthes' subtle equivocations.
[8]   Gallop (above, note 7) 124.

Pleasure of the Text is implicated in a common elitizing practice: indulgence in real, genuine pleasure (however its nature may be defined) is frequently justified by contrasting it pejoratively with the coarse amusements of the masses.[9] Barthes' textual *jouissance*, an experience proper to "*aristocratic readers*" (13; Barthes' italics) is defined in opposition to what Fitzgerald categorizes first as a "classical, bourgeois" and then as a "vulgar" reading pleasure; the polarization between them is epitomized by juxtaposed litanies summing up the two concepts "*pleasure of the text*" and "*texts of pleasure*" (51-52).[10] In rebuttal, Johnson argues that Barthes' concept of pleasure is actually not dichotomized but dialectical, involving a moment-to-moment interplay of classical pleasure and *jouissance*. Again, Barthes specifically repudiates the notion of a "class eroticism" by denying an appreciation of language first to the bourgeoisie, then to the People, and finally to the mandarinate (38).[11] At the outset, Johnson might have added, Barthes moves to subvert any facile attempts to politicize and elitize his idea of textual pleasure by branding as "a minor mythology" the notion that pleasure belongs to the right, morality to the left: "Pleasure, however, is not an *element* of the text, it is not a naïve residue; it does not depend on a logic of understanding and on sensation; it is a drift, something both revolutionary and asocial and it cannot be taken over by any collectivity, any mentality, any ideolect" (22-23). Johnson's claim that Barthes has no intention of associating a given form of pleasure with a given social class seems to be vindicated; contrariwise, Fitzgerald's reading appears reductionist. This is not, after all, a simple case of *Aphrodite Urania* versus *Aphrodite Pandemos*.

But Fitzgerald is onto something. Wily, protean, refusing to be subsumed under any neat political rubric, Barthes is nevertheless championing a supreme good, literary *plaisir/jouissance*, against—what? He never does say; but it might presumably be whatever the one out of two Frenchmen who does not read (46) prefers to reading. Furthermore, Barthes' anti-hero is a *highly trained* reader: he takes his pleasure from Severo Sarduy's *Cobra*, not from the sporting pages and certainly not from *Elle*. The training that permits the exceptional individual to savor the perverse "dismantling of language," especially at a historical moment when many of his poorly schooled fellow

---

9 W. Fitzgerald, "Horace, Pleasure and the Text," *Arethusa* 22 (1989) 81-103.
10 Fitzgerald (above, note 9) 83-84.
11 The mandarins are credited, though, with the possibility of enjoying pleasure (*plaisir*), if not *jouissance*. But, according to Johnson's formulation, can the one even operate independently of the potential presence of the other?

citizens are having a hard time putting it together, is not linked indissolubly to class but is linked, most definitely, to the possession of education, money and leisure. To that extent, Barthes' rhetorical posture, if not overtly class-bound, is still exclusionary and dangerously close to elitist.

In Johnson's paper, the dichotomizing tendency observed above is much more evident. His deployment of electronic mass amusements as a negative foil to the pleasure of reading makes an implicit appeal to class snobbery. Spoon-fed to wholly passive consumers, media entertainment is dispensed, he claims, in accordance with the self-serving agenda of "technocrats":

> I distinguish genuine pleasure (the kind that Barthes says no one is any longer pleased by), from another, unreal variety of pleasure that bureaucrats, that is to say the technocrats who administer technological societies, have no objection to: mechanical pleasures, electronic, mass-produced pleasures which are easily controlled and which both promote consumerism and conformity and induce temporary oblivion in the people whose labor fuels the elaborate mechanisms that the technocrats invent, reinvent and manipulate.

Later, Johnson qualifies this blanket indictment of popular culture by conceding that some "electronic poetry" does have artistic value. Even with that modification, though, his image of mass entertainment is hostile, impacted heavily by academic diatribes against television and rock music as devices to distract a working population and soothe it into docility.

While space does not permit me to reply at length, I would like to offer a brief rejoinder to this particular argument of Johnson's. To ascribe mass taste to a mysterious cabal of masterminds positioned beyond ideology in order to control it for their own sinister purposes is to indulge in a fallacious scapegoat fantasy. It is impossible for any group of individuals, no matter how powerful, to stand so completely outside culture as to be able to manipulate its ideological systems dispassionately. If all art mirrors its surroundings and is affected, to some degree, by cultural developments (to which, of course, it may likewise contribute), mass entertainment produced solely for commercial reasons must be particularly sensitive to audience concerns. Consequently, the myth of popular visual entertainment as a drug—either an opiate or a brainwashing tool—has been recently challenged by American critics who suggest that it is, instead, an effective medium for giving expression to unresolved cultural tensions, one that can, in some circumstances, even promote a heightening of personal consciousness.[12] In merely assuming, without evidence, the incomparably greater social value of literary texts, we academically trained readers show ourselves enmeshed in our own class-bound perspective. The example of Dickens is enough to prove that one generation's popular art can become the next generation's high art. From our present vantage point, we cannot foresee what twentieth-century cultural products the Program on Narratology at the University of Tokyo at Portland (deemed, in the year 2090, one of the Pacific Rim's premier research institutions) will elevate to canonical status. James Joyce, Robert Frost and Toni Morrison should undoubtedly make the list; but so, unless I badly miss the mark, will *Casablanca, Gone with the Wind, Star Trek* and the Beatles.

Class, then, is one subtext of Johnson's paper; the other subtext is pedagogy, and the two eventually converge. At the end of his presentation he turns his attention to the practical question addressed to all participants in this symposium: what work should classics as a discipline undertake during the next twenty years? His reply takes the form of a proposal for modifying the present American graduate curriculum. First-year graduate students should be given a solid grounding in classical Roman rhetoric. Having learned to focus upon what he terms the "surface" of the text, they would come to savor verbal point and ingenuity. Presumably they would eventually import that training into their own classrooms. Concentrating, along with these instructors, on the text's surface, undergraduates too would learn to cherish the subtle joys of the reading experience, and so become improved readers. Training graduate students in rhetoric would be pedagogically productive, then, for it would ultimately help to enhance the lives of yet other students, those at an earlier phase in their educational careers.

Johnson's proposition incorporates a standard defense of the traditional classical education: coming to grips with the great Greek and Latin

---

[12] See, for example, two studies of popular fictions, such as soap operas, directed toward exclusively female audiences: T. Modleski, *Loving with a Vengeance* (New York and London 1984) and J. Radway, *Reading the Romance* (Chapel Hill 1984). A programmatic comment by Modleski is instructive: "I propose not to ignore what is 'feminine' about soap operas but to focus on it, to show how they provide a unique narrative pleasure which, while it has become thoroughly adapted to the rhythms of women's lives in the home, provides an alternative to the dominant 'pleasures of the text' analyzed by Roland Barthes and others. Soap operas may be in the vanguard not just of T.V. art but of all popular narrative art" (87). Modleski's description of soap operas as episodic, ongoing, open-ended narratives could be applied, *mutatis mutandis*, to the oral Greek epic cycle. On the politics of critical reception of the ancient Greek romance, which furnishes another interesting parallel to contemporary popular narratives, see M. Williamson, "The Greek Romance," in J. Radford, ed., *The Progress of Romance* (London and New York 1986) 23-45.

masterpieces in the original language is a splendid means of personal self-
enrichment. Other speakers at this conference obviously share that view of
classics; indeed, both Michael von Albrecht and Elaine Fantham eloquently
appealed to the same doctrine in their own presentations. I too acknowledge its
validity, but with the cautious proviso that it assumes the economic freedom to
treat education as an end in itself, not as immediate preparation for earning a
living. Education in that sense has always been, and still is, a luxury not
available to everyone.

    While I do not think training in classical rhetoric is the ultimate panacea
for the present crisis in undergraduate education, I will stipulate that a sound
knowledge of the subject is both good for its own sake and professionally
useful. Where I really take issue with Johnson is at the point where he
connects theory, on the one hand, and rhetoric, on the other, to the two-tier
system that presently bisects the American classics community.[13] Some few
new Ph.D.'s, he surmises, will eventually be able to devote much of their time
to analyzing ancient literary texts, or even to generating theory about the
production and consumption of such texts; but the majority of future degree
recipients will spend their careers teaching beginning and intermediate Latin,
and maybe the occasional upper-division course. The latter will need much
less familiarity with theory, more training in close work with the surface of
the text.

    The argument sounds plausible, but let's unpack it a little further.
Johnson's first group, of course, will have found tenured places in the graduate
programs of other leading research institutions; his second group will teach in
the undergraduate programs of regional liberal arts colleges and "land-grant"
universities like my own. The latter schools provide higher education to a
pluralistic student body of mixed background, degrees of educational
preparation, and aspirations—very different in makeup from the still largely
homogeneous population of elite colleges and universities. In the second-tier
institutions, furthermore, the ancient languages, contrary to the impression
given by Johnson's paper, are not the central focus of classical studies
programs. Classics is instead supported and justified by massive enrollments in
civilization, literature in translation, and mythology courses, where

---

13   For descriptions of this system, see the following articles in Culham and Edmunds
(above, note 3): L. Edmunds, "Introduction," pp. xiii-xviii; S.G. Cole, "Taking Classics into
the Twenty-First Century: A Demographic Portrait," 15-23; J. Henderson, "The Training of
Classicists" 89-98; S.L. Spaar, *"Veni, vidi, spem abieci:"* A Report from the Provinces," 155-
62. The essay by Spaar is particularly chilling.

undergraduates make their acquaintance with the Greco-Roman world through a selected group of texts read in English and lectured upon by the instructor—often to classes of a hundred or more at one time.

Whatever its inherent limitations, theory is in Johnson's scheme the perk reserved for the select few, and pedagogy the function delegated to the masses. But that relation overlooks the actual role of theory within the American academic environment, particularly in classical studies. Theory has become both the discourse and the disciplinary posture of those intellectually and professionally marginalized. Its questioning of self-evident assumptions naturally extends to analysis of the mechanisms for the production and validation of academic knowledge. Since those mechanisms are so closely linked to the authoritative position of the great research centers, the radical inquiry we have been conveniently labeling "theory" has in general been undertaken by scholars affiliated with lesser-known institutions.

From the very beginning, theory in our field addressed itself, peripherally or directly, to the relationship between classical studies and issues of gender and class. Educational programs intended for the children of the privileged orders have customarily used select Greek and Roman texts, selectively interpreted, as media for imparting values and attitudes deemed appropriate for the rulers of a society. As W.R. Connor has demonstrated in an influential article, that was the rationale for the pivotal place accorded classics in the liberal arts education of the 1950's, which was intended to prepare future American leaders, the sons of the wealthy, for the responsible exercise of power.[14] But the curriculum designed for that purpose, which Connor terms the "Old Humanities," proved inadequate to meet the needs of students enrolled at second-tier institutions during the 1970's and 1980's. Perceiving the lack of ideological fit between accepted readings of classical texts and the values and concerns of those students, classicists at such schools eventually began to employ theory, especially feminist theory, as a tool for deconstructing and defusing fossilized ideology. Originating as a grass-roots movement on the part of isolated, individual scholars, the project has now become so extensive that Connor can legitimately speak of a "New Humanities."

The production of new readings of classical literature by theorists has altered our understanding of class and gender in antiquity. Contrary to first superficial impressions, it is becoming apparent that Greek and Roman literary

---

[14]   W.R. Connor, "The New Classical Humanities and the Old," *CJ* 81.4 (1986) 337-47.

texts, although produced chiefly by and for a male elite, betray a keen awareness of problems inherent in asymmetrical class and gender relations and consequently offer enlightening examples of the kind of dissonances secretly embedded in discourses on power. At the same time, a more sophisticated critical and pedagogical interest in authors previously slighted because of their primary focus on the private rather than the public realm—Sappho, Apollonius of Rhodes, Petronius and Apuleius, to name a few—has resulted in their increasingly widespread classroom use. Consequently, the so-called "classical canon" has now been broadened to include texts that make a direct, engaging appeal to the personal experiences and the concerns of working-class, female, and non-white college students.

In view of the attack presently being mounted on the standard classical canon by feminist and minority scholars outside the discipline, the development of the "New Humanities" has patently come just in time. As a next step, we must now bring those revisionist readings, readings that attempt to make works of Greco-Roman literature pertinent to the lives of a broader spectrum of students, to the attention of our radical academic colleagues in order to counter their charges that classics is an elitist and irrelevant subject. To overcome their hostility and convince them of the educational value of our texts, we will have to speak in the language of academic radicalism, which is theory. It is obvious, then, that for classicists, especially those at second-tier institutions, theory will continue to be as indispensable as rhetoric. In fact, the linkage between the two is reciprocal: if rhetoric provides the theorist with a firm foundation for exegetical inquiry, theory in turn has the potential to teach the rhetorician that aesthetic appreciation cannot be divorced from political awareness and that no text is composed, read or taught in a historical vacuum.

In taking Johnson's statements about reading, pleasure and theory at face value I may, however, have mistaken their intent. Permit me, if you will, to redeploy Charles Segal's intriguing concept of "boundary anxiety" along lines suggested by Frederick Ahl's responsive effort to apply it to the behaviors of our scholarly "guild." It is possible that Johnson's apocalyptic pronouncements are really metaphors for a sense of alienation—codes, that is, for articulating a malaise felt by certain members of the humanistic disciplines during this transitional period in American higher education, when the approach of a new, uncertain millenium seems to coincide with an extensive modification of traditional educational goals. In institutions where classical studies retains some of its old prestige, those changes are often perceived as a repudiation of former standards and lamented through nostalgic invocations of a vanished past and dystopic prophecies of future cultural collapse.

But we must be realistic and practical. The new breed of students— marginally prepared and, for the most part, far less committed to learning— will not go away, and if we classicists still take ourselves seriously as educators, we will have to modify our instructional methods and materials to accommodate them. What is more, the pressing problems facing our discipline are the business of us all. They will not be solved by pedagogues battling in the trenches while the dynasts of the profession retire to their crenellated Gothic towers and pull up the drawbridge: what is happening today in the classics program at Northern Illinois may happen at Texas within ten years, and begin to be felt at Chicago shortly after that. (Harvard can probably hold out for twenty years—they have a large endowment.) So perhaps it is time to forgo these keenings for the death of pleasure and the closing of the national mind. They are clarion calls to retreat.

In conclusion, I too would like to make one positive recommendation about the future direction of American classical studies; like Johnson's, it concerns graduate training. Granted that most new Ph.D.'s in classics will wind up teaching at places like Northern, how should those of you involved with major American doctoral programs prepare your students for such careers? As far as curriculum goes, perhaps a compromise is in order. Let them learn rhetoric, as Johnson advises. By all means, acquaint them with theory as well. But arm them, in addition, with skills more valuable than a mere knowledge of rhetoric, or theory, or any other block of information. Give them a sense of mission. Give them real, not token, classroom training. Above all, do not give them to understand that their professional lives are disposable because they will not be hired by a research institution. After describing the elitist operations of a two-tier system in classics, Edmunds observes that such elitism is not structural, but instead resides in "the attitude of the upper toward the lower tier."[15] That attitude has to change. What is happening out there in the provinces is too important to be dismissed as the job of losers, for it will play a large part in deciding whether classics survives into the twenty-first century.

Implicated so deeply in the hierarchical, agonistic mindset of past decades, our profession has spent tremendous energy trying to settle "whose team is No. 1" and who amongst us is "best of the Achaeans." The cost has

[15]   Edmunds (above, note 3) xiv.

been terrible: the virtual abdication of good teaching as a serious professional concern; the demoralization of a large number of our colleagues; and now, perhaps, from the evidence of Johnson's paper, feelings of disorientation even among the once proud few as the towers crumble and the ground shifts beneath their feet. It is time to give some thought to the rest of the Achaeans: to acknowledge their difficulties, celebrate their accomplishments, support their endeavors. If you, the representatives of the elite institutions, vouchsafe to do that, I promise that the rhetoric and the ideology, together with the theories, the philologies, and even the allegories, will eventually combine to produce a more comprehensive awareness of the past, and a heightened sense of the multiple reading pleasures it can afford us.

GRECIAN WONDERS AND ROMAN WOE: The Romantic Rejection of Rome and its Consequences for the Study of Latin Literature

The calling of this conference is evidence enough of the successful challenge to conventional interpretive strategies raised by the "theory revolution" in literary studies over the past few decades. Despite the implied opposition between hermeneutics, or theory, and empiricism, no Latinists, not even those who claim to be mere empiricists, can pretend to engage in an a-theoretical or un-ideological approach to literature. Indeed, the loss of innocence and public confession thereof have come to constitute a rite of passage for members of our profession. During such a period of paradigm shift in the history of a discipline it is useful to reflect on the origins of the paradigm that is being challenged. Awareness of the considerations that led our scholarly predecessors to construct the discipline in a particular way gives us a clearer picture of what we stand to lose and what we might hope to gain as we pursue the dictates of our new-found critical self-consciousness.

The key term in the development of Latin literary studies, as Professor Zetzel rightly observed in the opening paper of this conference, is "Romanticism." Whereas Zetzel regards the widespread use of the term, often in a way bordering on invective, as reason to dispense with it as a means of differentiating among critical stances, I would like to emphasize the historical and intellectual appropriateness of the term "Romantic" as a description of the assumptions and strategies shared by various conventional approaches to Latin literature. Latinists cringe when called Romantics not because the accusation is tiresome, but because it is true. Like most professional humanists, we are Romantics by pedigree and by predisposition. The modern university, in which criticism of Latin literature is still by and large carried out, is the product of the late German Romantic period, and most academicians, at least to some degree, fancy themselves inhabitants of a realm designed to realize the Romantic ideal of the aesthetic, a place where purer motives might expel the coarse instincts and base passions that supposedly characterize the other professions. While Romantic legacy is a mixed blessing for all humanists, its costs have been particularly acute for Latinists, for, as I shall argue, the construction of classical studies that arose during and immediately following the Romantic period involved the creation of a hierarchy between Greece and

Rome that privileged the former and denigrated the latter, and that worked, in particular, to aestheticize the study of Latin literature, removing it from a connection with Roman culture that might have made clear its relevance and intrinsic interest to contemporary society. Rome was suspect to the romantics for a variety of reasons, and if Latin literature was to be preserved as an area of study, it had to be removed as far as possible from the culture that enabled its production. Recognizing the suppression of Rome that lies at the heart of our discipline can make it easier for Latinists to accept the challenge of refashioning the discipline to respond to and take advantage of changes in the contemporary intellectual and social environment, and can also suggest some directions in which that refashioning might proceed.

Martin Bernal's book *Black Athena: The Afroasiatic Roots of Classical Civilization* advances the argument that the invention of modern notions of Greek history and culture by late eighteenth and early nineteenth century German Romantic writers was a process of exclusion and suppression as much as it was one of discovery and articulation.[1] Bernal's concern is with the exclusion of Semitic and Egyptian or African contributions to ancient Mediterranean civilization, but he could have written with equal zeal about the suppression of Rome. Winckelmann, who is the key figure in Bernal's account, went to Rome in more ways than one, becoming a Catholic, a priest, and librarian to Cardinal Albani, but he did so in order to have access to the treasures of his beloved Hellas. His notions of classicism and of a distinctively Greek artistic genius stand in marked contrast to the work of Montfauçon who just a generation earlier (1719-24 versus 1764) could present all of European art from antiquity through the Renaissance as part of a coherent generic and symbolic system.[2]

By the end of the eighteenth and beginning of the nineteenth centuries the paradigm shift evident in Winckelmann's neo-Hellenism had found expression in literary and historical studies as well. I take as a particularly subtle and sophisticated representative of this movement Friedrich Schiller's essay on "Naive and Sentimental Poetry," in which, among other things, we

1   Martin Bernal, *Black Athena: The Afroasiatic Roots of Classical Civilization*. Vol. 1: *The Fabrication of Ancient Greece 1785-1985* (New Brunswick 1987).
2   Winckelmann lived from 1717 to 1768. His *History of Ancient Art* was published in 1764. Bernard de Montfauçon's work *L'antiquité expliquée et representée en figures* appeared in five volumes 1719 to 1724. Cf. the concise remark of R. Pfeiffer, *History of Classical Scholarship from 1300 to 1850* (Oxford 1976) 170: "Only in the emulation of earlier masterpieces could new ones be created. Roman culture now appeared to be no more than an approach to that of Greece." I owe the reference to Montfauçon to Professor Daniel Selden.

learn that "even Rome in all its splendour, except it be transfigured by the imagination, is a limited greatness, and therefore a subject unworthy of poetry, which, raised above every trace of the actual, ought only to mourn over what is infinite."[3] Schiller's criticism is aimed at Ovid's exile poetry, and there is a specific point being made about the transcendent power of the imagination; but it is characteristic of Schiller's rhetoric that the negative example is drawn from Latin literature, and not from the writing of the Greeks, whose "impatient imagination," we are told, "only traverses nature to pass beyond it to the drama of human life. It [this Greek imagination] only takes pleasure in the spectacle of what is living and free."[4]

In a recent essay Paul Alpers has documented the persistence and vitality of Schiller's formulations in the criticism of pastoral poetry;[5] one can go further and trace the survival of Schiller's categories and hierarchies in criticism of Latin literature generally. To take but one example, a recent work on Vergil's *Georgics,* by a scholar who has himself taken issue with the romantic tendency in Latin literary criticism, begins with an *apologia* constructed around a set of oppositions characteristic of Schiller's text:

> Virgil is by no means an easy poet. The *Odyssey* is read by school children, and the *Iliad* can be understood by the average college student more easily and (I think) more accurately than any other work of classical literature likely to be encountered in survey courses. The *Aeneid,* however, often seems tedious and mechanical to these same students and more often than not frustrates the lecturer who tries to convey to a general audience some idea of the depth and beauty of Virgil's verse and the poem's profound power over mind and emotions.[6]

Even as the modern scholar seeks to defend the study of Vergil against a Romantic longing for the simple and the heroic, he reinforces Schiller's

---

3   Quotation is from Friedrich Schiller, *Aesthetical and Philosophical Essays*, edited by Nathan Haskell Dole, Volume 5.2 (London 1902) 12. Schiller lived 1759-1805. "Naive and Sentimental Poetry" was published in 1795-96; Schiller's correspondence with Goethe had begun in 1794.
4   Schiller (above n. 3) 5.1, 296.
5   Paul Alpers, "Schiller and the Modern Ideal of Pastoral," *Cabinet of the Muses: Essays in Classical and Comparative Literature in Honor of Thomas G. Rosenmeyer,* ed. M. Griffith and D.J. Mastronarde (Atlanta 1990).
6   D.O. Ross, *Virgil's Elements: Physics and Poetry in the Georgics* (Princeton 1987) 3.

oppositions between childhood and adulthood, Greek and Roman, emotion and reason, the special soul and the run-of-the-mill general public, with their implicit privileging of the former over the latter in each pair. The tedious and mechanical nature of the *Aeneid*, we learn, is a matter of appearances—the implication being that in reality the poem merits some such Schillerian laudatory epithets as "vital" and "organic." The momentary put-down of the Greek epics as fit for children, or at least college students, turns out to be an expression of the writer's failed ambition to make the Latin poem available to precisely such readers. Even the tone of frustrated melancholy that pervades the passage evokes Schiller's opposition, complete with erotic connotations, between the "scholastic spirit" that "enervates and blunts thought in order not to wound the reader" and "genius," wherein "expression gushes forth spontaneously from the idea," and "the spirit appears as if disclosed in a nude state."[7] The interpreter of Vergil presents himself as doomed to an enervated scholasticism while he longs for the joyous escapism associated with the Greeks.

The connection between Schiller and much recent criticism of Latin literature is not merely one of analogy. The characteristics that Schiller admired and that he and others identified with the Greeks were sought in Roman history by its earliest professional investigators. If Rome had no Schiller to unveil its spirit, it at least found a voice in the person of Berthold Niebuhr, who began lecturing at von Humboldt's newly established University of Berlin in 1810, a few years after Schiller's premature death.[8] The focus of Niebuhr's energy, however, was history, not literature, and specifically the history of early Rome with its folksongs, its *ager publicus*, its tribunes speaking in defense of a free and loyal peasantry, and its non-violent resolution of social conflict. Rome had remained independent longer than Greece, hence was from a strictly political standpoint a more appropriate paradigm for incipient nationalism, but instead of the suffocating, bureaucratized, and over-extended Rome of the Empire, Niebuhr and his disciples turned to early Rome, "young, vigorous, and hoping for a bright future."[9] Bernal reminds us that "Romantics longed for small, virtuous, and 'pure' communities in remote and cold places: Switzerland, North Germany, and Scotland"[10] and marvels at

---

7   Schiller (above n. 3) 5.1, 291-292.
8   R. Pfeiffer (above n. 2) 184ff. Cf. Zvi Yavetz, "Why Rome? Zeitgeist and Ancient Historians in Early 19th Century Germany," *AJP* 97 (1976) 276-296.
9   Yavetz (above n. 8) 295.
10   Bernal (above n. 2) 209.

their ability to transform Greece with its hot climate and seaward orientation into an ancient Switzerland. Niebuhr and others of the first generation of post-Romantic scholars performed the less imaginative, albeit equally influential, feat of transferring the Tiber to the Elbe.

But it was another instance of geographical legerdemain that had the profoundest impact on American classical studies, and thus on American Latinists: Basil Lanneau Gildersleeve's ability to see in the ancient Greeks prototypes of his beloved antebellum Southerners and eventually of all Americans resisting the homogenization and mongrelization of their society.[11] In an essay entitled "A Southerner in the Peloponnesian War,"[12] Gildersleeve manages to ascribe to the Confederacy the best qualities of both the Spartans and the Athenians, depending on whether he is emphasizing Southern resistance to Northern commercial power, or the bravery of the Southern homefront in the face of widespread hunger and privation: "The Northern Union, represented by Athens, was a naval power. The Southern Confederacy, under the leadership of Sparta, was a land power;"[13] but it was in the South, as in Aristophanes, that "hunger was the dominant note of life."[14] In "The Limits of Culture," written in 1867, Gildersleeve concluded his attack on progressive educators with a passage linking their criticism of classical education to the recent Yankee invasion of the South:

> We of the South have little left except our system of higher education, and it is our duty to meet the assault that [the North] is making on it—an assault which is a part of the grand attempt to crush all individuality of development into a homogeneous centralization. Already do we see the snares spread; already is the 'vast slave-net of mischief' preparing to draw all the educational institutions of the country into the meshes of a West Point system. In a few years the Minister of Public Instruction will send out his sergeants to drill the free citizens of this republic into passive tools

11 On Gildersleeve's life and contribution to American classical studies see the collection of laudatory essays entitled *Basil Lanneau Gildersleeve: An American Classicist*, ed. W.W. Briggs, Jr. and H.W. Benario, *AJP* Classical Monographs 1 (Baltimore 1986). W.W. Briggs, Jr. has also prepared a collection of Gildersleeve's letters: *The Letters of Basil Lanneau Gildersleeve* (Baltimore 1987).
12 The essay was originally published in the *Atlantic Monthly*, September 1897, and was reprinted in Basil L. Gildersleeve, *The Creed of the Old South: 1865-1915* (Baltimore 1915) 53-103.
13 Gildersleeve, *Creed of the Old South* (above n. 12) 73.
14 Gildersleeve, *Creed of the Old South* (above n. 12) 91.

of a great central power; and we can well understand why studies which stir so many earnest doubts of our present condition should be thrust into the background, so that none but dreamers may think of the wonders which Greek autonomy wrought or of the immeasurable woe which was the price of Roman unity and the cause of Roman ruin."[15]

Gildersleeve's view of Greece as positive exemplum, Rome as negative; Greece as the freedom-loving South, Rome as the domineering North was reinforced, perhaps even generated, by his fondness for the German Romantic writers. The editor of Gildersleeve's letters pictures him as entering the Civil War in response to "the call of Goethe,"[16] and Gildersleeve himself describes how he discussed Faust with a fellow officer moments before the latter was felled by a Yankee bullet.[17] Gildersleeve's Romanticism is especially evident in his fondness for heroes who have dedicated themselves to hopeless causes. "Are we such strangers to faithfulness that we cannot understand how men can be true to a cause foredoomed?" wrote Gildersleeve in a spirited appreciation of the recently assassinated emperor Maximilian of Mexico.[18] Gildersleeve likens Maximilian to Julian the Apostate (himself the subject of another lengthy eulogy),[19] calling one "the Romanticist on the throne of the Caesars," the other "the Romanticist on the throne of the Montezumas."[20] "In the month of June, the chivalric Emperor of Mexico fell with his faithful followers. In the month of June, the chivalric Caesar fell for his. Yet few mourned for the one; how many are sorrowing for the other."[21] Even in his defense of Latin as a field of study, at the conclusion of his address marking the tenth anniversary of Johns Hopkins, Gildersleeve resorts to a doubly Romantic argument, telling the

15   Basil L. Gildersleeve, *Essays and Studies: Educational and Literary* (Baltimore 1890) 3-40. An authorial note gives 1867 as the date of composition of the passage quoted in the text.
16   W.W. Briggs, Jr. "Basil L. Gildersleeve at the University of Virginia," in *Basil Lanneau Gildersleeve* (above 1) 10-20 (quotation from p. 15). Briggs goes on to state "Certainly he [Gildersleeve] may have needed a pocket Goethe less than a pocket Homer, for he appears to have nearly everything the German master wrote committed to memory." (p. 15).
17   "The Creed of the Old South" first published in *Atlantic Monthly* January 1892, reprinted in Gildersleeve, *The Creed of the Old South* (Baltimore 1915) 7-52. The episode referred to in the text is described pp. 12-15.
18   "Maximilian: His Travels and His Tragedy," *Essays and Studies* (above n. 15) 453-496 (quotation from p. 480) although the volume was published in 1890, an authorial note gives 1868 as the year of composition of the memoir of Maximilian.
19   *Essays and Studies* (above n. 15) 355-400.
20   "Maximilian," *Essays and Studies* (above n. 15), 494.
21   "Maximilian," *Essays and Studies* (above n. 15) 495-96.

story of a professor whose lecture on the vanishing of weak vowels in Latin managed to connect "the disappearance of the vowel with the downfall of a nationality . . . [G]reat linguistic, great moral, great historical laws marched in stately procession before the vision of the student, the airy vowels that had flitted into Nowhere seemed to be the lost soul of Roman life."[22] The Romantic assumption that the story of Rome *is* the story of loss coincides with the Hegelian claim that grammar grants access to a race's spirit.[23]

With allusions to lost greatness and to the innate spirit of a race, Gildersleeve's Romantic preference for Greece over Rome takes on a more sinister cast. Roman unity comes at the price of immeasurable woe and leads to ruin; yet earlier in the same essay "the old Greeks" are praised for holding on to their myths, thereby refusing "to break up the unity of their national life."[24] Unity alone cannot be the culprit in Rome's demise; nor, in light of the Greek history of intra- and inter-state strife, can the Romans be regarded as having an ancient monopoly on woe. What, then, makes Rome the target of criticism?

A set of passages in Gildersleeve's eulogy for Maximilian suggests a possible answer. Near the end of that work, Gildersleeve refers to Napoleon's plan of installing Maximilian as emperor of Mexico as evidence of a scheme "to restore to the Latin race on this side of the water its power and prestige, and so to check the invasions of the Anglo-Saxons."[25] He calls attention to the irony implicit in the use of "the most thoroughly German prince in Europe"[26] to carry out this scheme, then expatiates on the differences among Germans, Frenchmen, and other nationalities, in both his own view and that of Maximilian. "Frenchmen," we learn, "are not good judges of race, and show an incredible philosophy in the matter of amalgamation. Those nations that keep their blood pure, that refuse to blend with an inferior stock, are those that are destined to the mastery; and 'Latin' America owes most of its misery to the degradation of race."[27] There follows reference to a section of Maximilian's memoirs which describes "a strikingly handsome" Peruvian youth who, in

---

[22] "On the Present Aspect of Classical Study," delivered at Johns Hopkins April 26, 1886, printed in *Essays and Studies* (above n. 15) 500-508. Quotation from pp. 507-508.

[23] On the significance of this Hegelian notion for the institutionalization of language study in American universities, see the brief discussion by G. Graff, *Professing Literature: An Institutional History* (Chicago 1987) 28ff.

[24] "Limits of Culture," *Essays and Studies* (above n. 15) 24f.

[25] "Maximilian," *Essays and Studies* (above n. 15) 481.

[26] *Ibid.*

[27] *Ibid.*, p. 487.

Gildersleeve's words, exhibits a racial "combination which a Frenchman like Michelet might admire, which the good sense of a man of Germanic stock can regard only as a curiosity not deserving of repetition."[28] Gildersleeve's comment on the ethnographic *monstrum* continues: "But we of the United States are fast developing in this direction, and if reports tell the truth, the crosses in California of Indian, Chinese, Negro, Kelt and Anglo-Saxon promise results which will throw utter contempt upon Maximilian's specimen of mixed breed."[29] Empire, especially an empire dominated by foolish members of a Latin race, promotes the mingling of racial stocks, and such mingling leads to degradation and "misery." A related thought is applied to literature in a passage from the anniversary address that closely precedes the elegy for the lost vowels: " . . . I am not at all shaken by the self-satisfied edicts of those who rule so large a portion of the reading world, and I maintain with unwavering confidence that all healthy literature must be kept in communion, direct or indirect, with the highest exemplars of our Indo-European stock; and if anything could prove the necessity of a return to healthy human nature, with its compassed form, its fair red and white, it would be the utter wearisomeness of so much recent fine writing, in which there is no blood, no sap, nothing but division and subdivision of nerve-tissue. 'A pagan suckled in a creed outworn' is a joy and delight in comparison with the languid, invertebrate children of the great goddess Anaemia."[30] The unity that led to the loss of Roman soul was a unity, or mingling, of races, cultures, languages, and religions that stands in marked contrast to the preservation of distinctive national identity that Gildersleeve associates with the autonomous Greeks. The facts of Roman history were too obvious to permit it to serve the needs of those who sought ancient precedent for their own quest for national and cultural identity.

In his anxiety over the mingling and dilution of races and cultures Gildersleeve was a man of his times. The historian John Higham, in his classic study of American nativism, describes the varieties of "racial thinking" that circulated in nineteenth-century America.[31] One sort, predominantly literary and cultural in expression made a "vague identification of culture with ancestry [that] served mainly to emphasize the antiquity, the uniqueness, and the permanence of a nationality. It suggested the inner vitality of one's own

---

28   *Ibid.*
29   *Ibid.*, p. 488.
30   "Present State," *Essays and Studies* (above n. 15) 504.
31   John Higham, *Strangers in the Land: Patterns of American Nativism 1860-1925* (Westport, CT, 1981) [reprint of corrected edition (New Brunswick 1963)] 131ff.

culture, rather than the menace of another race."[32]   A second type, which expressed itself in a form of scientific discourse, focused on physical differences between races, often, but not exclusively, from a perspective of white superiority over other groups. The melding of these two types of "race-thinking," supplemented by a Darwinian focus on the survival of the fittest, produced a third, more potent ideology that explained in natural, "scientific" terms, the superiority of one race over another and was accompanied by deep anxiety over the mingling of races and consequent diluting of the strength of the superior race. Gildersleeve's writings show traces of all three types, ranging from the ascription of specific characteristics to members of different nationalities (e.g., the "slowness of Englishmen"[33] and the "want of personal cleanliness" attributable to Orientals)[34] to the medical metadiscussion of healthy versus enervated literature to the express concern over the blending of Anglo-Saxon with inferior stock—an early instance of Eastern fear of Californian innovations.

If for Gildersleeve the connection between ancient Rome and modern empire, ancient Greece and cultural purity was a matter of historical analogy, for others of his time the association was more direct. The practices of the ancient Roman heathens, as taken over by the Popes at Rome, had, in the view of American nativist propagandists of the 1850's, deformed Biblical Christianity;[35] hence contemporary Catholicism, with its suspect condemnation of slavery, its supposed insistence on dual political loyalties, and most important, its ability within the United States to forge an alliance between aristocratic descendants of early colonists and the masses of working-class immigrants could be treated as the obvious antagonist—political, social, and cultural—of Americans eager to protect their own embattled identity.[36] The

---

[32]   Higham (above n. 31) 133.

[33]   Letter to D.C. Gilman, dated 12/20/1875, published in *Letters of B.L. Gildersleeve* (above n. 11) 57.

[34]   Letter to D.C. Gilman, dated 6/30/1880, published in *Letters of B.L. Gildersleeve* (above n. 11) 112. Gildersleeve's letters are peppered with insults based on national origin. His view of unique national characteristics formed part of his public discourse as well: indeed, he argued for the likelihood of a significant American contribution to classical philology on the grounds that "an audacious, inventive, ready-witted people, Americans often comprehend the audacious, inventive, ready-witted Greek à demi-mot, while the German professor phrases, and the English 'don' rubs his eyes, and the savant appreciates the wrong half" ("University Work in America and Classical Philology," reprinted in *Essays and Studies* [above n. 15] 85-123, quotation from p. 105).

[35]   See R.A. Billington, *The Protestant Crusade, 1800-1860: A Study of the Origins of American Nativism* (New York 1938), chapter entitled "The Literature of Anti-Catholicism."

[36]   See the discussion of sources of Anti-Catholicism in the article "Nativism, American" in *New Catholic Encyclopedia* (Washington, D.C. 1967) vol. 10, pp. 245-250.

Romantic intellectual's disdain for ancient Rome and anxiety over the spread of a "Latin" empire thus marked the transition between a slightly earlier popular discourse in which "Rome" constituted the symbolic opposite of "America" and an emerging obsession with the diluted racial purity of American society.

Neither Gildersleeve's moral character nor the place of religious and ethnic minorities in nineteenth-century America is the issue here. My concern is to expose and analyze the ideological context in which the profession took its present shape, especially as regards the relative significance (or insignificance) attributed to Latin literary studies, and to consider the extent to which supposedly discarded ideology continues to affect the profession's representation of itself and its aims. It seems clear that in the early stages of American classical studies, at least as represented in the career and writings of Gildersleeve, the privileging of Greece over Rome was part of a larger, significantly more complicated project involving the emergence of national identity, the search for ancient prototypes of modern peoples, an essentialist view of the relationship between language and culture, the creation of an aesthetic realm within culture, and the self-aggrandizing heroization of supporters of doomed causes. Greece triumphed over Rome because it better served the needs of intellectuals, especially those who saw themselves as spokesmen for emerging, or, in Gildersleeve's case, embattled cultural identities. As in the writings of his Romantic intellectual forebears, so in the work of Gildersleeve, the relative evaluation of Greece and Rome is largely the product of contemporary hopes and anxieties.

In light of the comfortable fit between Gildersleeve's prejudices and the larger concerns of American society, it should come as no surprise that his construction of the profession survived him. Indeed, one of the most intriguing aspects of the story of Roman studies in America is the extent to which Latinists have acquiesced in their own subordination. Like colonized peoples everywhere, we have tended to mimic, even to exaggerate, the discourse and attitudes of the metropolitan power. In Roman studies that has meant the constant retreat into an ever more remote and esoteric version of the field, a shrinkage of the literary canon and of the methods applied to it, and adoption of self-defeating principles of pedagogy and scholarship. Niebuhr was not the last to seek in Rome the qualities admired in Greece.

On this matter, a single historical example must again suffice. In the late 1950's and early 1960's it must have seemed as if the literary study of Latin was at last coming into its own. The battle between critics and scholars that had been waged earlier within Departments of English was played out anew among classicists. Bernard Knox's essay on the imagery of the second book of the *Aeneid*,[37] although written by a scholar generally viewed as a Hellenist, and Steele Commager's work on Horace[38] seemed to offer a new way of talking about Roman poetry that was bound to the text without limiting the imagination of the interpreter. Again, as with Gildersleeve's professionalization of American classical studies, this revolution in critical studies, too, was prompted by unarticulated ideological considerations that from the vantage point of hindsight can only be regarded as problematical. On the one hand, the work of America's literary Latinists continued and developed the efforts of post-war European scholars like Curtius and Pöschl,[39] who sought to universalize the implications of classical Roman texts as a way of establishing literature as a force that could humanize and even transcend the terrifying world of national and racial hatred.[40] Equally important, however, was the example of the American New Critics of the 1930's, who for all their purported anti-Romanticism[41] nonetheless reinforced the view of literature as a realm independent of society and ideology in to which only the privileged few could enter. In the words of Roger Fowler, the writings of these New Critics "are an apologia for a privileged and unproductive elite, they deny literature any social responsibility, they mystify the practice of writing."[42]

Fowler's critique makes no mention of efforts to translate New Critical theory into a democratized pedagogy, bringing explication to the masses of middle-class college students. But his diagnosis of the attempt to split literature from society and of the mystification involved in much New Critical interpretation and terminology rings true for the Critics of English and American poetry as well as for their Latinist progeny. In the first few paragraphs alone of Commager's groundbreaking study of Horace we find an insistence on the importance of technique at the expense of meaning, reference to the "covenant" (restrictive, perhaps?) between critic and poet, and such tantalizingly oracular proclamations as "[Horace's] poems record only an

---

[37] B.M.W. Knox, "The Serpent and the Flame," *AJP* 71 (1950) 379-400, reprinted in *Virgil: A Collection of Critical Essays*, ed. S. Commager (Englewood Cliffs 1966) 124-142.
[38] S. Commager, *The Odes of Horace: A Critical Study* (New Haven 1962).
[39] E.R. Curtius, *Europäische Literatur und lateinisches Mittelalter* (Bern 1948); V. Pöschl, *Die Dichtkunst Virgils* (Innsbruck 1950). English translations were published in 1953 and 1962 respectively.
[40] On Curtius' aims, see F. Lentricchia, *Criticism and Social Change* (Chicago 1983) 127-28. On Pöschl, see the discussion of W.R. Johnson, *Darkness Visible* (Berkeley 1976).
[41] David Daiches, *The New Criticism*, Aquila Essays Number 5 (Portree, Scotland 1982).
[42] R. Fowler, *Literature as Social Discourse: The Practice of Linguistic Criticism* (Bloomington 1981) 55.

imaginative apprehension of the world" or "an *Ode's* meaning . . . inheres in the sounds, the figures, the tone, the emotional coloring."[43] Language of this sort illustrates what one writer has called New Criticism's tendency to resort to "declaration of literary infallibility" and to become a "technique by which literature is actually protected from criticism."[44] Or again, in an introduction to a collection of essays on Vergil, we encounter the New Critical assertion that "The *Eclogues*, despite their contemporary political and social allusions, are essentially an attempt to substitute a world of imagination for that of fact."[45] Such a view of literature and of the critic's role as a kind of *Doppelgänger* of the poet lays claim to the seductive vision of an aesthetic realm propounded by Romantics such as Schiller, without Schiller's refreshingly honest recognition of the political and social implications of his teachings.

The study of Roman culture, and of Latin literature in its relation to that culture, has thus been characterized by a prolonged process of self-dismemberment. The first limb to go, it would appear, was chronological extension. Greece had a classical period, so Rome needed one as well, and it should come as no surprise that Augustine and Prudentius lost out to Vergil and Cicero. But Cicero was hopelessly enmeshed in the culture of his time, a representative of an outmoded humanism that had been replaced by ideals of the aesthetic, and so he, along with Seneca, Quintilian, and others could be relegated to the task of teaching writers of the modern languages a clear understanding of linguistic structure.[46] The historians could remain, but only as historians: after all, someone had to bear witness to Rome's immeasurable woe. What remained was compact and homogeneous enough to be no threat to the Greeks and bear no resemblance to Papist Rome or Latin empire, but it was still not sufficiently polished to attain to classical standards of excellence. And so the canon was reduced further: in the words of Gildersleeve, "Away with Marcus Manilius, Valerius Flaccus, Silius Italicus . . . we earnestly hope that

---

43   Commager, *Odes of Horace* (above n. 38) pp. vii and viii.

44   G. Graff, "The University and the Prevention of Culture," in *Criticism in the University*, ed. G. Graff and R. Gibbons (Evanston 1985) 62-82 (quotation from p. 72).

45   S. Commager in *Virgil: A Collection of Critical Essays* (above n. 37) 2.

46   See Gildersleeve's remarks in "Limits of Culture," *Essays and Studies* (above n. 15) 24ff. It is interesting to note that when Gildersleeve accepted the Chair of Greek at Hopkins, it was with the stipulation that he not teach students below the senior undergraduate level. A Latinist was found to offer elementary instruction in both Greek and Latin. See H. Benario, "The Foundation of Johns Hopkins and the First Faculty," in *Basil Lanneau Gildersleeve* (above n. 11) 21-35. Gildersleeve's letters to President Gilman of Hopkins during his overseas trip to find a suitable Latinist for the faculty make suggestive reading. Gildersleeve has some objection or worry concerning every possible appointee. The attempt to recruit a Latinist in Europe seems doomed from the start. See *Letters* (above n. 11) 89ff.

professors of Latin do not generally deem themselves bound to read, as poor
Addison considered himself bound to quote, these vapid productions . . ."[47]
Now at last we had our perfect Greek torso of classical Latin poetry: unless,
of course, some of these Latin poets actually seemed to have and—worse—to
express a vested interest in the power relations inscribed in Roman politics and
society. What if they were implicated, embedded, compromised? Well then,
out with the fourth book of Horace's *Odes* and of Propertius' elegies (hadn't
Aristotle privileged the number three anyway?); farewell to the second half of
the *Aeneid*; goodbye to Aristaeus in the fourth book of the *Georgics*—that
poem ends, as nearly everyone but Vergil seems to know, with the death of
Orpheus and not the rebirth of the bees or the praise of Caesar.[48]

Even the organization of this conference exemplifies the tendency to
limit, rather than expand, the horizons of study. Invitations were issued under
the working title of "Roman Literature: Current Trends and Future
Prospects," suggesting an open-ended opportunity to reflect upon the state of
the field and to articulate the various points of conflict as well as consensus
among diverse representatives of the profession. As plans were formalized this
admirable goal was reduced and restricted, partly, one imagines, for practical
reasons, but also, I suspect, because of the longstanding Romantic tendency to
limit, marginalize, and aestheticize Roman studies. Literature became poetry,
and "current trends" became a reductionist opposition between empiricism and
hermeneutics. Gerald Graff has written that American universities strive to
minimize intellectual conflict, to hide it behind closed doors, and the same can
be said for professional societies and academic conferences.[49] In this respect,
we Latinists are no different from other members of the academic community.
Like Gildersleeve and our other Romantic predecessors, we fear that
mongrelization means loss of identity, that the public exposure of diverse and
seemingly incompatible heritages will destroy the myth of solidarity and
weaken us before our foes. If we are treated with disdain by others in the
humanities, and isolated from the larger discourse developing outside
Departments of Classics, it is because we have chosen such isolation for
ourselves, preferring the coolness and purity of Switzerland to the heat and
diversity of Rome.

---

[47] "Limits of Culture" in *Essays and Studies* (above n. 15) 8.
[48] T.N. Habinek, "Sacrifice, Society, and Vergil's Ox-Born Bees," in *Cabinet of the Muses* (above n. 5) 209-223.
[49] G. Graff, *Professing Literature* (above n. 23) 247ff.

To describe the ideological underpinnings of the works of Winckelmann and Schiller, Niebuhr and Gildersleeve, Curtius and Commager, is to engage in neither praise nor blame but to make some attempt at understanding. The view of classical literature and culture that these men developed responded to pressures, anxieties, and needs of their respective eras. The Romantic movement's emphasis on the reformative power of literature was a response to the perceived chaos of the French Revolution; its vision of liberation through classical studies is a highly charged one in the context of the Napoleonic Wars. Gildersleeve's *apologia* for slaveowners and his concern for racial purity fall on deaf ears today, but his anxieties about bureaucratic centralization and the leveling of all cultural differences are scarcely to be dismissed out of hand. The Romanticism these men developed was an ideology for its time; but their time is not our time and to hold fast to their views and to the patterns of professional behavior that they established is not a tribute to them, but a betrayal of their engagement in their own social and political environments.

What, then, might an un-Romantic Roman studies, or to borrow Karl Galinsky's term, a "postmodern" Roman studies look like? Instead of focusing on a narrow chronological band, it would surely embrace the broad sweep of Latin literature, and attend to the continuities—as well as discontinuities—in form and theme between various eras of pagan as well as Christian Latin. No longer would it enforce arbitrary and anachronistic barriers between poetry and prose, or history and literature. The terms "Roman" and "intellectual history" would come to seem redundant, rather than oxymoronic as they are treated today. There would be a genuine engagement with ancient culture, in all of its manifestations: religion, sexuality, social structure to name a few, not as a way of reinforcing the categorical distinction between literature and "real life," but in an attempt to understand the ways in which pressures—ideological, material, and personal—operate on literary texts and, concurrently, the ways in which literature works to create culture, to articulate or mystify privileges, to fossilize, naturalize, and at times even subvert the conditions that make its creation possible. An un-Romantic Roman studies would have no fear of theory, would never see an opposition between empiricism and hermeneutics or theory, recognizing as it would that empiricism itself is a theoretical construct created to meet the needs of a certain fraction at a certain moment in history. An un-Romantic Roman studies would embrace theory, not as a means of dispensing with ideology, but as a way of gaining perspective on it, dislodging it sufficiently to perceive its effects.[50] Finally, and perhaps most important, an un-Romantic Roman studies would struggle against its own institutionalization. Surely, the most important reason that Latinists today are Romantics is that the university as we know it is a Romantic institution, isolated from what Schiller calls the "evils of civilisation,"[51] full of individuals of "refined feeling,"[52] great souls set firmly on the path of individual contemplation. Compartmentalization of new approaches will simply repeat and extend the self-defeating pattern of isolation. Un-Romantic Latinists would seek more, rather than less contact with those outside the profession, and even within the charmed circle they would value collaboration, interaction, and open conflict as much as private and individualized achievement.

When an aristocrat of the Roman Republic wanted to know how he was regarded by the community at large, he turned to someone of lower rank rather than to a peer. This I take to be the social foundation of the institution of *amicitia*, as exemplified in Scipio's request that Polybius be with him always so that he might learn how to become worthy of his ancestors[53] or in Ennius' depiction of the good friend as one who listens unthreateningly to the hopes and anxieties of his more prominent acquaintance.[54] In the waning days of the Republic Cicero sought to revive the aristocracy by advancing a conception of friendship between equals.[55] One element of traditional, unequal friendship, however, he both maintained and highlighted: the insistence that a friend speak with complete candor. "But there is once cause of offence which must be encountered in order that the usefulness and loyalty of friendship be preserved; for friends frequently must be not only advised, but also rebuked, and both advice and rebuke should be kindly received when given in a spirit of goodwill . . . A troublesome thing is truth, if it is indeed the source of hate, which poisons friendship; but much more troublesome is obsequiousness, which by showing indulgence to [the sins of] a friend, allows him to be carried headlong

---

[50] Cf. the remarks of R. Fowler (above n. 24) 26: "Ideology cannot be removed. It can be replaced—by alternative. Criticism demonstrates that there are ideologies; compares their structural characteristics, their geneses, their consequences; cannot disperse them."
[51] Schiller (above n. 3) 5.1, 294.
[52] *Ibid.*, 278.
[53] Polybius, *Histories* 31.23-25.
[54] *The Annals of Q. Ennius*, ed. O. Skutsch (Oxford 1985) lines 268-287 with notes *ad loc.*
[55] T.N. Habinek, "Towards a History of Friendly Advice: The Politics of Candor in Cicero's *De Amicitia*," *Apeiron* 23 (1990).

away."[56] I trust that the foregoing mixture of admonition and rebuke will be taken in the Roman spirit of *amicitia* in which it is intended.

56   *Laelius* 88-89; Loeb translation with slight changes.

INDEX OF GREEK AND ROMAN AUTHORS

Aeschylus	126
Alcaeus	71, 108, 113
Anaximander	159
Apollonius	86, 129, 135, 224
Apuleius	60, 195, 224
Aratus	115
Aristophanes	231
Aristotle	104, 173, 200, 201, 202, 209, 211, 239
Augustine	60, 176, 187, 194, 238
Callimachus	34, 75, 84, 85, 86, 90, 91, 96, 108, 116, 118, 188
Catullus	26, 34, 43f., 46, 55f., 59, 111, 118, 131f., 157; (16), 60; (34), 48-50, 62-64; (51), 52f.; (68), 54; (85), 45; (101), 51f., 61.
Cicero	55, 160, 161, 172, 189, 194, 211, 238, 241
Claudian	165
Clement of Alexandria	84
Curtius	237, 240
Epicurus	137, 138, 139, 142, 143, 144, 145, 146, 148, 150, 152, 154, 155, 171, 172
Euripides	200
Dionysius of Halicarnassus	166
Festus	160, 161
Gallus	67, 85, 86, 87, 91, 116, 117, 131, 132, 133
Hesiod	159
Homer	4, 113, 166, 168, 183, 188, 205; *Odyssey*, 61; (*Il.* 19.418), 159
Homeric Hymns	84
Horace	2, 62, 173, 194, 201, 237, 239; (*Epode* 7), 159; (*C.* 3.30), 142; (*C.* 3.30.13f.), 29; (*Epist.* 2.1), 29, 113; (*A.P.* 268f.), 29; (*A.P.* 396-401), 30
Ilias Latina	182, 190
Juvenal	208, 212
Leonidas	128
Livy	66, 100, 186, 191
Lucan	153, 161, 162
Lucian	61, 122
Lucretius	35, 55, 115, 137-75, 194; (1.38f.), 148; (1.72-74), 144; (1.222f.), 143; (1.225f.), 139; ; (1.227f.), 143; (1.259-61), 143; (1.354f.), 148; (1.852), 139; (1.958-62), 160; (1.1028-34), 140; (1.1038-43),

141f.; (1.1102-10), 139; (2.7f.), 144; (2.645-60), 144; (2.1133-40), 140; (2.1145), 140; (2.1173), 144f.; (3.15f.), 145; (3.15-24), 161; (3.25-30), 144f.; (3.216-20), 140; (3.252-57), 140; (3.344-47), 147; (3.576f.), 148; (3.584f.), 140; (3.806-18), 141; (3.885-87), 151; (4.1016f.), 150; (4.1108-11), 151; (4.1120), 151; (5.73f.), 151; (5.97), 142; (5.99), 142; (5.259), 143; (5.305), 146; (5.346f.), 141; (5.351-63), 141; (5.466-70), 147; (5.777f.), 149; (5.990-93), 149f.; (5.1440)f.), 151f.; (6.121-23), 146; (6.121-23), 146; (6.772), 149; (6.951), 148; (6.954), 148; (6.955), 149; (6.958), 149; (6.1141-43), 149; (6.1151-53), 149

Macrobius   74, 81, 85, 87, 101
Martial   7
Menander Rhetor   20
Nicander   115, 135
Origo Gentis Romanae 70, 87
Ovid   29, 35, 45, 56, 99, 111, 120, 172, 176-199, 201, 229; *Heroides,* 117; *Metamorphoses,* 138, 153; (*Amores* 1.1), 134; (1.14), 46f.; (*A.A.* 3.346), 113; (*R.A.* 381), 119; (*Her.* 15), 119; (*Fasti* 1.147-58), 101; (1.543-86), 100; (2.8), 120; (2.126), 120; (4.836-48), 159; (*Met.* 1.151-62), 197; (1.452ff.), 107; (1.192ff.), 187; (1.533ff.), 187; (1.539), 187; (2.332), 185; (2.731f.), 125-29; (2.735f.), 125-29; (4.122ff.), 187; (Book 5), 180; (6.1ff.), 181; (9.454-665), 163; (Book 9), 192; (Book 10), 180f.; (10.1ff.), 183; (10.3), 184, 196; (10.5), 184; (10.10), 184; (10.11), 184; (10.12), 184; (10.22-24), 184, (10.40), 184, 196; (10.41-43), 184; (10.45), 184; (10.49), 184; (10.58), 196; (10.58f.), 184; (10.80f.), 185; (10.298-502), 163; (11.1ff.), 181; (11.591f..), 188; (12.39ff.), 188; (Book 14), 192; (Book 15), 181; (15.680-82), 199; (*Tristia* 2.427-30), 60
Pausanias   84
Persius   114
Petronius   195, 224
Pindar   71, 74, 97, 167; (*Paean* 6.1-6), 70; (7-8), 78; (6.9), 98; (7-11), 72; (12-18), 73; (13-14), 75; (58-65), 78; (122), 73; (128), 79; (*Ol.* 8.9f.), 76.
Plato   163, 166, 167, 168, 205

Plautus 126
Plutarch 138, 159, 160, 163, 172
Polybius 241
Propertius 34, 43, 46, 108, 113, 120, 124, 178, 194, 239;
(1.2), 47; (1.8.5ff.), 132; (2.1.3-4), 45; (2.12), 129;
(3.1.3), 108; (3.1.6), 108; (3.3), 118; (3.3.5), 108);
(3.3.51f.), 108; (3.5), 118; (4.1.135), 118; (4.6),
91; (4.9) 65-103; (4.9.13f.), 73; (4.9.15-18), 73;
(4.9.16-20), 69; (4.9.21), 84; (4.9.21f.), 68;
(4.9.23-26), 74; (4.9.23-29), 68; (4.9.26), 98;
(4.9.32), 80; (4.9.33), 78; (4.9.34), 80; (4.9.35),
78, 84; (4.9.47-50), 89; (4.9.53), 80; (4.9.57f.), 84;
(4.9.63f.), 86; (4.9.69), 100
Prudentius 238
Quintilian 209, 211, 238
Sappho 52, 77, 88, 119, 224
Scipio 241
Seneca 153, 158, 162, 205, 238
Servius 194
Silius Italicus 164, 182, 238
Simonides 130
Sophocles 166
Statius 164, 165, 172
Theocritus 34, 88, 112, 126, 132
Theophrastus 34
Tibullus 178, 208
Timander 51
Varro 85, 87, 101
Vergil 4, 7, 25f., 111f., 124, 129, 154, 161, 163, 166,,
195, 197, 239; Eclogues, 192; Georgics, 135, 229;
Aeneid, 230; (Ecl. 6.45-73), 132; (Ecl. 10), 116-18,
131f.; (Geo. 4.501f.), 196; (Aen. 1.92), 9; (1.94-
101), 162; (2.601-3), 162; (2.604-18), 162; (6.721),
162; (6.851), 198; (8.184ff.), 100, 102; (9.607f.),
128; (9.609f.), 127; (12.919-52), 9-11

INDEX OF MODERN AUTHORS

Adorno, T.	177, 178
Alpers, P.	229
Arnold, M.	207
Bartenbach, A.	180, 181, 189
Barthes, R.	22, 26, 209, 211, 212, 215, 217, 218, 219, 220, 221
Bate, W.J.	28
Becker, C.	16
Beckford, W.	47
Belsey, C.	4, 8, 12
Benjamin, W.	24
Bernal, M.	228, 230
Bernbeck, E.	198
Bloom, H.	20, 22, 25, 28, 29
Boeckh, A.	1, 4, 8, 15, 17, 42, 43, 45, 60
Bowles, W.L.	46, 47, 50
Bowra, C.M.	27
Börner, F.	126, 180, 194
Butler, M.	43, 44, 46, 55, 56
Byely, A.	182
Byron, G.	208
Cameron, A.	35
Cavafy, C.	201
Coleman, R.	191
Commager, S.	237, 238, 240
Connor, W.R.	223
Copley, F.	65, 72, 76
Crabbe, A.	191
Crane, R.S.	6, 33, 41, 42, 43, 48, 50, 53, 54
Crews, F.	8, 26
Curran, S.	43, 44, 45, 46, 47, 50, 54, 55
Dante	194
de Man, P.	7, 27, 209
de Saussure, F.	5
Derrida, J.	26
Deubner, L.	116
Douglas, M.	138, 139, 152
Dryden, John	4, 16
Duckworth, G.E.	182, 189
Dürrenmatt, F.	165
Eagleton, T.	14, 15, 22, 24, 32
Eco, U.	176

Ellul, J.	203
Felperin, H.	5, 15, 26, 27
Fish, S.	3, 7, 12, 25, 209
Fisher, S.	137, 138, 152
Fitzgerald, W.	218, 219
Fowler, R.	237, 241
Frazer, J.	160, 161
Froesch, H.	177
Frost, R.	221
Gadamer, H.G.	5
Gallop, J.	218
Giamatti, A.	24
Gildersleeve, B.	209, 231, 232, 233, 234, 235, 236, 237, 238, 239, 240
Glatt, M.	177, 178
Goethe, J.W.	16, 229, 232
Graff, G.	3, 5, 6, 7, 8, 12, 13, 14, 15, 23, 32, 42, 199, 204, 233, 238, 239
Green, P.	6
Greenblatt, S.	17
Hardie, P.	198
Heath, M.	71, 76, 91
Heinze, R.	1, 19, 23, 180
Heisenberg, W.	211
Herbert, G.	201
Higham,	234, 235
Hinds, S.	180, 181, 190, 192, 193, 195, 198
Hirsch, E.D.	5, 7, 8, 17, 34
Hofmannsthal, H. von	205
Housman, A.	21, 42, 201
Hubbard, M.	54, 130
Hubbard, T.	54
Huyssens, A.	26
Iser, W.	8, 177, 188, 190
Jacobson, R.	209
Jameson, F.	30
Jauss, H.	8, 27, 178, 190
Jencks, C.	18
Joyce, J.	7
Kafka, F.	155
Keats, J.	201
Kenney, E.J.	195
Klingner, F.	135
Knapp, S.	21, 27

Knox, B.	14, 193, 196, 197, 237
Konstan, D.	154, 216
Kroll, W.	116
Kubrick, S.	137
Lacan, J.	209
La Capra, D.	31
Leach, E.	19
Lentricchia, F.	4, 7, 13, 19, 20, 25, 29
Leo, F.	180
Lobsien, E.	6, 7
Lodge, D.	58, 60
Lyotard, F.	18
Mallarmé, S.	201
Michaels, W.B.	21, 27
Miller, H.	16, 17, 60
Milton, J.	201
Montaigne, M.	176, 207
Montfauçon, B.	228
Morrison, T.	221
Möhler, G.	182, 183, 184, 185, 190, 196
Niebuhr, B.	230, 231, 236, 240
Nietzsche, F.	209
Nisbet, R.	130
Norden, E.	48, 49, 180
Nugent, G.	193
Ong, W.	158
Otis, B.	176, 178, 180, 190, 195
Pasquali, G.	186
Peradotto, J.	21
Podossinov, A.	177
Popper, K.	53, 54
Porson, R.	209
Postal, S.	138
Powell, A.	59, 60
Pöschl, V.	237
Putnam, M.	2, 9
Ricoeur, P.	30
Rodin, A.	179
Rorty, R.	6
Ross, D.	192
Said, E.	15, 16, 23, 32
Santini, C.	194
Scaliger, J.C.	112

Scherer, A.	186, 190
Schiller, F.	228, 229, 230, 238, 240, 241
Schmidt, E.A.	2, 3
Scholes, R.	4, 7, 8, 22, 24, 30
Searle, J.	26
Shakespeare, W.	205, 208
Shorey, P.	209
Sidney, P.	177
Slater, W.J.	71, 89, 90
Smith, K.F.	209
Snow, C.P.	204, 212
Solodow, J.	186
Spenser, E.	201
Stern, R.	26
Sullivan, J.P.	7
Syme, R.	18, 176, 177, 190, 197
Szondi, P.	5
Tate, A.	14
Thomas, R.	18, 20, 66, 75, 77, 192
Todorov, T.	3, 5, 15, 22, 26, 27, 30, 50, 51
Tompkins, J.	27
Updike, J.	25
Valéry, P.	202, 212
Väisänen, M.	157, 158
Veyne, P.	193
Vickers, B.	209, 211
Vico	189
Voss, J.H.	182
West, D.	28, 33
Whatmough, J.	16, 26, 27
Whitman, W.	172
Wilamowitz, U. von	6, 21
Williams, G.	19, 31, 49, 195
Wilson, E.	60, 61
Wimsatt, W.	5, 30
Winckelmann, J.J.	228, 240
Winkler, J.	3, 19, 195
Wlosok, A.	8
Woodman, T.	28, 33
Wyke, M.	193
Yeats, W.B.	201, 212
Zanker, P.	12

STUDIEN ZUR KLASSISCHEN PHILOLOGIE

Herausgegeben von Michael von Albrecht

Band   1 Ulrike Kettemann: Interpretationen zu Satz und Vers in Ovids erotischem Lehrgedicht. 1979.

Band   2 Walter Kißel: Das Geschichtsbild des Silius Italicus. 1979.

Band   3 Peter Smith: Nursling of Mortality. A Study of the Homeric Hymn to Aphrodite. 1981.

Band   4 Änne Bäumer: Die Bestie Mensch. Senecas Aggressionstheorie, ihre philosophischen Vorstufen und ihre literarischen Auswirkungen. 1982.

Band   5 Christiane Reitz: Die Nekyia in den Punica des Silius Italicus. 1982.

Band   6 Markus Weber: Die mythologische Erzählung in Ovids Liebeskunst. Verankerung, Struktur und Funktion. 1983.

Band   7 Karin Neumeister: Die Überwindung der elegischen Liebe bei Properz. (Buch I - III). 1983.

Band   8 Werner Schubert: Jupiter in den Epen der Flavierzeit. 1984.

Band   9 Dorothea Koch-Peters: Ansichten des Orosius zur Geschichte seiner Zeit. 1984.

Band 10 Bernd Heßen: Der historische Infinitiv im Wandel der Darstellungstechnik Sallusts. 1984.

Band 11 Cornelia Renger: Aeneas und Turnus. Analyse einer Feindschaft. 1985.

Band 12 Reinhold Glei: Die Batrachomyomachie. Synoptische Edition und Kommentar. 1984.

Band 13 Nikolaos Tachinoslis: Handschriften und Ausgaben der Odyssee. Mit einem Handschriftenapparat zu Allen´s Odysseeausgabe. 1984.

Band 14 S. Georgia Nugent: Allegory and Poetics. The Structure and Imagery of Prudentius´ *Psychomachia*. 1985.

Band 15 Anton D. Leeman: Form und Sinn. Studien zur römischen Literatur (1954-1984). 1985.

Band 16 Wolfgang Hübner: Die Petronübersetzung Wilhelm Heinses. Quellenkritisch bearbeiteter Nachdruck der Erstausgabe mit textkritisch-exegetischem Kommentar. (Band I-II). 1986.

Band 17 Roland Glaesser: Verbrechen und Verblendung. Untersuchung zum Furor-Begriff bei Lucan mit Berücksichtigung der Tragödien Senecas. 1984.

Band 18 Fritz-Heiner Mutschler: Die poetische Kunst Tibulls. Struktur und Bedeutung der Bücher 1 und 2 des Corpus Tibullianum. 1985.

Band 19 Rismag Gordesiani: Kriterien der Schriftlichkeit und Mündlichkeit im homerischen Epos. 1986.

Band 20 Madeleine Mary Henry: Menander´s Courtesans and the Greek Comic Tradition. 1985. 2. Auflage 1988.

Band 21 Bernd Janson: Etymologische und chronologische Untersuchungen zu den Bedingungen des Rhotazismus im Albanischen unter Berücksichtigung der griechischen und lateinischen Lehnwörter. 1986.

Band 22 Ernst A. Schmidt: Bukolische Leidenschaft - oder Über antike Hirtenpoesie. 1987.

Band 23 Pedro C. Tapia Zúñiga: Vorschlag eines Lexikons zu den Aitia des Kallimachos. Buchstabe "Alpha". 1986.

Band 24 Eberhard Heck: MH ΘEOMAXEIN oder: Die Bestrafung des Gottesverächters. Untersuchungen zu Bekämpfung und Aneignung römischer religio bei Tertullian, Cyprian und Lactanz. 1987.

Band 25 Manfred Gerhard Schmidt: Caesar und Cleopatra. Philologischer und historischer Kommentar zu Lucan. 10,1-171. 1986.

Band 26 Wolfgang Jäger: Briefanalysen. Zum Zusammenhang von Realitätserfahrung und Sprache in Briefen Ciceros. 1986.

Band 27 Lewis A. Sussman: The Major Declamations Ascribed to Quintilian. A Translation. 1987.

Band 28 Klaus Kubusch: Aurea Saecula: Mythos und Geschichte. Untersuchung eines Motivs in der antiken Literatur bis Ovid. 1986.

Band 29 Helmut Mauch: O laborum dulce lenimen. Funktionsgeschichtliche Untersuchungen zur römischen Dichtung zwischen Republik und Prinzipat am Beispiel der ersten Odensammlung des Horaz. 1986.

Band 30 Karl Meister: Studien zu Sprache, Literatur und Religion der Römer. Herausgegeben von Viktor Pöschl und Michael von Albrecht. 1987.

Band 31 Hubert Müller: Früher Humanismus in Oberitalien. Albertino Mussato: Ecerinis. 1987.

Band 32 Andrea Scheithauer: Kaiserbild und literarisches Programm. Untersuchungen zur Tendenz der Historia Augusta. 1987.

Band 33 Carlos J. Larrain: Die Sentenzen des Porphyrios. Handschriftliche Überlieferung. Die Übersetzung von Marsilio Ficino. Deutsche Übersetzung. 1987.

Band 34 Catherine J. Castner: Prosopography of Roman Epicureans from the Second Century B.C. to the Second Century A.D. 2nd unchanged edition. 1991.

Band 35 Gabriele Möhler: Hexameterstudien zu Lukrez, Vergil, Horaz, Ovid, Lukan, Silius Italicus und der Ilias Latina. 1989.

Band 36 Clara-Emmanuelle Auvray: Folie et Douleur dans Hercule Furieux et Hercule sur l'Oeta. Recherches sur l'expression esthétique de l'ascèse stoïcienne chez Sénèque. 1989.

Band 37 Thomas Weber: Fidus Achates. Der Gefährte des Aeneas in Vergils Aeneis. 1988.

Band 38 Waltraut Desch: Augustins Confessiones. Beobachtungen zu Motivbestand und Gedankenbewegung. 1988.

Band 39 Maria-Barbara Quint: Untersuchungen zur mittelalterlichen Horaz-Rezeption. 1988.

Band 40 Eugene Michael O'Connor: Symbolum Salacitatis. A Study of the God Priapus as a Literary Character. 1989.

Band 41 Michael von Albrecht: Scripta Latina. Accedunt variorum Carmina Heidelbergensia dissertatiunculae colloquia. 1989.

Band 42 Werner Rutz: Studien zur Kompositionskunst und zur epischen Technik Lucans. Herausgegeben und mit einem bibliographischen Nachwort versehen von Andreas W. Schmitt. 1989.

Band 43 Henri Le Bonniec: Etudes ovidiennes. Introduction aux Fastes d'Ovide. 1989.

Band 44 Stefan Merkle: Die Ephemeris belli Troiani des Diktys von Kreta. 1989.

Band 45 Michael Gagarin: The Murder of Herodes. A Study of Antiphon 5. 1989.

Band 46 Joachim Fugmann: Königszeit und Frühe Republik in der Schrift De viris illustribus urbis Romae. Quellenkritisch-historische Untersuchungen. 1990.

Band 47 Sabine Grebe: Die vergilische Heldenschau. Tradition und Fortwirken. 1989.

Band 48 Bardo Maria Gauly: Liebeserfahrungen. Zur Rolle des elegischen Ich in Ovids Amores. 1990.

Band 49 Jörg Maurer: Untersuchungen zur poetischen Technik und den Vorbildern der Ariadne-Epistel Ovids.1990.

Band 50 Karelisa V. Hartigan: Ambiguity and Self-Deception. The Apollo and Artemis Plays of Euripides. 1991.

Band 51 Hermann Lind: Der Gerber Kleon in den 'Rittern' des Aristophanes. Studien zur Demago-
genkomödie. 1990.

Band 52 Alexandra Bartenbach: Motiv- und Erzählstruktur in Ovids Metamorphosen. Das
Verhältnis von Rahmen- und Binnenerzählungen im 5., 10. und 15. Buch von Ovids Metamorphosen. 1990.

Band 53 Jürgen Schmidt: Lukrez, der Kepos und die Stoiker. Untersuchungen zur
Schule Epikurs und zu den Quellen von *De rerum natura*. 1990.

Band 54 Martin Glatt: Die 'andere Welt' der römischen Elegiker. Das Persönliche in
der Liebesdichtung. 1991.

Band 55 John F. Miller: Ovid's Elegiac Festivals. Studies in the *Fasti*. 1991.

Band 56 Elisabeth Vandiver: Heroes in Herodotus. The Interaction of Myth and History. 1991.

Band 57 Frank-Joachim Simon: Τά κύλλ ' ἀείδειν. Interpretationen zu den Mimiamben des Herodas. 1991.

Band 58 Arthur J. Pomeroy: The Appropriate Comment . Death Notices in the Ancient historians.
1991.

Band 59 Martina Kötzle: Weibliche Gottheiten in Ovids Fasten. 1991.

Band 60 Glynn Meter: Walter of Châtillon's Alexandreis Book 10-A commentary. 1991.

Band 61 Burghard Schröder: Carmina non quae nemorale resultent. Ein Kommentar zur 4. Ekloge
des Calpurnius Siculus. 1991.

Band 62 Michele V. Ronnick: Cicero's Paradoxa Stoicorum. A Commentary, an Interpretation and a
Study of Its Influence. 1991.

Band 63 Mary Frances Williams: Landscape in the *Argonautica* of Apollonius Rhodius. 1992.

Band 64 Christine Walde: Herculeus labor. Studien zum pseudosenecanischen Hercules Oetaeus.
1992.

Band 65 Anna Elissa Radke: Harmonica vitrea. 1992.

Band 66 Werner Schubert: Die Mythologie in den nichtmythologischen Dichtungen Ovids. 1992.

Band 67 Karl Galinsky (Hrsg.): The interpretation of Roman poetry. Empiricism or hermeneutics?
1992.

Band 69 Peter Prestel: Die Rezeption der ciceronischen Rhetorik durch Augustinus in De doctrina
Christiana. 1992.

Band 70 Ursula Hecht: Der Pluto furens des Petrus Martyr Anglerius. Dichtung als Dokumentation.
1992.

Bestellungen: Verlag Peter Lang AG, Jupiterstr. 15, CH-3015 Bern, Switzerland

John F. Miller

Ovid's Elegiac Festivals
Studies in the *Fasti*

Frankfurt/M., Berlin, Bern, New York, Paris, Wien, 1991. IX, 192 pp.
Studien zur klassischen Philologie. Vol. 55
Edited by Michael von Albrecht
ISBN 3-631-43392-1   pb. DM 63.--

Until recently, Ovid's *Fasti* has been the most neglected of his major poems. The present study aims to contribute to the rehabilitation of the *Fasti* as a work of art by analyzing Ovid's depictions of religious ceremonial in the light of the elegiac tradition, especially the tradition of Ovid's own earlier elegies. After introductory studies of the *Fasti's* poetics and of sacred rites in the *Amores*, the author explicates eleven of the poetic calendar's versions of festivals. Special attention is devoted to the poem's polytonality and shifting personae.

Contents: The Poetics of the *Fasti* - *Sacra* in the *Amores* - Ovid's versions of the consuls' installation - Robigalia, Megalensia, Caristia - The merchants' feast of May 15 - Magic at the Feralia - Ovid's popular festivals and Tibullus

Verlag Peter Lang Frankfurt a.M. · Berlin · Bern · New York · Paris · Wien
Auslieferung: Verlag Peter Lang AG, Jupiterstr. 15, CH-3000 Bern 15
Telefon (004131) 321122, Telex pela ch 912 651, Telefax (004131) 321131
- Preisänderungen vorbehalten -